PROVIDING EMPLOYMENT
SUPPORT FOR PEOPLE WITH
LONG-TERM MENTAL ILLNESS

PROVIDING EMPLOYMENT SUPPORT FOR PEOPLE WITH LONG-TERM MENTAL ILLNESS
Choices, Resources, and Practical Strategies

by

LAURIE HOWTON FORD
Western Washington University

·P·A·U·L·H·
BROOKES
PUBLISHING C°

Baltimore • London • Toronto • Sydney

Paul H. Brookes Publishing Co.
Post Office Box 10624
Baltimore, Maryland 21285-0624

Typeset by Signature Typesetting & Design, Baltimore, Maryland.
Manufactured in the United States of America by
The Maple Press Company, York, Pennsylvania.

The case studies and examples used in the text are based on real individuals with mental illness and other disabilities. Identifying information has been changed to protect confidentiality; and, in some cases, individual stories have been combined or slightly altered to produce a stronger illustration.

All of the cartoons in this book have been drawn by John McClure. They appear on these pages with his permission.

Library of Congress Cataloging-in-Publication Data
Ford, Laurie Howton.
    Providing employment support for people with long-term mental illness: choices, resources, and practical strategies / Laurie Howton Ford.
        p.   cm.
    Includes bibliographical references (p.   ) and index.
    ISBN 1-55766-190-1
    1. Mentally ill—Employment.   2. Mentally ill—Rehabilitation.   I. Title.
HV3005.F67   1995
808'.06665—dc20   95-3724
                                                                                         CIP

British Library Cataloguing-in-Publication data are available from the British Library.

CONTENTS

ABOUT THE AUTHOR

Laurie Howton Ford, M.S., is the Director for Community Rehabilitation Training Programs at the Center for Continuing Education in Rehabilitation (CCER) at Western Washington University. She manages continuing education programs in employment services for people with long-term mental illness and other disabilities, community building approaches to enhancing employment opportunities for people with disabilities, and community rehabilitation program administration. She has worked as a job coach, placement coordinator, prevocational trainer, program developer and manager, and consultant.

FOREWORD

Employment for people with long-term mental illness has become increasingly more accepted over the years. Increased advocacy efforts, perfected employment technologies, and understanding of business cultures are leading to dramatic results. Supported employment is a relatively new approach to employment for people with mental illness. Its inclusion in the Rehabilitation Act Amendments of 1986 (PL 99-506) implied an accepted employment service strategy for individuals with severe disabilities. Supported employment then emerged from research and practice with people with developmental disabilities. These individuals required support to obtain and maintain competitive employment. As the successful results of early demonstration programs were publicized, so was the message that employment technology could easily be generalized from one group of people to another. From the onset, those who were not part of the developmental disabilities system expressed concerns about the efficacy of supported employment for people with mental illness. These concerns were primarily expressed by mental health (MH) and vocational rehabilitation (VR) professionals who believed that a person had to be "cured" before he or she could be employed.

The MH and VR systems have a history of operating on parallel tracks. Shrouded in stigma, prescriptive drugs, and an array of treatment modalities, the world of mental health stood apart from other disability groups who were grappling with the problems associated with disability and employment. Although supported employment was based on the foundation of competitive work, many MH professionals questioned this value and wondered about its harmful effects. Because supported employment technologies were designed by people with little experience in the provision of support to individuals with mental illness, there were not many answers to the many questions regarding people with mental illness and employment and therefore professionals were told to adapt the early trainings and writings as they saw fit.

Service provider organizations often found their niche in providing services to specific groups of individuals. There were not many organizations that offered their services to an "eclectic" clientele. Therefore, the staff may not have had personal experience in providing services to people with disabilities other than the specific groups with which they were familiar. When VR agencies in some states began advocating for individuals with more severe and varied disabilities to receive supported employment, doubts arose concerning how to provide services, especially for people with long-term mental illness.

Continuing education programs began offering supported employment training as a result of federally funded, state supported employment systems change projects. Initially, these trainings did not offer skill building as an area in which to provide support for individuals with different disabilities. Such support was not made available until trainees began asking questions or making comments such as, "When and how do you make disclosures about the disability?", "What happens when the person stops taking medication? What do I do?", "How can I train him or her on the job?", and "She has been employed before as a paralegal and I don't have those skills." Comments like these led to the redesigning of staff development specifically targeting employment for individuals with mental illness and people with physical disabilities, sensory disabilities, and brain injury.

Supported employment is based on an individualized service approach. Services vary according to the abilities and requirements of the person receiving them, regardless of the person's disability. Service providers have learned from practice and are more confident about what is needed to provide quality supported employment to people with long-term mental illness.

Although a diagnosis does not predict employability, it is necessary to understand mental illness and how it affects functioning. For example, the medications an individual is taking can positively or negatively influence employment. A number of questions should be asked. What are the individual's family dynamics? What natural supports are available? What is the status of benefits and how will they be affected by employment? What is the individual's current living situation? Other staff development areas include the theory and best practices of job development, behavior management, skills training, and career development. Related factors include knowledge of the MH system and its relationship (or lack thereof) to the VR system, and service coordination strategies that may be necessary for maintaining employment.

Professionals must understand the peaks and valleys that characterize mental illness and how to track them, provide interventions and supports when needed, and advocate to the employer when the employee is not able to work for a period of time. Because the symptoms of mental illness are frequently intermittent, long-term employment in one job may not be possible. Yet, an individual with a psychiatric disability who wants to work (despite the severity of the disability) is a candidate for supported employment. The challenge is making this a reality. These considerations and the employment specialist's role in coordinating services and facilitating supports are extremely complex. Effective strategies should be included in every continuing education program and product that addresses supported employment for people with mental illness.

During the mid-1980s, the outcomes of quality staff development programs and federally funded state supported employment, systems change activities have resulted in more people with severe disabilities becoming employed. An understanding of the effectiveness of vocational options for people with severe disabilities has grown among people with disabilities, their families, and service providers. The consumer advocacy movement, with its emphasis on informed choice and control, is having a profound influence on how staff respond to the needs of people with disabilities. Service providers are *expected* to offer and negotiate a richer variety of services and supports.

The success of supported employment is reflected in the data. More than 100,000 people with a variety of disabilities have received supported employment services since 1986. It is also known that supported employment has been successful across disability groups. In 1991, 22.2% of all people in supported employment were individuals with mental illness (Revell, Wehman, Kregel, West, & Rayfield, 1994).

What lies ahead? During the 1990s the number of people in supported employment and competitive employment has not increased significantly, even with the passage of PL 101-336, the Americans with Disabilities Act of 1990. For many individuals, not working is the primary disability. Over two thirds of people with disabilities are not employed, yet three fourths of these people show a willingness to work (Harris and Associates, Inc., 1994). The United States has a growing economy, a proven service technology, and a civil rights law for people with disabilities. Stigma and fear are combated with familiarity and understanding. As more is learned about the beneficial effects of employment for people with mental illness, we must continue to advocate for employment opportunities. The challenge that we all face is to make our workplaces reflect our diverse society, which means substantial employment of people with disabilities.

Karen Flippo, M.R.A.
Training Associate
Rehabilitation Research and
Training Center on Supported Employment
Virginia Commonwealth University
Richmond

REFERENCES

Americans with Disabilities Act of 1990 (ADA), PL 101-336. (July 26, 1990). Title 42, U.S.C. 12101 et seq: *U.S. Statutes at Large, 104,* 327–378.

Harris and Associates, Inc. (1994). *N.O.D./*Harris survey of Americans with disabilities. New York: Author.

Rehabilitation Act Amendments of 1986, PL 99-506. Title 29, U.S.C. 701 et seq: *U.S. Statutes at Large, 100,* 1807–1846.

Revell, W.G., Wehman, P., Kregel, J., West, M., & Rayfield, R. (1994). Supported employment for persons with severe disabilities: Positive trends in wages, models, and funding. In P. Wehman & J. Kregel (Eds.), *New directions in supported employment* (pp. 30–39). Richmond: Virginia Commonwealth University, Rehabilitation Research and Training Center on Supported Employment.

FOREWORD

Supported employment (SE) is a flourishing rehabilitation concept in the United States, with more than 90,000 people participating in community employment through this strategy (Inge, 1994). Although closely linked with the field of developmental disabilities, principles now associated with supported employment (e.g., on-site support, no prerequisites, in vivo training) have been utilized in psychiatric rehabilitation for many years. Examples include the Fairweather Lodge model (Fairweather, 1980), rehabilitation clubhouses such as the Fountain House (Malamud & McCrory, 1988), and assertive community treatment (Russert & Frey, 1991). However, people with mental illness still fare poorly in the labor market (MacDonald-Wilson, Revell, Nguyen, & Peterson, 1991) and often require extensive support to hold and maintain employment.

This book examines SE concepts, philosophy, and methodology as they apply to people with long-term mental illness. The exposition offered by the author is important because some misconceptions, which are particularly prevalent among mental health practitioners, have hindered the expansion of this form of employment opportunity to a major group of potential beneficiaries. The genesis of this mythology is attributable to the following two primary factors: 1) mental illness in Western society generates social stigma and discrimination; and 2) supported employment as a part of rehabilitation social policy has been linked, in the public image, with day programming for individuals with developmental disabilities (Marrone & Gold, 1994). Only after an initial research and development phase from 1978 to 1986 was the concept of supported employment seen as useful for individuals with mental illness. Even then, it was seen as a means to transfer a knowledge base from one realm of disability-specific intervention to another (i.e., from the mental retardation field to the psychiatric field). Controversy has arisen over whether the SE approach can be generalized from the developmental disabilities field to other populations without significant modifications.

The clinical concepts inherent in the SE method of rehabilitation service delivery owe as much to past work in the field of psychiatric disabilities as to that of developmental disabilities. These core principles have been cornerstones of the psychiatric rehabilitation movement since the mid-1960s, although never articulated within this typology. These concepts include the following:

- In vivo learning (i.e., site-based training)
- On-site support
- Support as a healthy, not dysfunctional, need

- Zero-reject policy (i.e., a presumption of suitability for services)
- Integration into the work force
- A new definition of success (i.e., the extra support a person may need is seen as an obligation for the service system to address; working with intensive on- or off-site support has come to constitute a desirable outcome, not a failure, as it had been viewed prior to the passage of the Rehabilitation Act Amendments of 1986 [PL 99-596], which defined supported employment as an acceptable vocational rehabilitation [VR] outcome [Marrone & Gold, 1994])

The SE movement has advanced the concept of employment services from a strictly clinical issue to one of civil rights and societal inclusion, involving both social and work integration. Supported employment was a radical departure from the norm of day programs for people with developmental disabilities. Day programs serving people with developmental disabilities were an outgrowth of school- and institution-based services developed by special educators. Therefore, these programs often were designed on a special education model (i.e., one based on sequential skill acquisition or what has been labeled a continuum of services). However, day programs for people with mental illness were usually developed on a medical model (i.e., one focused on psychiatric pathology and treatment) and were usually created by adult services providers.

Before a person can understand the phenomenon of the wave of rehabilitation programming occurring in the 1990s, which was labeled "supported employment for people with mental illness," he or she must understand the broader historical context that formed the background for these important developments. In the field of mental retardation, the panoply of SE options has sprung from pioneers in the field, including Marc Gold, Lou Brown, Wolf Wolfsenberger, and vocational leaders such as Tom Bellamy, Madeleine Will, and Paul Wehman. Their respective contributions have been well chronicled in the literature since the early 1980s. Supported employment has come out of a specific social, historical, and political context from which other public laws and acts have grown; these laws include the following: the Education for All Handicapped Children Act of 1975 (PL 94-142) and its reformulation as the Individuals with Disabilities Education Act of 1990 (IDEA) (PL 101-476) for students with "special" educational needs, the Civil Rights Act of 1964 (PL 88-352) for members of ethnic and/or racial minority groups, and the Americans with Disabilities Act of 1990 (ADA) (PL 101-336). All of the above are elements of an increasingly overt commitment to ensure integration of all people throughout American society and a desire to improve rehabilitation innovations.

I first met the author at a SE conference in Washington state in 1990. At that time, she had recently moved from working primarily with people with developmental disabilities to assisting others in helping people with mental illness find and retain community employment. Our first conversation illustrated to both of us that although we had different perspectives, came from different backgrounds, held different roles, and could disagree on many items, we shared one elemental common belief. Namely, supported employment, in its essence, involves a personalized, relationship-based response to individual employment needs and should transcend disability labels.

This book is the culmination of years of work by the author, which have made her more knowledgeable and caused her to shape her views through the prism of increased experience. However, the reader will sense the core value that the author and I shared in our initial conversations emanating clearly from this book—that is, support offered to people with mental illness must be personal and caring, not technical in nature. This book weaves together knowledge bases from the mental health, developmental disabilities, and SE disciplines within this overall humanistic context. The author presents a wealth of information, covering all the topics that people involved in supported employment want to know about. These topics are covered extensively, yet in a way that staff without specialized clinical skills can understand and use.

My colleagues at the Institute for Community Inclusion in Boston and I can appreciate the amount of effort and expertise required to complete the task Laurie Howton Ford set out to do. She has synthesized the information available without trivializing it or presenting it as a recipe to be followed blindly; however, she makes it accessible so that personnel with limited experience in the field will not be daunted by letting it guide them through their in-service or preservice training. This book nicely dovetails a multiplicity of facts, values-driven content, and user-friendly language and format. She has done what every author must do—she has added to the body of knowledge available to the field, in a manner that illuminates, not obfuscates for the sake of demonstrating an author's erudition or grasp of minutiae. The author has truly helped advance the work of those interested in assisting people with mental illness to achieve jobs and careers in the community, rather than just providing enhanced vocational programming. She is not able to answer all the questions this challenge poses but, for that matter, no one is. But, in the words of the artist Emil Nolde, "Clever people master life; the wise illuminate it and create fresh difficulties." Rather than retreat from these difficulties, the author has taken the advice of another, more contemporary artist, Andy Warhol, "They say that time changes things, but actually you have to change them yourself."

Joe Marrone
Coordinator, Technical Assistance
Center on Promoting Employment
Boston, Massachusetts

REFERENCES

Americans with Disabilities Act of 1990 (ADA), PL 101-336. (July 26, 1990). Title 42, U.S.C. 12101 et seq: *U.S. Statutes at Large, 104,* 327–378.

Civil Rights Act of 1964, PL 88-352. (July 2, 1964). Title 42, U.S.C. 1971 et seq: *U.S. Statutes at Large, 78,* 241–286.

Fairweather, G.W. (1980). *New directions for mental health services: The Fairweather Lodge: A twenty-five year retrospective* (No. 7). San Francisco: Jossey Bass.

Individuals with Disabilities Education Act of 1990 (IDEA), PL 101-476. (October 30, 1990). Title 20, U.S.C. 1400 et seq: *U.S. Statutes at Large 104,* 1103–1151.

Inge, K.J. (Ed.). (1994). *Conversion: The time is now.* Richmond: Virginia Commonwealth University, Rehabilitation Research and Training Center on Supported Employment.

MacDonald-Wilson, K.L., Revell, W.G., Nguyen, N.H., & Peterson, M.E. (1991). Supported employment outcomes for people with a psychiatric disability: A comparative analysis. *Journal of Vocational Rehabilitation, 1*(3), 30–44.

Malamud, T.J., & McCrory, D.J. (1988). Transitional employment and psychosocial rehabilitation: A community model for the vocational rehabilitation of individuals with prolonged mental illness. In J.A. Ciardello & M.D. Bell (Eds.), *Vocational rehabilitation of persons with prolonged psychiatric disorders* (pp.150–164). Baltimore: The Johns Hopkins University Press.

Marrone, J., & Gold, M. (1994). Supported employment for people with mental illness: Myths and facts. *Journal of Rehabilitation, 60*(4), 38–47.

Rehabilitation Act of 1973, PL 93-112. (September 26, 1973). Title 29, U.S.C. 701 et seq: *U.S. Statutes at Large, 87,* 355–394.

Rehabilitation Act Amendments of 1986, PL 99-506. Title 29, U.S.C. 701 et seq: *U.S. Statutes at Large, 100,* 1807–1846.

Russert, M.G., & Frey, J.L. (1991). The PACT vocational model: A step into the future. *Psychosocial Rehabilitation Journal, 14*(4), 7–18.

PREFACE

This is an exciting time to be involved in the field of vocational rehabilitation. The acceptance of employment as an appropriate and vital part of the lives of all people, including those with mental illness, is changing the way in which services are designed and delivered. The consistent message from people with long-term mental illness is that they want to work and they want vocational services to assist them in accomplishing that goal. This is forcing many professionals to reexamine and modify their roles.

Most supported employment procedures were developed around and continue to be used with individuals with developmental disabilities, especially mental retardation. The extension of these procedures to the population of individuals with long-term mental illness has not been without its difficulties, and many of these difficulties involve a lack of information. Several excellent manuals and books have been written about job coaching for people with developmental disabilities (Botterbusch, 1989; DiLeo, 1993; Fadely, 1987; Mcloughlin, Garner, & Callahan, 1987; Moon, Goodall, Barcus, & Brooke, 1986; Moon, Inge, Wehman, Brooke, & Barcus, 1990; Powell et al., 1991). Applications for use with people who have long-term mental illness have not been as well documented. Job coaches who are well experienced with workers who have mental retardation are often hesitant to apply their knowledge and experience to workers whose primary difficulty may not be in learning the job but in long-term job maintenance and illness management. Similarly, mental health professionals have a thorough understanding of the issues surrounding mental illness, but may be just beginning to look at employment as a viable and reasonable activity for their clients. Thus, they may lack the training technologies and business viewpoint that have made supported employment successful with other populations. In many, if not most, cases, the education that prepared people to provide mental health counseling and case management within the confines of the mental health center did not address the challenges of providing services on the job.

There is a recognition that one of the major roadblocks to reinvolvement in the "normal" world has been the very low expectations that employment specialists have had for their clients and their capabilities. For example, after examining several long-term research studies, Harding, Zubin, and Strauss (1987) suggested that increasing deterioration may not be a function of mental illness per se but rather of how the person with the illness is treated in his or her environment. It is clear that service providers need to quickly raise their standards and learn the skills needed to assist people in fulfilling their potential.

This book has been developed for professionals who are directly involved with assisting individuals with long-term mental illness to obtain and maintain community-based employment. These professionals have titles such as job coach, employment specialist, vocational coordinator, case manager, occupational therapist, supported employment specialist, or community support program coordinator; they work for mental health centers, rehabilitation facilities, adult learning programs, independent supported employment agencies, clubhouses, and so forth. The jobs they help their clients find may be part- or full-time, transitional or permanent, paid or volunteer. Although they answer to different titles and work in different settings, they share a commitment to the right of individuals with disabilities to have access to employment.

This book is intended to help fill the gaps in knowledge about employment for people with long-term mental illness. Experienced job coaches will find information about the functional effects of mental illness and the modifications of standard approaches that have been successful for people with mental illness. Mental health practitioners will find information about supported employment and the training and support techniques that have been adapted from earlier successes.

The primary audience for this book is the person who is directly involved in supporting people with long-term mental illness as they move into community-based employment activities. For the sake of continuity, throughout the book I call this person the "employment specialist." His or her role typically involves some combination of job exploration and development; teaching skills; case management; troubleshooting and counseling; advocacy; informing and/or supporting employers, co-workers, and family members; behavior management; record keeping; and networking with other professionals and agencies who are also involved with the client.

The first and second sections of the book provide background information about the clients served and the systems that serve them. The third section then addresses client screening and assessment; job development, seeking, analysis, structuring, and modification; and client–job matching. The fourth section focuses on issues that arise after employment, including teaching tasks and adult learning, social skills and integration, behavior management, natural supports, self-management, and advocacy. The fifth section then addresses long-term issues, such as routine follow-up, troubleshooting and crisis intervention, and dealing with job loss. The book concludes with a useful list of references.

Recognizing that the language we use powerfully shapes the way we see things, I must include a few comments about the terms used in this handbook. Throughout the book, I have followed The Association for Persons with Severe Handicaps (TASH) guidelines in using language that emphasizes the humanity of people with psychiatric disabilities; thus, for example, "individuals with schizophrenia" is used, rather than "schizophrenics." In the ongoing debate over which word best describes people who receive our services, I side with those who see the label "consumer" as stereotyping and somewhat degrading. Accountants, hairstylists, fitness trainers, employment counselors, lawyers, talent agents, and other professionals who provide services do not call the people without disabilities whom they serve their "consumers." Therefore, throughout the book I have used the term "clients" to describe individuals with long-term mental illness when considering aspects of their relationship with the employment specialist. In other settings, they may be referred to as "workers," "individuals," "people," "family members," or any other descriptor that addresses their role at a given time. The label *long-term mental illness* has been used to indicate a psychiatric disability that is both severe and long lasting; the term *chronic* mental illness (CMI) is considered by consumer groups to be unnecessarily stigmatizing and pessimistic (Anthony, Cohen, & Farkas, 1990).

Gender specifications for both clients and employment specialists are alternated by chapter; thus, in Chapter 1 the client is male and employment specialist is female, in Chapter 2 the client is female and the employment specialist is male, in Chapter 3 the client is male and the employment specialist is female, and so forth.

As employment providers strive to make their services client centered, at many agencies the title "case manager" is giving way to that of "service coordinator." This new title more properly reflects the professional's role as one of coordinating services along with and on behalf of people with disabilities and avoids labeling people with disabilities as "cases" needing management by someone else. However, this paradigm has yet to shift in most mental health settings in which case managers often provide the majority of direct services. Because case managers are an important audience for this book, I have retained the "case manager" title for those mental health service providers, although I feel strongly that we need to reexamine the meaning implied in the words and continue the move away from language that dehumanizes the people we serve.

We are a long way from the full inclusion of people with long-term mental illness in the everyday world of work. Changes in service systems, client self-advocacy, and public awareness about mental illness have only just begun to change long-established paradigms regarding whether an individual has the ability and stability to be employed.

I have developed a profound respect for people who strive to get and keep jobs while at the same time deal with mental illness, as well as those professionals and family members who struggle to provide quality client-centered services in an environment of increasingly limited public resources. It is my hope that by presenting a broad range of information about both mental illness and employment approaches, this book will support and encourage all those who believe in the right of people with disabilities to live and work in their communities.

REFERENCES

Anthony, W., Cohen, M., & Farkas, M. (1990). *Psychiatric rehabilitation.* Boston: Center for Psychiatric Rehabilitation, Boston University.

Botterbusch, K.F. (1989). *Understanding community based employment and follow-up services.* Menomonie: Research and Training Center, Stout Vocational Rehabilitation Institute, University of Washington–Stout.

DiLeo, D. (1993). *Enhancing the lives of adults with disabilities: An orientation manual* (2nd ed.). St. Augustine, FL: Training Resource Network.

Fadely, D.C. (1987). *Job coaching in supported work programs.* Menomonie: Materials Development Center, Stout Vocational Rehabilitation Institute, University of Washington–Stout.

Harding, C.M., Zubin, J., & Strauss, J.S. (1987). Chronicity in schizophrenia: Fact, partial fact, or artifact? *Hospital and Community Psychiatry, 38,* 477–486.

Mcloughlin, C.S., Garner, J.B., & Callahan, M. (1987). *Getting employed, staying employed.* Baltimore: Paul H. Brookes Publishing Co.

Moon, M.S., Goodall, P., Barcus, M., & Brooke, V. (1986). *The supported work model of competitive employment for citizens with severe handicaps: A guide for job trainers* (rev. ed.). Richmond: Rehabilitation Research and Training Center, Virginia Commonwealth University.

Moon, M.S., Inge, K.J., Wehman, P., Brooke, V., & Barcus, J.M. (1990). *Helping persons with severe mental retardation get and keep employment: Supported employment issues and strategies.* Baltimore: Paul H. Brookes Publishing Co.

Powell, T.H., Pancsofar, E.L., Steere, D.E., Butterworth, J., Itzkowitz, J.S., & Rainforth, B. (1991). *Supported employment: Providing integrated employment opportunities for persons with disabilities.* New York: Longman.

ACKNOWLEDGMENTS

I offer my appreciation to the experienced rehabilitation practitioners who read the first draft of this book and offered some very helpful feedback. They were Mary Denevan, Delaunay Mental Health, Portland, Oregon; Linda Jones, S.W.I.F.T., Pocotello, Idaho; Janice Moore, Moore and Associates, Spokane, Washington; Nick Codd, Community Psychiatric Clinic, Seattle, Washington; and John McClure, Olympic Mental Health, Everett, Washington.

A special thank you goes to John McClure whose cartoons fill these pages. Ideas for several of the cartoons in this book began when Mr. McClure was a student in one of my workshops. After several years as an employment specialist in the mental health field, Mr. McClure is now the director of the New Frontier Club in Everett, Washington, and is a faculty member at the International Center for Clubhouse Development.

Thank you also to my CCER colleagues for their patience during the months of revision; and especially to John Dineen, who codeveloped the training sessions from which the book grew, as well as provided advice and support during its development.

To my family: Eric, Jay, Brian, and Elizabeth;
and to my mother, Guinevere Foley Howton

I
THE PEOPLE

1

PEOPLE WITH MENTAL ILLNESS

Michelle was worried. Since she had taken the position of employment specialist 2 years ago, she had grown to enjoy the variety of challenges that came with the job. Over time, she had gained confidence that she provided good service to the clients in her caseload—helping them to identify interests and skills, find job opportunities, learn their jobs, get to know their employers and co-workers, and maintain stable employment. The problem was that most of Michelle's clients had mental retardation, and now the agency was going to start working with people with mental illnesses.

"How will I work with someone who has a mental illness?" Michelle wondered. "I don't know anything about mental illness. What if they get stressed out and lose it on the job? Will they act crazy? Hear voices? Use drugs? What if they need support that I don't know how to provide?"

THE VALUE OF INFORMATION ABOUT MENTAL ILLNESS

Service providers whose backgrounds and experiences come from working with people with developmental disabilities often feel that they need a great deal of general information about mental illness before they can do a good job serving an individual with mental illness. A common question for a person teaching service providers how to support people with mental illness is "What kind of a job *should* you find for someone with schizophrenia?" The answer, of course, is that although schizophrenia may significantly interfere with an individual's performance of ordinary life functions—it is only a part of what and who the person is and does not determine the type of job in which he would be successful. People with long-term mental illness are as diverse as the population in general. They are men and women of every race; they may be married, divorced, or single; and they may have good work histories, terrible work histories, or no work histories. Some have exhibited violent behavior in the past, but most have not. Some will experience significant impairments for the rest of their lives, while others will return to nearly their original level of functioning.

Neither diagnostic categories nor symptom patterns are good predictors of future work performance. In fact, there is strong evidence that there is no relationship between diagnosis and future independent living and vocational functioning (Anthony, Cohen, & Farkas, 1990). Traditional psychiatric diagnoses have been more concerned with deficits than strengths and abilities (Black, 1988). In contrast, the task of the employment specialist is to build and capitalize on each client's strengths and abilities. Even the functional limitations that are often experienced by people with mental illness and that are meaningful in the context of arranging employment are only moderately associated with diagnostic types. A person with schizophrenia is likely to have hallucinations, but many people with schizophrenia do not.

The bottom line is that diagnoses actually provide very little information that will help the employment specialist support the client's move into employment. Knowing only that a person has schizophrenia tells someone very little about his specific skills, interests, or limitations.

However, a basic understanding of psychiatric syndromes and their usual treatment modalities will give the employment specialist a common language and framework to use in dealing with the mental health caseworker, the medical staff, and the client himself. Although a diagnosis gives little information about the effects of a particular disease on a given individual, it can prompt the employment specialist to investigate issues typically associated with that diagnosis. For example, a diagnosis of schizophrenia is very likely to imply ongoing drug therapy, and a diagnosis of antisocial personality disorder does not imply such treatment. Because

People with long-term mental illness are as diverse as the population in general.

clients usually have been diagnosed long before they are involved in vocational services, employment specialists will not generally be in the position of diagnosing mental illness. However, employment specialists will need to interact with other professionals who think in traditional psychiatric terms, and diagnostic labels provide a common language.

It is also important for the employment specialist to be aware of the treatment approaches that are being used with a given individual so that rehabilitation efforts can be coordinated with other routines. For example, an understanding of the type of medication being used and the potential side effects allows the employment specialist to be aware of any signs that these side effects are developing or changing. In addition, employment specialists who routinely update their knowledge about new treatment possibilities may be able to effectively advocate for their clients who might benefit from such treatment.

In learning about long-term mental illness and the people it affects, employment specialists should keep in mind that they may work with people who do not have recognizable symptoms of their illness on a routine basis. Symptoms may be effectively controlled through medication and other treatment, and there may be no way to tell that the worker has a mental illness. In these situations it becomes even more important to develop a relationship with the worker in which the employment specialist spends time learning about the illness and the unique way it is manifested (Furlong, Jonikas, Cook, Hathaway, & Goode, 1994).

DEFINITIONS OF LONG-TERM MENTAL ILLNESS

Long-term mental illness is identified by the presence of a psychiatric diagnosis and significant functional limitations in living, learning, and working environments (Fifteenth Institute on Rehabilitation Issues, 1988). This disability or impaired functioning may be evidenced by unemployment or limited skills and a poor work history, a prolonged need for public financial assistance and the inability to apply for such assistance without help, an inability to establish or maintain a personal social support system, difficulty with basic living skills, and inappropriate social behavior that results in a demand for intervention by the mental health and/or judicial system (Anthony et al., 1990). During the 1970s, mental illness was defined largely through the number and frequency of psychiatric hospitalizations. Since 1980 there has been a movement toward more functional definitions that do not rely on the number and length of hospitalizations; this is important because people diagnosed with mental illness now tend to spend less time in hospitals and to be discharged more quickly with referrals to community-based outpatient care.

The categorization system that is usually followed in the diagnoses and description of mental illness is summarized in the *Diagnostic and Statistical Manual of Mental Disorders* (4th ed.) (DSM-IV) (American Psychological Association [APA], 1994). The DSM-IV attempts to describe clinically significant behavioral or psychological syndromes or patterns (i.e., diagnoses) typically associated with problematic symptoms or impairment in one or more areas of functioning. Some of these syndromes are those commonly called mental illness (e.g., schizophrenia, bipolar disorder), but many of the mental problems described in the DSM-IV involve other issues such as mental retardation, Alzheimer's disease, and sleep disturbances. People with some DSM-IV diagnoses (e.g., agoraphobia) might be dealt with by psychologists or other mental health professionals but are rarely seen by employment specialists.

The DSM-IV system generally describes *what* a disorder is without considering *how* or *why* the disorder came about or how it can best be treated (although in some cases discussion of causative and treatment factors is included). As noted previously, a diagnosis does not provide any specific information about a person's rehabilitation potential; thus, diagnoses have limited predictive value for vocational rehabilitation (Anthony et al., 1990).

To make a diagnosis in accordance with DSM-IV guidelines, symptoms are noted in terms of five distinct categories, or axes. Subcategories under each axis are classified by number. For example, under Axis I a diagnosis of schizophrenia would be assigned a different number code than a diagnosis of bipolar disorder. A person can be assigned more than one code number per axis—for example, both depression and alcohol dependence would be noted on Axis I. In theory, a diagnosis across all five axes should represent a comprehensive evaluation of the individual.

The five axes are as follows:

Axis I: Clinical disorders and other conditions that may be a focus of clinical attention and treatment (e.g., marital problems, noncompliance with medical treatment, uncomplicated bereavement). Alcohol dependence is also an Axis I diagnosis.

Axis II: Mental retardation and personality disorder(s) (i.e., dependent personality). Axis II disorders generally begin in childhood and persist into adult life, while Axis I disorders are generally considered to originate in adolescence or adulthood.

Axis III: General medical conditions (e.g., diabetes, paraplegia).

Axis IV: Psychosocial and environmental problems that affect the diagnosis, treatment, and prognosis of mental disorders. These include problems with the primary support group or the social environment, education, occupation, housing, economic, and legal problems.

Axis V: Global assessment of functioning. On this axis, two ratings are made— one for current status and one for highest level of functioning during the past year. The scale goes from 1 to 100, with a score in the 90s indicating absent or minimal symptoms with good functioning in all areas; a score in the 50s representing serious symptoms or impairment in social, occupational, or school functioning; and a score less than 10 indicating persistent danger of hurting oneself or others, or a persistent inability to maintain minimal personal hygiene.

The DSM system is constantly being revised to try to reflect more accurately the people it describes. For example, the functional and environmental factors were added to try to take into account the importance of outside events (Axis IV) and the fact that not everyone is affected identically by the same disease (Axis V). *However, the employment specialist is still strongly advised to remember that even the best diagnosis provides only limited information.*

DEMOGRAPHIC CHARACTERISTICS
OF PEOPLE WITH LONG-TERM MENTAL ILLNESS

In 1994, the National Institute of Mental Health (NIMH) estimated that 42 million people in the United States had psychiatric impairments that limited one or more major functional areas (Rutman, 1994). Estimates of the number of people in the United States with severe, long-term mental illness generally fall somewhere between 1.5 million and 2.8 million (Farkas, Anthony, & Cohen, 1989; Tashjian, Hayward, Stoddard, & Kraus, 1989). Tashjian et al., in a vocational rehabilitation study of best practices in vocational services to people with mental illness, estimated that 40% lived in nursing homes, 40% in their own households, 9% in supported community residences, 5% were homeless, 4% lived in long-term mental health facilities, and 4% in short-term mental health facilities. (When added, these figures equal 102% as a result of rounding.) The subjects of this study were people with mental illness who were thought to be appropriate for vocational rehabilitation services and who probably represented individuals with less severe disabilities in the population. Therefore, these numbers may not accurately describe the general population of people with long-term mental illness. In his study of 175 participants in supported employment programs, Coiner (1990) reported that 61% lived in their own home or apartment, 17% in supervised apartments, 15% with parents or other relatives, and 7% in group homes. Studies examining the educational achievement of people with long-term mental illness estimated that 50%–90% were high school graduates, and 15%–60% attended college (Farkas et al., 1989; Tashjian et al., 1989).

Although people with mental illness come in all shapes, sizes, and socioeconomic statuses, a few generalizations may be made. Many people with mental illness (30%–40%) continue to live with their families, while many others are cared for in nursing facilities or other community housing, such as group homes. They tend to be relatively well educated compared to people with other disabilities, although not compared to people without disabilities. People with mental illness often have other significant problems such as substance abuse or physical illness. Most are unmarried. The average age of people involved in vocational programs tends to fall in the early to mid-30s, and more men than women are involved. In looking at people served by vocational programs specifically, schizophrenia is by far the most common diagnosis, followed by the combined mood disorders (i.e., depression and bipolar disorder), schizoaffective disorder, and others (chiefly personality disorders) (Danley, Rogers, & Nevas, 1989). Compared to other vocational rehabilitation clients, people with mental illness tend to be a bit older, are more likely to have finished high school, and are much less likely to be married. They do not differ on measures of race or gender.

THE USE OF MEDICATION TO TREAT MENTAL ILLNESS

Medication is used to treat the symptoms of diseases and also to avoid or ameliorate the side effects of other medication. For example, some of the antipsychotic medication commonly used to treat schizophrenia may cause physical symptoms similar to Parkinson's disease; thus, antiparkinsonian medication is added to the treatment plan. The best way to determine which medication will work best, and at what dose, is through trial and error.

Ideally, drug therapy is used as only one aspect of treatment that includes other components such as counseling, skill training, support building, and vocational rehabilitation. There is little evidence that drug therapy alone increases a client's strengths and assets, although it does allow the person to take advantage of other treatment procedures. Therefore, compliance with drug therapy does not eliminate the need for other rehabilitation activities. In fact, rehabilitative support can assist with successful drug therapy. A survey of discharged psychiatric patients revealed that more than half of the patients (56%) could not state the name and dosage of their medication, or the reason they were taking it (National Alliance for the Mentally Ill, 1994). Employment specialists may be able to provide valuable support in assisting individuals in understanding and monitoring their medication regimen.

Issues of compliance with medication regimens frequently arise when people move into employment activities because their symptoms are less severe than when they originally became ill, and medication and/or side effects may be seen as an interference with vocational performance. In fact, there are a number of research studies showing that medication may impair work capacity while at the same time controlling symptoms (Mintz, Mintz, & Phipps, 1992), causing the individual to feel that he would perform better without the medication. Psychotropic medication takes several weeks to have a full effect, which may result in an individual not feeling any negative effects for quite a while after he has stopped taking his medication. Then once the level of medication in the body drops and symptoms return, the individual may not associate the symptoms with the lack of medication. Once the medication regimen is resumed, it will once again take a substantial period before the full effect is felt.

Many people report experiencing unpleasant side effects while taking antipsychotic medication. Some side effects are hazardous and need to be attended to quickly and others can be ameliorated with other drugs, but many must be tolerated (Owen, 1982). Sometimes people stop taking medication because they do not like the side effects, they miss the enhanced sensations associated with the illness, they wish to avoid the stigma associated with taking psychotropic medication, or they are denying the illness and their need for medication. In other cases, people stop taking their medication because they do not clearly understand the function of the medication.

The bottom line for employment specialists is understanding that no matter what the diagnosis, medication regimens *must* be individually developed for the highest effectiveness, and each client's treatment plan must be studied and the medication effects and side effects reviewed to identify potential employment and support issues. Careful adjustment of medication types and dosages can greatly improve the functioning level of many people with long-term mental illness. Employment specialists can have an important role in helping to plan for medication changes and in monitoring the effects of medication on performance and comfort levels.

SCHIZOPHRENIA

Schizophrenia is a broad descriptive term that is applied to gross personality disorganization, disruption of thought processes, and severe impairment in psychosocial function. Although the word "schizophrenia" comes from Greek words meaning "split mind," schizophrenia is not related to the disorder commonly called "split personality" (i.e., multiple personality disorder). Schizophrenia is thought to be experienced at some time by about 1% of the U.S. population, involving 2 million people at any one time. According to the *NAMI Advocate* (1994), at any given time 25% of the hospital beds in the United States are occupied by people with schizophrenia. Common myths about schizophrenia are shown in Table 1.

Table 1. Common myths about schizophrenia

- Schizophrenia is a result of bad parenting.
- People with schizophrenia are prone to unpredictable acts of violence.
- Schizophrenia is a single disorder with a known cause.
- Schizophrenia is the same as split personality.
- Someone with a diagnosis of schizophrenia cannot be responsible for his actions.

PROFILE: ALAN

Alan grew up in a big city, where he was an average student and played in the school orchestra. Upon graduating, he began his studies at a small college. His freshman year started well, and his first quarter grades were great. However, when he went home for Christmas his parents noticed that he had lost a lot of weight and spent most of the vacation alone in his room sleeping or staring at the ceiling. Alan had begun to hear voices in his head that told him he would never be successful and the devil was coming to torment him.

He returned to school and stumbled through another quarter of classes. That spring, however, he became convinced that the devil was controlling him through radio waves broadcast via the street lights outside the dorm. His roommate called the student health service when Alan refused to get out of bed for 2 days, alternately muttering to himself and babbling about the devil.

Alan was diagnosed with schizophrenia and hospitalized for 2 months while the doctors identified which medication would best control his symptoms. He was discharged to his parents' home and referred to the local community mental health clinic for outpatient treatment including medication

A common myth is that schizophrenia is the same as split personality.

management and counseling. Now 25, he has been hospitalized twice since his initial psychotic break. He has scars on his hands and wrists as a result of the voices telling him to put his hands in scalding water. He continues to take antipsychotic medication and irregularly attends activities at the mental health center. He has never had a job. Mostly he just hangs around at home. When people meet him, he seems passive and unmotivated and responds slowly to others, but is usually tuned in to the events around him. He reports that he still has hallucinations occasionally, when he is tired or under stress.

Diagnosis of Schizophrenia

Because there is no direct way of testing for schizophrenia, clinicians must rely on symptom patterns for diagnosis. DSM-IV (American Psychiatric Association, 1994) guidelines for diagnosing schizophrenia are as follows:

1. Two or more of the following:
    a. Delusions
    b. Hallucinations
    c. Disorganized speech
    d. Grossly disorganized or catatonic behavior
    e. Negative symptoms (e.g., flattened affect)
2. One or more major areas of functioning such as work, interpersonal relations, or self-care markedly below previous levels
3. Symptoms of illness for at least 6 months
4. Schizoaffective disorder and mood disorder, substance abuse, and medical conditions ruled out as possible causes for the behavior changes

One of the most widely known writers and researchers on schizophrenia, E. Fuller Torrey (1988), suggested the following, simpler guidelines for diagnosing schizophrenia: "Alterations of the senses; an inability to sort and interpret incoming sensations and respond appropriately; delusions and hallucinations; an altered sense of self; and changes in emotions, movements, and behavior" (p. 18).

Most people show "slow and gradual development of symptoms such as social withdrawal, loss of interest in school or work, deteriorating hygiene and grooming, unusual behavior, and/or angry outbursts" (American Psychiatric Association, 1994, p. 282) as they become ill with schizophrenia. It is not always easy to discriminate between schizophrenia and mood disorders, such as bipolar disorder. The DSM-IV definition above requires that other mental disorders be ruled out before a diagnosis of schizophrenia is made. According to Pope and Lipinski (1978), classic schizophrenic symptoms are reported in 20%–50% of validated cases of bipolar disorder. Problems with misdiagnosis can be significant because of the differences in the antipsychotic medication used to treat thought disorders and mood disorders. A person who is mistakenly given Thorazine for misdiagnosed bipolar disorder may experience no improvement, whereas the correct medication may cause rapid improvement.

Schizophrenia is the most common diagnosis for individuals with mental illness involved in employment programs, probably because the residual symptoms experienced by many people with schizophrenia continue to cause difficulties in employment. For example, a study of the Oregon State Supported Employment Programs for people with psychiatric disabilities reported that 52% of the participants were diagnosed as having schizophrenia (Coiner, 1990). In addition, a diagnosis of schizoaffective disorder, which is considered a thought disorder like schizophrenia but also involves some symptoms typical of mood disorders, was the third most common diagnosis, involving an additional 16% of the participants. Danley et al. (1989) profiled four psychosocial rehabilitation programs providing vocational services to people with long-term mental illness and found that 43%–70% of those served had a primary diagnosis of schizophrenia (mean = 56.5%).

Causes of Schizophrenia

The specific cause of schizophrenia is not known, but the following factors are generally regarded as important.

Chemical Imbalance Brain chemicals called *neurotransmitters* are essential for the transfer of messages between nerves that enable people to think and feel in a normal manner. In schizophrenia some of these chemicals, such as dopamine, are out of balance. There is either too much dopamine or the nerves are too sensitive to it. Although the exact cause of chemical imbalances is unknown, the major effect is thought to lie in the limbic system of the brain, which is the system that filters stimuli, decides whether or not they are important, and routes them to the appropriate part of the brain. When the limbic system is not functioning well, the result is that too many messages are experienced at the same time, are received in a garbled fashion, or are not properly routed. A common metaphor for the limbic system is the old-fashioned switchboard operator who physically moves plugs and wires to receive and forward calls. The schizophrenic "switchboard" ignores some calls, overemphasizes others, and sends still others to the wrong receiver. This causes the person to do things like hear mysterious voices, have false and absurd beliefs, and be unable to think logically.

Heredity About one third of the people who get schizophrenia have a close blood relative who also has it. It is thought that this cause involves genetic factors that affect the ability of the brain to maintain a normal chemical balance, rather than indicating dysfunctional parenting styles. Another possible cause is that a slow virus (i.e., one that takes years to cause damage) is transmitted among family members. Other researchers believe that prenatal or birth trauma is the cause of schizophrenia. Researchers at the University of California at Los Angeles (UCLA) identified characteristic signs exhibited by infants who later developed schizophrenia, including a distinct pattern of spurts and lags in weight gain, bone growth, and mental development ("Infants May," 1992).

Stresses Schizophrenia usually begins between the ages of 16 and 30, just when a person is trying to gain emotional and financial independence. It is unclear what role environmental stress plays in the development of schizophrenia because many people live through difficult periods without developing a long-term mental illness. It may be that high levels of stress trigger the disease in people who are already genetically disposed to develop it.

Because it develops at a crucial stage in a person's life, schizophrenia interferes with important stages of maturation, individuation, separation, and educational/vocational development, therefore making vocational rehabilitation a critical part of treatment.

Schizophrenia is more often diagnosed among lower socioeconomic groups (American Psychiatric Association, 1994). This may be related to a lack of upward mobility, the higher stress associated with poverty, or a bias on the part of professionals making the diagnoses. Schizophrenia affects men and women in equal numbers, although the age of onset is earlier with men and their long-term adjustment rate is poorer (American Psychiatric Association, 1994).

Symptoms of Schizophrenia

Schizophrenia typically causes changes in the way the individual interacts with and responds to the environment, including the following:

1. Alterations of the senses [blunted or more acute]
2. Inability to sort and interpret incoming sensations, and an inability therefore to respond appropriately [to incoming stimuli]
3. [Responded to nonexistent stimuli, for example,] delusions and hallucinations
4. Altered sense of self [e.g., being confused about where the body stops and the rest of the world begins]
5. Changes in emotions [i.e., exaggerated, inappropriate, or flattened]
6. Changes in [physical] movements (Torrey, 1988, p. 18)

These internal changes result in changed behaviors, which are then recognized as symptoms of the disease.

The symptoms associated with schizophrenia play three different roles. During the acute phase they are used for diagnostic purposes and their decrease is used as evidence that the chosen treatment is effective. Symptoms that continue after the acute phase (i.e., after treatment has stabilized or reduced the symptoms as much as possible) are called *residual* symptoms. These symptoms may decrease or stay the same over time. It is important for the employment specialist to remember that the presence of residual symptoms is not necessarily an insurmountable obstacle to employment. Many people continue to experience hallucinations, for example, but learn to deal with them on the job and are thus able to maintain employment.

People with schizophrenia are prone to sleep disturbances.

Symptoms that appear or intensify before a relapse or period of decompensation are called *prodromal* symptoms. These differ from person to person, and identifying individual prodromal symptom patterns can be an important step in obtaining employment. One study showed that 70% of people with schizophrenia and 93% of their family members could predict decompensation by changes in behavior (Herz, 1984).

Common symptoms experienced by people with schizophrenia are listed in Table 2.

Treatment of Schizophrenia

The unusual chemical sensitivity of the neurotransmitters in the brain can be partially corrected by the use of antipsychotic medications called *neuroleptics*. The best medication to use and the amount required at a given time will vary depending on the intensity of the illness and the individual's body chemistry. Many people with schizophrenia benefit from medication when the dose adjustments and side effects are properly handled. People who are able to and encouraged to monitor their own symptoms and reactions to medication have a better chance of avoiding negative side effects.

Medication is generally more effective at improving what are known as *positive* symptoms (i.e., those that are added to the person's life, such as hallucinations, aggressive or bizarre behavior, and delusions). *Negative* symptoms (i.e., those missing from the person's life, such as apathy, ambivalence, poverty of thought, and flattened affect) are less responsive to medication and tend to remain as residual effects. However, there is increasing evidence that the newer drugs used to treat schizophrenia (e.g., Clozaril, Risperidone) have a stronger impact on negative symptoms than the more traditional medications.

Most people with acute schizophrenia are hospitalized when first diagnosed because of the time needed to identify the best medication regimen. Once the person is stabilized and the medication is identified, most people return to their communities for ongoing care. Because the mere suppression of symptoms is not usually enough to enable people to successfully reenter the community, supportive counseling and skill rebuilding are also important in the treatment of people with schizophrenia. Much like a person who experiences a physical injury resulting in a long-term disability must deal with both the psychological effects of having a disability as well as the practical aspects of developing compensatory strategies and getting on with life, assistance is needed in adjusting to the residual effects of schizophrenia.

Table 2.   Common symptoms experienced by people with schizophrenia

Bizarre behavior	Social withdrawal
Regression	Fatigue (as a result of sleeplessness)
Agitation	Talking and laughing to self
Hallucinations	Flat emotional response
Delusions	Loss of ego boundaries
Anxiety	Blunted affect
Illogical thinking	Inappropriate affect
Lability	Low motivation
Fear	Poor concentration
Low self-esteem	Suspiciousness
Sleep disturbances	Poor adaptive skills

An analysis of 25 long-term follow-up studies (Stephens, 1978) suggested that over a long period of time (30 years), 25% of people with schizophrenia will recover completely, 35% will be greatly improved and relatively independent, 15% will be improved but require intensive support, 10% will remain the same, and 15% will die (many by suicide). Thus 75% of people with schizophrenia will show substantial improvement over time, with 60% experiencing great improvement and living independently. With the development of new medical treatments along with the increased emphasis on providing support in the community and avoiding institutionalization, it is likely that this percentage rate will rise in time.

The treatment of schizophrenia can be considered to have three phases: acute, continuation, and maintenance and prevention.

The Acute Phase   During the acute phase of the illness, the individual may become psychotic, literally out of touch with reality. During the first acute episode, treatment emphasizes diagnosing the illness, protecting the safety of the individual and those around him, and identifying the most appropriate and effective medical treatment. Medication is usually effective for relieving symptoms, although some people may show only partial recovery and others very little improvement. There is no known reason why medication works on one person and not another, and there are no rules about which medication to try first with a given individual, often causing a delay in identifying the most effective medication. After an effective medication is found, it generally takes 4–6 weeks to provide the full benefit.

The Continuation Phase   The continuation phase begins when maximum improvement has been achieved. During this phase, attempts are made to fade medication levels in order to minimize the impact of side effects such as restlessness (i.e., akathisia), fogged thinking, slurred speech, and tremors of the hands and feet. For individuals who make the greatest improvement on medication during the acute phase, fading their medication levels works better than for those who showed less improvement (Kane, 1988). Some individuals may need to remain at continuation levels indefinitely.

The Maintenance and Prevention Phase   Studies show that continued medication dramatically decreases the risk of relapse. However, there are concerns about side effects that have prompted two approaches to minimizing the amount of medication used: 1) low dose approaches attempt to lower the medication levels as far as possible without the return of symptoms; and 2) targeted or intermittent approaches involve prophylactically increasing medication levels in response to or anticipation of temporary life stresses, while keeping levels as low as possible or discontinuing medication at other times. Some researchers, including Torrey (1988), believe that the danger from the side effects of antipsychotic medication is grossly overstated and that people are much more likely to be undermedicated than they are to experience severe side effects.

Medication for Schizophrenia

Many people with schizophrenia are left with significant residual impairments despite treatment with medication during the acute phase. The goal of ongoing medication therapy is to continue to control symptoms and ward off new acute episodes, while allowing the person a chance to rebuild his skills and his life support structures.

Antipsychotics, the drugs used to treat schizophrenia and other thought disorders, were discovered in France in 1952. Antipsychotics are used to decrease or occasionally eliminate hallucinations, delusions, and agitation during an acute psychotic episode. At lower doses, antipsychotics may continue to reduce symptom levels. Although antipsychotic medications are not tranquilizers, they may appear to have a tranquilizing effect on some people (Torrey, 1988).

Antipsychotics can be taken as tablets or liquids or by injection, depending on the particular drug and the needs and preferences of the individual. Commonly used antipsychotics are Thorazine, Mellaril, Prolixin, Stelazine, Trilafon, Navane, and Haldol. It is important for the employment specialist to assist the individual in communicating with the medical staff regarding doses and timing, because people vary enormously in their sensitivity to these drugs and in the side effects they may develop.

Some side effects, such as drowsiness, restlessness, dry mouth, weight gain, erectile difficulty, and constipation, may be relatively minor, and in some cases, may even be helpful to the medical staff and people with schizophrenia in deciding which drug to prescribe. An individual who is sluggish may benefit from an antipsychotic that sometimes causes restlessness, while another person who is restless may do best on a drug that is associated with drowsiness.

However, other side effects such as tardive dyskinesia (TD), an involuntary movement disorder usually affecting the face, trunk, and limbs, may be severe and disabling. TD occurs more in people who are older and/or have had some brain damage; the longer medication is taken, the more likely TD is to develop (Gorman, 1990). Considered one of the most serious side effects of antipsychotics associated with neuroleptics, TD is generally irreversible. It is impossible to predict who will develop TD, although the prevalence increases with age. Antiparkinsonian medication (e.g., Cogentin) taken to alleviate or prevent tremors and restlessness can also mask the symptoms of TD and make it more difficult to diagnose. Because it is a serious development, clients who are at risk should be routinely examined for evidence of the disease. Although there is no established treatment for TD once it is established, some individuals with TD have improved when switched to another medication (e.g., Clozaril).

Two other common side effects are akinesia (i.e., rigidity and immobility, stooped posture, shuffling gait) and akathisia. These are usually treated with antiparkinsonian agents such as Cogentin, Benadryl, Kemadrin, and Artane or by trying different medication or dosage levels.

A new drug for treating schizophrenia, clozapine (Clozaril), has been successful with many clients who were not helped by traditional antipsychotics. Clozapine has been used in Europe and China for many years and is increasingly being used in the United States. Clozapine's major drawback is that it can cause a dangerous decrease of the white blood cell count (i.e., agranulocytosis), which can be fatal if not detected. Although it has not been proven, clozapine is not thought to cause TD. Therefore, people taking clozapine must be monitored frequently with blood tests. In addition, clozapine is more expensive than other drugs, partly due to the required blood testing. At first Clozapine may cause heavy drowsiness. As of 1995, it is primarily used with people who have not responded well to other medication because of the cost ($4,500–$7,000 per year) and the potentially fatal side effects.

Another new antipsychotic has been approved for use with schizophrenia and is being recommended as first-line therapy for many people (Judd & Rapaport, 1994). Like clozapine, risperidone blocks two neurotransmitter chemicals found in the brain (serotonin and dopamine), whereas traditional medications like Haldol act only on one neurotransmitter. Reports on this medication have been very positive and clinical trials showed improvements in both positive and negative symptoms, with fewer side effects (National Alliance for the Mentally Ill [NAMI], 1994).

For more information on common medications for schizophrenia, there are handbooks available at major bookstores or through NAMI. In addition, mental health centers often have reader-friendly handouts about the medications used by their clients. It is important that employment specialists are knowledgeable about the medication used by an individual and the possible side effects that may have an impact on the person's health and/or employability. The *NAMI Advocate* (available by joining NAMI, 2101 Wilson Blvd., Suite 302, Arlington, VA, 22201; 1-800-950-NAMI) is a source of up-to-date news on medications and other treatment options.

MOOD DISORDERS: MAJOR DEPRESSION AND BIPOLAR DISORDER

Diagnosis of Mood Disorders

The essential feature of mood disorders is disturbance of mood. These mood disturbances can involve depression (i.e., a depressed mood and diminished interest or pleasure in most activities), mania (i.e., a distinct period of elevated, expansive, or irritable mood), or both. Depressive disorders are diagnosed when there are two or more episodes of major depression (i.e., loss of interest and pleasure, depressed mood for 2 weeks, plus other symptoms such as weight loss or gain, sleep disturbances, and loss of energy), or 2 years of ongoing depression without manic episodes. Bipolar disorders are defined as one or more manic episodes, with or without depression (Bipolar I), or a history of major depression along with one or more manic episodes (Bipolar II) (American Psychiatric Association, 1994). Some individuals are considered "hypomanic," experiencing only mild elevation alternating with deep depression. Others are "rapid cyclers," with shorter periods of stability (four or more intense mood episodes per year).

NIMH (1993) estimated that 1.2% of the U.S. adult population have bipolar disorder, and people with major depression or bipolar disorder account for about 12% of those hospitalized for psychiatric disorders. NIMH figures from 1990 showed 5% of the U.S. population (9.2 million) experienced major depression at some time during that year. Many of these 9.2 million individuals are able to maintain stable lives with medical treatment and counseling and do not need or use intensive employment services. Therefore, individuals with mood disorders who are served in employment programs tend to be those who experience greater residual problems from their illness. The Oregon study cited previously showed that of the 24% of supported employment participants diagnosed with mood disorders, 18% had bipolar disorder, and 6% had major depression (Coiner, 1990). In psychosocial rehabilitation vocational programs it is reported that about 15% of the clientele have bipolar disorder and 10%–20% have depression (Danley et al., 1989).

PROFILE: BOB

Bob is a 50-year-old man with a doctorate in education who has bipolar disorder. Since his initial diagnosis 15 years ago (after 10 years of increasingly wide swings between depression and "hyper" behavior), he has been hospitalized several times. He also has obtained and lost several teaching jobs, been married and divorced twice, been evicted from several apartments (either for loud parties or for damaging property), made and lost great deals of money in various business ventures, and been arrested and jailed briefly for contacting his ex-wife who had a restraining order against him.

Bob is generally reliable about taking his lithium, but confesses to enjoying the "hypomania" (i.e., the period of high energy and creativity that occurs just short of true mania) he experiences when he does not take his medication. He is highly intelligent but has difficulty finding and maintaining a job due to his uneven behavior as well as his psychiatric label. When hypomanic, Bob has difficulty completing even one task when he normally could be working on many things. He is currently trying to have his teaching certificate reinstated by the state so he can again apply for teaching jobs. Although uninterested in day treatment or prevocational activities available through the mental health center, he has been enthusiastic about his volunteer placement editing a newsletter produced by the local United Way.

Causes and Symptoms of Mood Disorders

Similar to schizophrenia, it is generally thought that mood disorders (both bipolar and major depression) stem from chemical imbalances. There also seems to be a genetic link to mood disorders, with a higher incidence among people whose family members are also affected. Bipolar disorder occurs equally in women and men while major depression is more commonly diagnosed in women. However, it is not clear whether women actually experience depression more than men or if women are more likely to seek treatment. Some researchers believe that depression is the same disease as bipolar disorder but in a milder form (Andreason, 1984).

Mood disorders usually begin before a person is 30 years old. People with bipolar disorder may experience delusions or hallucinations (especially during a manic phase) simulating schizophrenia, which may result in a misdiagnosis. Most people with bipolar disorder experience cycles of mania and depression with periods of stability in between. It is very unusual to cycle between mania and depression without stable periods, and many people with mood disorders are able to function well during these stable phases. The symptoms commonly experienced by people with mood disorders are outlined in Table 3.

Table 3. Common symptoms experienced by people with mood disorders

Depressive symptoms	Manic symptoms
Decreased sociability	Hyperactivity
Panic	Rapid speech
Phobic reactions	Loud, hard-to-understand speech
Withdrawal	Inflated self-esteem
Inability to concentrate	Reduced need for sleep
Indecisiveness	Increased and flagrant sociability
Slowed thinking	Distractibility
Lethargy	Grandiose feelings
Insomnia or hypersomnia	Buying sprees
Excessive crying	Reckless driving
Feelings of worthlessness	Foolish business investments
Expressions of hopelessness	Atypical, risky sexual behavior

Treatment of Mood Disorders

Like schizophrenia, mood disorders are treated with a combination of psychotropic medication and support counseling. Acute manic episodes with psychotic symptoms may be treated with lithium or antipsychotic medications like those used for schizophrenia. Chronic depression or depressive bipolar phases are generally treated with antidepressant medication. In situations in which antidepressants have not been effective, electric convulsive (i.e., shock) therapy may be tried. Medication is also used between acute episodes of bipolar disorder to maintain stability and avoid relapse.

Medication for Major Depression People with major depression are usually given *antidepressant* drugs, which sustain the action of serotonin and norepinephrine, two chemicals that transmit impulses through the nervous system. Tricyclic or heterocyclic drugs (e.g., Elavil, Tofranil) block the resorption of these messengers by the nerve cells that release them; monoamine oxidase inhibitors (MAOIs), such as Nardil and Parnate, interfere with enzymes that break down the messengers.

Side effects of these medications include drowsiness, lowered blood pressure, heart disturbances, blurred vision, impaired concentration, dry mouth, constipation, nervousness, and dizziness. Due to changes in brain chemistry, people taking MAOI-type medications are unable to metabolize an amino acid called tyramine, found in such common foods as dairy products, red wine, pickles, chocolate, raisins, coffee, and avocados. Eating these foods, or using some types of common over-the-counter medications (e.g., cold or allergy medication) can cause extremely high blood pressure and result in headaches, nausea, strokes, or even death. These foods and substances must be strictly avoided, which may be difficult for individuals who do not remember or focus well. For this reason, MAOIs are less commonly prescribed than other types of medication (Gorman, 1990).

Another common drug used to treat depression, Prozac (fluoxetine), works similarly to the tricyclics but only targets serotonin. Compared to traditional medication used for depression, Prozac has fewer potentially disabling side effects (e.g., insomnia, nausea, diarrhea, headaches, nervousness) and a higher margin of safety from overdoses, and is also effective in relieving anxiety disorders, panic attacks, and obsessive-compulsive behavior. Since its introduction in 1988, Prozac has become one of the most commonly prescribed medications for the treatment of depression (Yudofsky, 1991).

Medication for Bipolar Disorder As mentioned previously, acute manic or depressive episodes are often treated with antipsychotic or antidepressive medication, whereas lithium is often used on an ongoing basis to maintain stability and avoid relapse. Lithium, a salt found in rock deposits and mineral waters throughout the world, does not cause addiction and the body does not develop a tolerance to it. Common types of lithium are Lithium Carbonate, Lithane, Eskalith, and Lithobid. Side effects often include drowsiness and hand tremors, but may be ameliorated with side-effect medication.

It should be noted that lithium has a relatively narrow *therapeutic window*, meaning the difference between an effective dose and a toxic dose is fairly small. People taking lithium are advised to have their blood levels tested frequently. Those taking lithium and those around them must be aware of the signs of toxicity: weakness, lack of coordination, staggering, muscle twitching, or fainting. Once a person has become stabilized at the therapeutic level he can decrease his blood level monitoring.

Research has shown that divalproex sodium, a drug commonly used to treat seizure disorders, is effective in relieving the symptoms of acute mania and may be used as an alternative treatment for the 30%–40% of individuals with bipolar disorder who do not respond to or cannot tolerate lithium (National Alliance for the Mentally Ill [NAMI], 1994).

PERSONALITY DISORDERS

Personality disorders involve "an enduring pattern of inner experience and behavior that deviates markedly from the expectations of the individual's culture, is pervasive and inflexible...is stable over time, and leads to distress or impairment" (American Psychiatric Association, 1994, p. 629). These patterns usually originate in childhood, develop in adolescence, and persist through adult life despite treatment. For this reason, the employment specialist needs to identify specific jobs and work environments that accommodate the individual's functional limitations.

Personality disorders are much less prevalent than schizophrenic or mood disorders, but they are typically so debilitating that they cause impairment throughout a person's life (McCue & Katz-Garris, 1983). It is not known what causes personality disorders although some types are associated with childhood abuse. People with personality disorders have difficulty seeing their maladaptive behavior, and are therefore unwilling to change their behavior patterns. They tend not to be insightful regarding their illness. Some individuals are characterized as having both an Axis I diagnosis (e.g., schizophrenia) and an Axis II diagnosis involving a personality disorder (e.g., compulsive personality disorder).

According to Beck, Freeman, and Associates (1990), people with personality disorders are among the most difficult to treat because of the long-term nature of their problems, their frequent participation in rehabilitation through pressure from others (e.g., family, the legal system), and their reluctance or inability to change. Common approaches to treating personality disorders include psychotherapy and the provision of therapeutic, structured settings (e.g., residential programs). With the exception of antisocial, schizotypal, and borderline personality disorders, people with personality disorders rarely require hospitalization (American Psychiatric Association, 1994). Psychotropic medication is sometimes used with people who have schizotypal and borderline types of personality disorders. Because by definition people with personality disorders have dysfunctional behavior patterns that are inflexible and enduring, attempts to make major changes in these behaviors are rarely successful. As a result, careful job matching and/or restructuring may be a more effective approach.

The DSM-IV groups personality disorders into three clusters based on the primary behavior pattern.

Cluster A includes paranoid, schizoid, and schizotypal disorders. People with these disorders often appear odd or eccentric.

Cluster B includes antisocial, borderline, histrionic, and narcissistic personality disorders. People with these disorders often appear dramatic, emotional, or erratic, and have little sense of right or wrong.

Cluster C includes avoidant, dependent, obsessive-compulsive, and passive-aggressive disorders. People with these disorders often appear anxious or fearful.

Paranoid Personality Disorder

Paranoid personality disorder is characterized by suspiciousness and mistrust, hypersensitivity, and restricted affect (i.e., an inability to show emotion of any kind). These individuals interpret other peoples' motives as malevolent, are often argumentative, and may fixate on ideas that have no basis in reality. They read hidden meanings into common words or acts, bear grudges, and usually think someone is out to get them. In general, these people are not particularly insightful.

People with paranoid personality disorder highly desire independence and self-sufficiency. Improving coping skills, increasing confidence in different situations, learning to realistically evaluate potential threats, and learning to identify those in the environment who can be trusted are all important approaches in supporting people with this disorder. The APA (1994) reported that 2%–10% of those served in mental health centers were diagnosed with paranoid personality disorder.

Schizoid Personality Disorder

Schizoid personality disorder is characterized by emotional aloofness, indifference, and detachment from social relationships. People with this disorder show little enthusiasm, energy, or motivation, and are often indifferent to the approval or criticism of others. They may have difficulty becoming involved in the employment process and respond best to approaches that are direct, simple, unemotional, impersonal, and to the point. Ongoing contact by the employment specialist is often necessary to sustain the involvement of the client in the job.

Schizotypal Personality Disorder

People with schizotypal personality disorder generally experience magical thinking, social isolation, recurrent illusions, odd speech, inadequate rapport, suspiciousness, undue social anxiety, and/or a pattern of discomfort with close relationships. They look, sound, and act eccentric and odd. Challenging their belief system is usually ineffective. It may be helpful to use structured sessions to teach socially appropriate behaviors and techniques for ignoring bizarre thoughts, rather than trying to change the person's internal belief system through logical discussion. Clarifying and emphasizing reward systems (e.g., work results in pay) may also be useful.

Antisocial Personality Disorder

Antisocial personality disorder is characterized by continuous and chronic antisocial behavior in which the rights of others are violated, including running away, fighting, cruelty to animals or people, stealing, lying, fire setting, recklessness, forced sexual activity, and property destruction. It is associated with low socioeconomic status and urban settings. The APA (1994) estimated 1% of women and 3% of men have antisocial personality disorder in the general population. This figure increases from 3% to 30% in clinical settings, and much higher in substance abuse treatment centers and the prison system.

A person with antisocial personality disorder is distrustful of authority and often deceitful, but civil, engaging, and charming when he wants something. Symptoms often decrease somewhat when the client reaches his 40s.

PROFILE: DAN

Dan, 26, was referred to the mental health center when he was released from jail after serving time for assault. It was his third arrest in as many years (although the charges were dropped in the other cases). Dan's history shows a pattern of disruptive, aggressive behavior since childhood. His parents stated that they "never could handle him." Dan was disruptive in school—frequently skipping school and getting in fights—although his IQ score was above average. He also started drinking and using marijuana and other drugs while in his teens and quit school when he was 16.

After quitting school, Dan joined the army where he got his general equivalency diploma and was trained as a cook, but was discharged early because of drinking, missing work, and fighting. He then returned to his hometown and got a job at a restaurant managed by a friend. Within a few months he quit the job because of an argument with his friend about coming to work late.

Dan continued to get high on alcohol and drugs several times a week and held 5 jobs over the next 3 years. In each case, he would quit after an argument with the boss or would be fired for poor attendance or his "bad attitude." Dan says he doesn't worry about finding another cooking job because they are easy to get, although he has currently been unemployed for several months.

Dan's personal life is no better than his employment situation. He has lived with two different women. He left the first because he "was bored with her," although she was pregnant. He has never seen his child and has no interest in doing so. His second partner left him after several abusive episodes. Dan denies that his behavior is unusual or problematic and typically blames others for the problems he encounters. He does not feel that his use of drugs and alcohol is a problem, and he is quick to point out that he has maintained employment in the past for up to 18 months while using.

The most effective way to work with people who have antisocial personality disorder is to identify the person's goals (even if they do not match the employment specialist's goals), and specifically relate actions to the likelihood of achieving them. For example, a person may not be interested in learning to respond appropriately to feedback from the boss just because it is a good work skill until the skill is related to the person's goal of moving into a promotional position. It often works well if the employment specialist helps the person develop a list of pros and cons related to several possible courses of action and together they can go over the possible consequences rather than the employment specialist prescribing action.

Davis (1990) suggested that to work effectively with an antisocial person, the employment specialist should possess self-assurance, objectivity, a relaxed and nondefensive personal style, a clear sense of limits, and a strong sense of humor.

Borderline Personality Disorder

Borderline personality disorder is perhaps the most common personality disorder seen in vocational programs, and clients who have it are some of the most difficult with whom to work (Beck et al., 1990). It should be noted that *borderline* in this disorder refers to the border between neurosis (e.g., mild mental illness) and psychosis (i.e., major mental illness), not between illness and wellness.

People with a diagnosis of borderline personality disorder show instability in mood, interpersonal behavior, and self-image. They are impulsive, often appear lost, lack a cohesive and stable sense of self, and have a pattern of unstable and intense relationships. They are very sensitive to environmental circumstances,

becoming fearful and angry when faced with separation or a loss of external structure. Many people with borderline personality disorder are survivors of childhood
abuse or neglect. They can attack others with intense anger and physical fights, or
turn their anger on themselves and become suicidal. The abuse of drugs and/or
alcohol is common; as is undermining positive changes just as a goal is within
reach. Of those diagnosed with this disorder, 75% are women (American Psychiatric Association, 1994).

Arguing with or confronting a person with borderline personality disorder is
not the answer. They generally need people in the workplace who can stay neutral
and provide calm, methodical support rather than responding to each crisis. It is
important to establish trustworthiness by communicating clearly, assertively, and
honestly. Making sure that verbal and nonverbal cues are consistent and following
through on agreements (Pretzer, 1990) are two additional factors an employment
specialist needs to address. Consistency and limit setting are key approaches.

Histrionic Personality Disorder

People with histrionic personality disorder exhibit overly dramatic behavior, ex-
cessive emotions, problems with interpersonal relationships, and difficulties with
sustained attention to detail. Meinz (1988) pointed out that people with histrionic
personality disorder may be charming in brief contact and usually do well in jobs
that involve brief contact with customers, such as hostessing.

Narcissistic Personality Disorder

Narcissistic personality disorder involves an inflated sense of self-importance and
the exaggeration of achievements and talents. Narcissistic people tend to be overly
sensitive to defeat, criticism, and evaluation by others. The individuals may also
be preoccupied with fantasies of success, power, beauty, and brilliance, and will
generally lack empathy. The APA (1994) reported that 50%–75% of those with
narcissistic personality disorder are men. It may be helpful to relate activities to
the person's sense of self-importance, as well as to provide structure and clear
expectations.

Avoidant Personality Disorder

Because of low self-esteem, people with avoidant personality disorder are hyper-
sensitive to rejection, unwilling to enter into interpersonal relationships, often feel
inadequate, and withdraw socially. Usually underachievers who are very sensitive
to criticism and frightened to make decisions, people with avoidant characteristics
tend to present themselves as evasive, secretive, and unrevealing, and will make a
commitment only when they are assured of a favorable outcome that protects their
fears. These individuals often have a history of brief employment experiences.
However, when they find a job in which they feel safe they are likely never to
leave. People with avoidant personality disorder need support that respects their
need for distance and allows them to avoid criticism.

Dependent Personality Disorder

Dependent personality disorder is one of the most common personality disorders
seen in mental health centers (American Psychiatric Association, 1994). As the
name suggests, a common characteristic of this disorder is a pervasive and exces-
sive need to be taken care of. The client allows others to assume the responsibility

for major life areas because he is unsure of his own decision-making ability and does not trust his own thinking. Because of his fear of loss of support or approval, the client is often vulnerable to abuse. He may volunteer to do things that are unpleasant or demeaning in order to get others to like him. Besides being alert to the possibility of exploitation, the employment specialist should provide support and a safe environment while setting limits on the relationship.

Obsessive-Compulsive Personality Disorder

Symptoms of obsessive-compulsive personality disorder include the persistent ritualized thought and behavior patterns often involving emotional restriction, dominance, indecisiveness, and preoccupation with orderliness, perfection, and control. Obsessive-compulsive people are ruled by shoulds and musts, and may also have Axis I diagnoses of depression or anxiety. They manage time poorly and attend to detail and rules to the point where the reason for doing the activity is lost. Of those served in mental health centers, 3%–10% have this disorder, with twice as many women as men represented (American Psychiatric Association, 1994).

Antidepressant drugs (notably Prozac) are sometimes used to treat obsessive-compulsive disorder. The employment specialist may need to help the person list the pros and cons of fixed beliefs in order to alter or reinterpret underlying assumptions about behavior and emotions.

Passive-Aggressive Personality Disorder

Indirect resistance to demands for adequate performance in occupational or social functioning is a common characteristic of passive-aggressive personality disorder. People who have passive-aggressive disorder often use "yes, but ..." phrasing, are difficult to please, and have a sullen demeanor. They resent, oppose, and resist demands by others, and respond with procrastination, forgetfulness, stubbornness, and intentional inefficiency.

A collaborative approach that involves analysis of the potential costs and benefits of possible plans may allow employment specialists to work around the resistance typically shown by people with passive-aggressive personality disorder. It may also be useful to include the client in as much decision making as possible.

VOCATIONAL OBSTACLES RELATED TO SYMPTOMS AND SIDE EFFECTS

Long-term mental illness affects emotional, cognitive, social, and basic task functions. Having active symptoms does *not* mean that a person is unable to work, but the nature of the symptoms being experienced provides important information to use in identifying appropriate employment situations for an individual. Many people with long-term mental illness experience some combination of the following symptoms that affect their ability to maintain employment.

Delusions and Hallucinations

Delusions and hallucinations are very common symptoms associated with schizophrenia and also can be found with bipolar disorder. *Delusions* involve the individual believing and acting on false assumptions about himself or things and people in the environment. For example, a common delusion is that an individual is being controlled through thoughts broadcast by others. *Hallucinations* involve nonexistent sensory input (e.g., hearing voices, seeing things, smelling scents that are not detected by others in the environment). Hallucinations can affect any of the senses although auditory hallucinations (i.e., hearing voices) are more common than those involving other senses. In some cases a stimulus may actually be present in the environment but the individual inaccurately interprets it (e.g., he sees an approaching car as a demon).

By diverting attention to internal stimuli, delusions and hallucinations interfere with both the client's work tasks and personal life. Discussing hallucinations or delusions with others in the workplace can also inhibit acceptance and limit social integration. Many people continue to experience delusions and hallucinations past the point where other symptoms are stable, but they may learn to ignore or otherwise control these stimuli while in the work environment. Some people enjoy their hallucinations and delusions and may be reluctant to have them controlled. This can lead the person to discontinue taking medication in order to continue hearing the voices or seeing intense colors.

Distractibility

Distractibility is associated with many diagnoses and can be either the result of the illness or a side effect of the medication taken to treat the illness. Distractibility makes it difficult to attend to the tasks involved on the job. The employment specialist may need to provide additional structure and/or stronger cues on the job to assist the individual in being successful. For example, a worker who has difficulty concentrating on a filing task may need to have clear cues so that if he is taken off the task he can regain his place quickly. Changes in distractibility levels are also important feedback for the worker and/or the employment specialist to give the medical consultant regarding levels of medication or possible decompensation.

Distractibility makes it difficult to attend to the tasks involved on the job.

Social Isolation or Withdrawal

Social isolation or withdrawal is associated with many diagnoses and interferes with the individual's interpersonal relationships. It may also cause problems with task completion because the worker who is focusing on how uncomfortable he feels while interacting with others often is distracted and performs poorly. In addition, workers who are socially isolated miss out on important information regarding the behavioral rules (usually unwritten) of the workplace. Most of us learn how to dress, where and when to eat lunch, and common topics of coffee-break conversation from talking with co-workers. People then can earn reinforcement (or at least escape punishment) by following those rules. People who have difficulty establishing or maintaining personal relationships may be capable of meeting the job requirements but might still lose their jobs because they are not meeting the social requirements.

Peculiar or Bizarre Behaviors

Peculiar behavior is mainly associated with schizophrenia or personality disorders, although people with bipolar disorder can exhibit unusual behaviors while in a manic phase. Peculiar or bizarre behaviors can present problems with co-workers, employers, and customers, and should be an important consideration in identifying possible jobs. As with hallucinations, many people can learn to control peculiar behavior patterns while in the work environment.

Suspiciousness and Paranoia

Paranoia, associated mainly with schizophrenia and personality disorders, interferes with the worker's ability to perceive and integrate praise and/or criticism. The employer who stops to compliment the worker on completion of a task may think she is providing positive attention, but the worker may interpret the employer's comments as a veiled threat to fire him. Therefore, the worker with paranoia is unable to understand and enjoy what is a major source of reinforcement on the job for most people—the positive attention of co-workers and supervisors. In addition, paranoia may cause people to behave in suspicious or bizarre ways, presenting a significant barrier to establishing interpersonal relationships on the job.

Decreased Concern for Hygiene

Poor hygiene is associated with all categories of mental illness and has detrimental effects on job acquisition and interpersonal relationships. As with many of the functional effects, changes in hygiene levels are important precursors of decompensation for many people.

Physical Restlessness

Physical restlessness is generally associated with the manic phase of bipolar disorder, but it can also occur as a side effect of neuroleptic drugs taken for schizophrenia or other disorders. It can prevent a client from performing steadily and consistently, especially in jobs that demand steady performance, yet do not provide outlets for physical activity. Adjustments in medication and dosage may control or lessen physical restlessness.

Sleep Disturbances

Common in both schizophrenia and mood disorders, sleep disturbances create a physiological barrier to good performance. This symptom may take the form of insomnia or oversleeping. A marked change in sleeping patterns is often an early warning of decompensation. Employment specialists must take special care in considering shift work that will change sleeping patterns.

Dysfunctional Personality Traits

Emotional coldness, disturbances in interpersonal relationships, antisocial behaviors, lack of control, and self-destructive urges are all examples of dysfunctional traits that occur in personality disorders. Many of them are behaviors incompatible with work activity or establishing relationships on the job. These behaviors are difficult to control and the employment specialist must work around them when assessing and modifying jobs, although some practitioners have reported success in using a cognitive therapy approach to help individuals with personality disorders modify their behavior (Beck et al., 1990).

Impairment of Insight and Judgment

Impairment of insight is common to all classifications of mental illness and is a major reason for needing employment support. A person with poor insight and judgment may have difficulty with problem solving, understanding the cues present in the environment or provided by other people, setting occupational goals, and selecting behavior that is appropriate to a given setting. For some individuals, these problems are caused or exacerbated by their medication and adjusting the dosage may improve functioning levels. However, in others the difficulties are a reflection of the illness and must be compensated for. The employment specialist can often assist by building structure into the job in order to minimize the insight and judgment required.

Slowed Gait, Awkward Movements, and Blurred Vision

People with long-term mental illness may walk slowly and/or awkwardly because of their impaired ability to process environmental cues or as a side effect of medication. Physical manifestations vary across individuals; clients may experience bizarre-looking movements including goose stepping or pronounced waddling, poor motor coordination, hand tremors, or blurred vision. Employment specialists should assist clients to identify physical limitations before doing career development and job matching.

The functional limitations described have been summarized to encourage the employment specialist to look at each client as an individual who brings unique strengths and challenges with him in his search for employment, rather than as a collection of static symptoms associated with a particular diagnosis. Each of the limitations listed above presents an obstacle worth considering in the employment process. The skilled employment specialist can address each obstacle with a combination of skill building, reinforcement, adjustment in medication, judicious job development and selection, and support on the job.

CONCLUSION

In many cases, the most disabling factors associated with mental illness are not the primary symptoms (e.g., hallucinations, paranoia) but the secondary symptoms that result from reduced levels of functioning and increased social withdrawal (McGurrin, 1994). Lack of motivation and goal-directedness, hopelessness, poverty, fear of failure, difficulty with social relationships, low self-esteem, poor job-seeking and job-keeping skills, and poor work habits pose significant barriers to employment for many people with mental illness. Professionals whose training and experience have involved people with mental illness will be familiar with all these issues through nonvocational contacts with their clients. Employment specialists whose vocational experience comes from working with people with developmental disabilities will notice that although the disability label is different, many of the issues are the same, including distractibility, poor hygiene, poor work history, social isolation, and poor judgment and decision making. Following chapters illustrate specific effective approaches to providing employment support, some adapted from techniques used with people with developmental disabilities and some that have been developed specifically for the support of people with long-term mental illness.

2

MENTAL ILLNESS AND SUBSTANCE ABUSE

The term *dual diagnosis* is often used to describe individuals who experience concurrent problems with mental illness and substance abuse. These clients present a unique challenge to the employment specialist and to the service system as a whole.

Substance abuse and mental illness share many characteristics. They are both considered chronic, treatable, and episodic problems that are socially stigmatizing and create an impact on the individual's family. Both mental illness and substance abuse have an effect on cognitive abilities as well as emotions, and both can have life-threatening consequences. Treatment for both involves a combination of medication, education, skills training, counseling, family involvement, and peer support.

It is not always easy to separate the symptoms of substance abuse and mental illness. Some people experience psychotic symptoms solely as a result of their substance abuse. These generally remit once the person stops using substances for a period of time. Other people with mental illness may use substances in amounts that most people would not find particularly problematic, but have major functioning problems because of the effect of the drugs on an already damaged brain.

PROFILE: FRAN

Fran was referred to the local mental health center by a vocational rehabilitation (VR) counselor who was trying to help Fran get a job but believed Fran needed ongoing mental health services. Fran was diagnosed with schizoaffective disorder and given medication to control hallucinations. She has been unsuccessful in finishing college after becoming ill and has returned to her hometown in search of employment and to "start her life over." She is currently living with her parents.

At first Fran denied using alcohol or other drugs. Missed appointments (especially right after Social Security checks came), increased confusion, and a lack of productive activities led the case manager to suspect otherwise. When

29

confronted, Fran admitted to drinking "a few beers every once in a while and maybe smoking a little dope," but she said that all her friends did these things and they helped her have a good time and not feel like a "mental." In addition, Fran feels that using marijuana alleviates many side effects (e.g., restlessness, anxiety) caused by the medication she takes, and she does not see what is wrong with it. Using has enabled Fran, and her parents, to avoid dealing with the fact that she has a mental illness that makes it necessary to reconsider the plans Fran had made for her future (i.e., go to college, get an M.B.A. and a management position in business, marry, raise a family while enjoying a comfortable income). Fran has attempted suicide twice, both times while intoxicated.

People with mental illness abuse substances for many of the same reasons other people do, but some reasons are more prominent, including the following:

- People with mental illness may be more susceptible to the addictive effect of substances because of the abnormalities in their brain chemistry (Evans & Sullivan, 1990).
- People with mental illness may feel that using substances helps them deal with some of the products of their illness (e.g., social awkwardness, anger, stress, anx-

"People in this town are out to get me!"

It is not always easy to separate the effects of substance abuse and mental illness.

iety, physical sensations, depression, voices, paranoia) or with the side effects of prescribed medication (e.g., stiffness, restlessness, a feeling of mental or emotional numbing) (Wingerson, 1994). These individuals are often described as *self-medicating.*

• People with mental illness may have difficulty understanding the difference between legal and illegal drugs or the dangers presented by substance abuse. Some, particularly those with antisocial personality disorder, may find the dangerous lifestyle of the drug scene to be attractive because they seek and enjoy high-risk behavior.

• Because of limited access to healthy peers, people with long-term mental illness may spend time with individuals who use or abuse substances. For example, a person whose delusions or poor social skills make her unwelcome at the local bowling alley may find acceptance on a bar stool or street corner with others who are using.

Many practitioners say clients with dual diagnosis are their most difficult for several reasons. First, the disorders have a synergistic effect on each other: Many residual symptoms of mental illness (e.g., slowed thinking, flattened affect) tend to increase with substance abuse. Clients with dual diagnosis use hospital emergency rooms and require hospitalization more than people with mental illness who do not use drugs (Evans & Sullivan, 1990).

Second, it is very difficult for a practitioner to diagnose the symptoms experienced by an individual with both mental illness and a substance abuse problem, which makes it difficult to determine appropriate treatment. A person with an undiagnosed mental illness often has a poor response to substance abuse treatment, just as a person with a substance abuse problem may not respond well to treatment for mental illness.

Third, at times the treatment for mental illness and the treatment for substance abuse can be in direct opposition, and it can often be difficult to determine which treatment should take precedence. Substance abuse counselors have sometimes advised clients who take antipsychotic medication for schizophrenia to avoid any medication. As a result, clients may not follow through on treatment for their mental illness (Evans & Sullivan, 1990).

Fourth, using a substance (e.g., alcohol) changes how the liver and other body systems metabolize medication, making it difficult to adjust the dosage accurately to get the strongest effect on psychiatric symptoms with the fewest side effects.

Some service providers may establish guidelines that set requirements (often 90 days) for sobriety to be considered for employment services. Other programs may allow access to some services by those who are still using substances (although not on site) or whose abstinence is more recent. These services may be day treatment activities, or participation in work crews or other, more sheltered work environments. This flexibility engages the client who may be struggling with substance abuse by providing structure and support while she participates in substance abuse treatment, but at the same time limits access to job placement and support until sobriety is reached. In either case, it is important to define and communicate agency policy clearly with regard to substance abuse and users (e.g., criteria to receive services, types of substance abuse treatment available by the agency or referral, the consequences of relapse ineligibility for services).

IMPLICATIONS FOR ASSESSMENT AND EMPLOYMENT ACTIVITIES

Assessing for Substance Abuse: Part of Every Mental Health Evaluation

Because substance abuse is very common among people with long-term mental illness (Wingerson [1994] stated that nearly 50% of people with schizophrenia abuse alcohol and/or other drugs), evaluation of substance abuse is critical when it becomes apparent that a problem does exist, and should then continue on an ongoing basis. An evaluation should include the determination of the amount of the abused substance(s), frequency, duration, current use and circumstances of use, type of substance(s), the client's family history, and hospitalizations (if any). Assessment should include not only alcohol and illegal drugs, but also over-the-counter medications, prescription medications, nicotine, and caffeine. These are often overlooked, although they can have serious effects on symptoms and treatment. Mental health centers (and work settings) are full of people who consume multiple cups of coffee each day without acknowledging the negative effect of high doses of caffeine, such as increased paranoia (Torrey, 1988). In most cases this assessment will have happened well before the individual is referred for vocational services, but the employment specialist should be aware of the signs of substance abuse so that appropriate support can be provided.

Understanding Problems in the Dual Disability Context

Mental health treatment and substance abuse treatment must be done in a dual diagnosis context (i.e., with full consideration of the dual diagnosis situation) to be

"Hey, who drank all the coffee?"

Mental health centers are full of people who consume multiple cups of coffee each day without acknowledging the negative effects.

effective. The following considerations are recommended by Evans and Sullivan (1990) and Nikkel and Fujita (1991) for employment specialists. Table 1 summarizes the general considerations with clients with dual diagnosis.

Focus on Specifics   People with mental illness and substance abuse problems often benefit from a structured, behavioral counseling approach that involves setting specific short-term goals, rather than holding out for insight or enlightenment. This is especially true when both disorders are present and the client may have significant cognitive impairment. Goals may include stability and small improvement rather than long-term change.

Education Must Be Concrete and Repetitive   Clients with dual diagnosis often need repeated and concrete input before learning can take place. A highly structured environment that provides consistent and frequent feedback is often the most effective. This is true on the job as well as in the employment specialist's office.

Emphasize Clear Communication   People with long-term mental illness frequently have difficulty accurately interpreting and understanding other people's attempts to communicate with them. Past or current substance abuse does nothing to enhance communication skills and generally makes things worse. Therefore, the employment specialist working with clients with dual diagnosis should communicate rules, goals, plans, information, and feedback as clearly as possible. Using different modalities may help (e.g., providing written reminders of agreed-upon goals and activities as a follow-up to discussion). The need for clear communication must be considered in the job matching and employer education process, as well as in provision of employment support.

View Client Behavior as Functional   It may be useful to examine the function of the using behavior when attempting to help people with mental illness change their abuse of substances by asking the following questions: Is it to seek attention? Reduce symptoms? Escape anxiety or boredom? Earn the respect of peers? Teaching alternative approaches and improving skills may be an important part of treatment for a person with dual diagnosis, even after she is stable enough to consider employment.

Confrontation May Need to Be Gentle   People with mental illness may not be able to tolerate the level of confrontation often used in substance abuse treatment. This may be a result of being stressed by expressed emotion (common with schizophrenia, which causes difficulty in filtering and organizing input); an inability to recognize and deal with the trauma of past abuse (common with borderline personality disorder); or other, similar reasons. Rather than intense confrontation, people may benefit most from a gentler, repetitive level of work (Nikkel & Fujita, 1991).

Table 1.   General considerations with the client with dual diagnosis

- Focus on specifics. Goals must be explicit and gradual.
- Education must be concrete and repetitive. Maintain a lot of structure.
- Emphasize clear communication.
- Look at client behavior as functional.
- Confrontation may need to be gentle.
- Progress may be slower than for other populations. Efforts must be consistent and persistent.
- Emphasize positive feedback rather than negative sanctions.
- Never cover up for a client who has been using substances.
- Coordinate with others providing treatment and/or support.

Sources: Evans & Sullivan (1990); Nikkel & Fujita (1991).

Progress May Be Slower than for Other Populations People who are struggling to deal with both mental illness and substance abuse may only be capable of slow and sporadic progress. The cyclical nature of mental illness, as well as the impaired judgment and cognition impede the client's ability to benefit from substance abuse treatment, while continued substance abuse may interfere with stabilizing the symptoms of mental illness. Insight-oriented therapy might be very beneficial for other clients but is ineffective with clients whose illness may preclude insight. The employment specialist must assume that resolving issues through a meaningful counseling or problem-solving session does not necessarily mean that he will not have to repeat the whole thing next week.

Consequently, treatment and support efforts must be consistent and persistent. Employment specialists should actively reach out to clients and avoid depending solely on the client's ability to initiate participation and recognize that people may need to drop in and out of treatment. Progress may be obvious with a long-range perspective but invisible in the short run. Employment specialists must be prepared for inconsistent participation and try not to use this manifestation of the disability as a reason to drop participants or deny services.

Emphasize Positive Feedback Rather than Negative Sanctions Many clients have limited sources of positive reinforcement in their lives and cannot afford to lose access to the ones they have. The best treatment should provide both corrective feedback and opportunities to increase reinforcement.

Never Cover Up for a Client Who Has Been Using If an employment specialist suspects substance abuse, it is important to ask the client about it and confront her with the problem. To do otherwise enables the client to avoid taking responsibility for her actions and may jeopardize her employment or her participation in vocational programs (Furlong et al., 1994).

Coordinate with Others Providing Treatment and/or Support Because the disability cuts across most areas of functioning, most people with long-term mental illness and substance abuse problems benefit when services and the efforts of service providers are coordinated. This is especially true when dealing with an individual with dual diagnosis because the type of treatment used for substance abuse may be antithetical to the mental illness treatment.

Identifying Appropriate Substance Abuse Treatment

It may be difficult for the employment specialist, whose area of expertise is not substance abuse, to identify appropriate treatment or support for clients with dual diagnosis. Some individuals (e.g., those whose bipolar symptoms are currently well controlled) can profit from traditional substance abuse treatment. However, it is important to make sure that the treatment emphasizes the difference between prescribed and nonprescribed drugs and the value in continuing medical treatment of the mental illness (Evans & Sullivan, 1990). Self-help groups (e.g., Alcoholics Anonymous) can be useful if the sponsor and group are knowledgeable about the client's mental illness and the prescription distinction is made.

However, some people with long-term mental illness may not do well in groups because of the important role of self-analysis, the possible discomfort with disclosure, and their need to sustain attention over an extended period (Evans & Sullivan, 1990). The decision either to seek specialized treatment or try generic programs depends on the need and functioning level of the individual concerned, as well as the resources available in the community. Evans and Sullivan (1990) offered suggestions on modifying the standard 12-step approach developed by Alcoholics Anonymous (AA) to accommodate people with various diagnoses. In many cases it will be beneficial to provide a great deal of support for the individual joining a group by describing what the meetings are like, helping her find a sponsor who understands the dual issues, accompanying her to open meetings, and role playing how to participate in the meetings.

There are some situations in which clients will need specially coordinated treatment for both mental illness and substance abuse. These are often situations where the mental illness interferes with the person's ability to comprehend information and translate it into behavior change. Occasionally, traditional substance abuse treatment approaches (e.g., demands to bring up and confront past events) may increase the severity of symptoms and destabilize the individual. In other cases, a person with mental illness may disrupt the other substance abuse clients, or the substance abuse treatment program may not have the resources to help the individual also manage her mental illness (e.g., there is no psychiatrist on staff to prescribe and monitor antipsychotic medication).

IMPLICATIONS FOR LONG-TERM STABILITY AND SUPPORT

In theory, most people with mental illness and substance abuse problems will be relatively stable before becoming involved in vocational activities (although there may be individuals with undiagnosed substance abuse problems who are employed). Therefore, the employment specialist may have a very significant role in relapse (i.e., decompensation) prevention planning. Long-term care and support are important components of both mental illness and substance abuse treatment.

Developing a relapse prevention plan starts with identifying the specific patterns of behavior that typically precede relapse. Evans and Sullivan (1990) wrote that the best predictors of relapse are stressful life events (e.g., losing an important person to death, divorce, or moving); increased thinking errors or distorted thinking; the lack of positive activities; positive expectations for using substances (e.g., "I'm going to enjoy drinking champagne at Susie's wedding this weekend"); peer pressure; and interpersonal conflict. For many people, having access to money (whether expected or unexpected) is a reliable precursor of using. Individuals may also have other idiosyncratic behaviors or life events (e.g., anniversary of the hospitalization, changes in schedules, special events) that tend to precede relapse. It is often helpful for the client and the employment specialist to identify these specific triggers and develop positive ways to deal with the impulse to use. These procedures can be reviewed often and summarized on cue cards.

Skills training may be an important component in helping clients achieve a balanced lifestyle. Having access to healthy activities with nonusing peers helps clients avoid the individuals and environments that were supporting their substance abuse.

Involving as many people as possible in providing support for stability will increase the likelihood of success. This may include getting the client involved in 12-step support groups, setting up or gaining access to pro-recovery peer groups, and working with family members. Arranging for the client to check in with one other person (besides the counselor, the employer, or family member) each day has been a successful treatment component in helping people avoid relapses (Nikkel & Fujita, 1991). This person could be a volunteer from church, a neighbor, another client, or anyone who is willing to have a brief daily chat about the issues of staying sober and dealing positively with mental illness. Family members may be able to provide support, or they may be dealing with their own substance abuse issues. If the whole family drinks or uses drugs, becoming sober may mean separating from the family.

It is important to help the client, and other significant people in her life, make a plan for dealing with relapse. Who gets called first? What are early treatment options? What are the fall-back approaches? What will the employer's role be? These are all important questions the employment specialist must be prepared to answer. Hoping that relapse will not happen is not enough. It is much smarter to assume that things will eventually fall apart, and set up a safety net that will limit the long-term impact of the relapse by minimizing its duration. Support plans need to be made around the client's average or worst likely level of functioning rather than around what she can do at her best level of functioning.

CONCLUSION

Working with people who have both a mental illness and substance abuse problems presents a special challenge to the employment specialist. The synergistic effect of the disorders tends to increase the severity of symptoms and to slow the response to treatment. The coordination of multiple service systems and treatment programs may require a significant investment of time and energy. Appropriate treatment for individuals with dual diagnosis may not be available in a given community. Nonetheless, supportive vocational programs and skilled employment specialists can play a major role in promoting recovery and stability.

3

FAMILIES AND CULTURAL INFLUENCES

Ever since Alex came home from his lengthy hospitalization 5 years ago, his family had watched him shuffle and sleep through the days. In the beginning, they had encouraged him to attend activities at the mental health center, but stopped because it did not seem to help him and it was a lot of work to get him to go. Soon it became easier for his family to let Alex do whatever he chose, which usually was watching television, smoking cigarettes, and napping. Occasionally, he did simple household chores (at his mother's request) and dutifully attended family or neighborhood gatherings. His parents felt he took pretty good care of himself (i.e., grooming), and he rarely argued with them.

Alex's parents were both teachers and had been very proud of his accomplishments at school and in the orchestra. They had assumed Alex would graduate from college, find a job, get married, and raise a family. His mental illness had changed all their plans. When Alex's brother went away to college, it was just Alex and his parents.

Alex's parents were skeptical when they went along with him to the mental health center to meet with the employment specialist. It sounded like a great idea for Alex to get a job, but what about the stability in his life? Wouldn't working be stressful and maybe cause decompensation? And what kinds of jobs were available? They had seen people with mental disabilities working at the local McDonald's, but somehow they couldn't see their son clearing tables or frying burgers. And what kind of support would they have to provide? They already had their hands full with their jobs and taking care of Alex.

Like other participants in employment programs, people with long-term mental illness are likely to have contact with their families. Because most people with long-term mental illness are unmarried, this contact often involves the family of origin (e.g., parents, siblings). However, some individuals with mental illness live with their spouses and children or at least interact with them regularly.

Family members can have a very significant effect on the success or failure of a vocational plan. Their confidence (or lack of it), as well as their instrumental support, may be the crucial link in successfully managing employment. Coiner (1990) found that supported employment participants in Oregon who lived with their parents, families, or spouses were more likely to remain involved in employment services and be successful in their jobs than people who lived alone or with roommates.

Although many family members enthusiastically support vocational rehabilitation and employment services, others may be hesitant to jeopardize hard-won stability for an uncertain benefit. This chapter presents information about common family concerns and positive family roles.

COMMON FAMILY CONCERNS ABOUT EMPLOYMENT

Family members of people with long-term mental illness experience concerns about employment that may vary according to the length of time the family has been dealing with the illness and the activities or roles the individual has held. For a young person who has recently become ill, family concerns may center around the different career path the person must look forward to and on the ways to help him be as independent as possible, while making long-term plans for needed supports. For the individual who has had mental illness for a long time and has been seen by the family as a "patient" in need of medical treatment and case management, considering employment means a paradigm shift for the family as well as for the individual. Table 1 summarizes some common family concerns.

Most family members will naturally have concerns and questions about the individual's changing role. Many of these concerns are often due to a lack of consistent information; living with a person who has a mental illness can be unpredictable and confusing, and the role of vocational rehabilitation in mental health services has changed rapidly over the past few years. Since the development of supported employment approaches in the 1970s, there has been a realization that people with mental illness need not be free of symptoms to be successfully employed. Although initial concerns were that employment might have a destabilizing effect, multiple studies have shown that involvement in vocational programs actually assists people to remain stable (Razzano, 1993). Family members need consistent and up-to-date information about appropriate expectations for the individual and about the services that are available. Being asked to provide such information often puts the employment specialist in conflict, wanting to give family members what they need to provide support while respecting the confidentiality and independent adult status of the client. These issues are areas to explore with the client early in

Table 1.   Common family concerns

- The need for information about mental illness
- The job selection process
- Jeopardizing access to unearned benefits
- Risking relapse due to work stress
- Dealing with leisure time
- Dealing with relapses and other crises
- Changes in the individual's role in the family
- The individual's safety in the community

the employment process, as the client and employment specialist discuss the effect working has on different areas of the client's life. Joint decision making between the client and the employment specialist concerning the role of his family and the type of information to be disclosed will ensure that the employment specialist is honoring the client's wishes in these areas.

The Need for Information About Mental Illness

Families may want and need information about mental illness and on what they can expect to happen with the individual in regard to symptoms, prognosis, treatment, and relapse. Although most clients involved in vocational services have been in mental health treatment for some time and have families who have already dealt with these early concerns, an employment specialist may also work with clients recently diagnosed with mental illness or whose families have just recently become involved in providing support. Families may have a difficult time accepting the individual's impaired vocational development and may make critical comments about the person's negative symptoms and functioning (e.g., not helping out at home, having difficulty starting new activities or employment).

The Job Selection Process

Family members of a client who is considering employment are often concerned about the job selection process, specifically whether there are jobs that the individ-

"I'll have her home by 5 P.M. Mrs. Johnson!"

Considering employment means a paradigm shift for the family and the individual with mental illness.

ual can handle and profit from. Family members often do not understand the process of job analysis and matching for an individual with mental illness, and are therefore worried that the individual will be working in a job that is too difficult, too boring, or otherwise inappropriate. They also may be comparing possible job placements with the types of jobs they expected the person to do before he became ill. To the parents of a young adult who was in medical school before he became ill, a job as a file clerk may not sound like a good placement even though it matches his current vocational goals, interests, and capabilities.

Jeopardizing Access to Unearned Benefits

One of the most common concerns family members have about employment relates to the client jeopardizing access to unearned benefits, such as Social Security. This is a realistic concern given that a recipient of Social Security Disability Insurance (SSDI) risks losing his benefits if he earns more than $500 a month, unless he is aware of and able to use one of the special work incentive programs (see Chapter 9). It is true that not all people with disabilities are better off financially when working. In some cases, people may actually lose money by going to work. Therefore, it is very important for the employment specialist to have a solid understanding of local benefits, current work incentive programs, and other information that can be shared with the family to make good decisions about working for pay.

Risking Relapse Due to Work Stress

Many family members who have invested a lot of time and energy helping the individual achieve stability are concerned that the stress of employment will cause a relapse. It may not be obvious to family members that unemployment is also stressful, and that people with mental illness (like most individuals) do better when engaged in routine, purposeful activity than when they spend their time doing nothing. As mentioned previously, many studies have shown that the risk of relapse is reduced by participation in vocational programs.

Dealing with Leisure Time

When people get to the point where they have been employed for a period of time, the issue of dealing with leisure time often arises. Family members may be concerned that even though the person manages work time well, he might have no idea what to do on days off. This issue is often the responsibility of the family, particularly if the person is doing well on the job and is therefore not getting a lot of attention from the employment specialist. Social clubhouses may fill this role for some individuals by providing a place where people can spend time participating in leisure activities or just hanging out and socializing (see Chapter 6).

Dealing with Relapses and Other Crises

Another area that remains a concern even after stability in employment is reached is that of dealing with a relapse or other crisis. How will this affect employment? What services will be available if a relapse or other crisis does occur? What should family members do to avert the crisis or deal with issues as they arise? Discussing and planning for these issues before they arise will both assuage the client's concerns (and the concerns of his family) and increase the likelihood of dealing effectively with crises as they do occur.

Changes in the Individual's Role in the Family

As a client makes the transition to employment, family members also need to make a change in the individual's role in the family. Some family members who have become accustomed to providing intensive and extensive support to a person with mental illness may have difficulty seeing him as an employable and independent person. However, other families may see the move to employment and the consequent need for support as yet another demand on their time and energy.

The Individual's Safety in the Community

Many families, particularly families of individuals who have been in the mental health system for some time, may feel that the community is not a safe place for the individuals to work and that they should remain in a more sheltered setting. Family members may believe that although the individual may be ready for employment in the future, he first needs more training, experience, therapy, and stability (anything to postpone employment). Family members may also be concerned that trying a job and failing (or experiencing other stresses) will cause the person to lose ground in his recovery and may precipitate a relapse. Families who have worked hard to help the person gain stability, perhaps through adjusting medication and therapy over an extended period of time, may be hesitant to risk this improvement for the unknown benefits of employment.

WAYS FAMILIES CAN HELP

Although families vary in their level of involvement in the employment process and in the amount and type of support they are able to provide, they do have some things in common. Families often provide needed vocational and nonvocational support directly to an individual. Bellamy, Rhodes, Mank, and Albin (1988) stated "However well-funded or well-provided, [paid] services can never substitute for the range of supports available from families and friends" (p. 65). This support can range from maintaining a positive, nonjudgmental, and noncritical atmosphere at home to providing direct daily assistance (e.g., preparing for work, advocating with a landlord, taking the person to and from therapy and other appointments). Although at times providing this level of support places a heavy burden on families, many family members are eager to participate in activities that will lead to more independence.

It may also be important for family members to participate in developing short- and long-range vocational plans and identifying desirable outcomes. The employment specialist must balance the client's right to confidentiality and independence with the family's interest in being involved and the possible support they can supply. However, families can easily sabotage employment efforts by not understanding the long-term goals developed by the client and the employment specialist. The family's work ethic and level of occupational success (i.e., the other family members' success and stability in their jobs) may predict whether they will be able or willing to support the client's efforts to become employed.

Bellamy et al. (1988) stated that families can also have a powerful, although indirect, influence on the services available by advocating for program development and funding at the agency, community, state, or national level. Many of the significant changes in rehabilitative services have come about under pressure from individuals with disabilities and their families. People with long-term mental ill-

ness have lacked a strong, effective advocacy base like that provided by The Arc
and other parent groups for individuals with developmental disabilities, although
mental health consumer and family advocacy groups are increasingly more visible
and vocal (Campbell, 1991).

Families can also provide mutual support by becoming involved in support
groups and information sharing. Other families with members who have a mental
illness can often offer firsthand knowledge and a credibility that not even the most
experienced paid service providers can match.

WAYS TO HELP FAMILIES PROVIDE SUPPORT

DiLeo (1991d) provided several recommendations for working with families of people involved in employment programs. Based on his list, along with a few areas of
particular concern to families of individuals with long-term mental illness, the following considerations (summarized in Table 2) seem to be most important in helping families provide support.

Ensure that Families Have Access to Information

An employment specialist must make sure that families have access to the information they need about mental illness and the disabilities that often result from it.
This information must be easy to understand and include concrete and practical
advice about taking care of the person and his symptoms at home. It often helps if
the family members understand that the person with mental illness will most likely experience repeated phases of acute illness, improvement, and stability as he
goes through a period of recovery that may stretch out for 20 or more years. The
employment specialist must make family members aware that what may look like
laziness or lack of motivation is at least partly due to the mental illness, and that
becoming frustrated at his lack of effort will only make things worse. Family members may need counseling themselves to deal with the disappointment, frustration,
anger, and grief that go along with accepting long-term mental illness.

Invest Time in Understanding Concerns and Hesitancies

The employment specialist must invest time in acknowledging and understanding
the concerns and hesitancies families may feel about the family member with
mental illness becoming employed. Blaming families (even covertly) for the
client's illness, lack of progress, false starts, or other difficulties only cause problems. The employment specialist should help clients and their families look at the

Table 2.   Ways to help families provide support

- Ensure that families have access to information.
- Invest time in understanding concerns and hesitancies.
- Communicate with the family members.
- Include family members as an active part of the support team.
- Support information-sharing and family-to-family support groups.
- Provide education, training, and assistance with benefit planning, communication skills, problem solving, residential planning, and so forth.
- Develop back-up plans.
- Remember that most families have a lifetime of commitment and responsibility.

Source: DiLeo (1991d).

whole picture and determine how work fits in. In addition, it is important to realize that many families find the mental health system frustrating and ineffective. According to Hyde and Goldman (1993), "most families have had a long, dismal experience with the mental health system—both private and public and usually in that order—as their insurance and savings have run out" (p. 64). Other issues include dealing with untreated side effects, financial demands, and having to repeat family histories for each new service provider without apparent coordination among agencies. Often, providing good service to the client includes supporting the family as well.

Communicate with the Family Members

The employment specialist must communicate with family members about her role as a service provider and the support she can provide. It is important to explain the values and approaches that characterize supported employment, and keep family members current on the progress and the challenges in the employment process while respecting the client's right to privacy. The employment specialist should try to share good news with the family on a routine basis and limit sharing bad news to only those situations that are essential or that the family can help resolve.

"It's Sue's employment manager...I didn't know she had one!"

Many family members of individuals with mental illness only hear from employment professionals when a problem has occurred.

Many family members hear from professionals only when problems occur (Powell et al., 1991).

Include Family Members as an Active Part of the Support Team

The employment specialist should include family members (if they are able and interested and the client is willing to have them) as an active part of the support team. It works best when the employment specialist emphasizes joint problem solving and avoids an "us versus them" (i.e., professionals versus families) mentality. An employment specialist may want to provide skill-building workshops to help teach families how to provide employment support. Many researchers have found that teaching coping skills to family members is a powerful way of indirectly providing support to people with mental illness (Marshall, 1989).

Support Information-Sharing and Family-to-Family Support Groups

If information-sharing and family-to-family support groups are already available in the community, the employment specialist should work with them to share information (e.g., success stories, problems and solutions) about employment efforts. If support groups are not available in the community, the mental health center or employment program should consider working to get one started. NAMI is a good resource for contacting support groups in a particular state. They can be reached at 1-800-950-NAMI.

Some programs report good results from doing program presentations to generic groups (i.e., service organizations, business groups, church groups). This activity raises the community's level of awareness about workers with mental illness and also publicizes a resource for audience members who may be involved with a person with mental illness.

Provide Education, Training, and Assistance

Assisting with any area (e.g., benefit planning, communication skills, problem solving, residential planning) that affects the client's employment might involve the employment specialist making referrals to other services, providing classes or groups, or providing individual support. Mueser and Liberman (1988) reported success in teaching family members skills such as listening empathetically, expressing positive feelings, making positive requests for behavior change, and expressing negative feelings constructively to alleviate tensions. These improved communication patterns practiced at home were beneficial in supporting the worker in his recovery.

Develop Back-Up Plans

The employment specialist must work with clients and their families to develop back-up plans for loss of employment, crisis management, rehospitalization, and any other contingency that is likely for that individual. These plans address issues such as who is called if the individual needs to miss work or is rehospitalized, whether or not the person's job and/or residential services will be held open, what kinds of support would be available should the person lose his apartment or have problems with Social Security, and so forth. Having these plans in place will help the employment specialist alleviate some of the concerns family members are likely to have about the individual moving into employment.

Remember that Most Families Have a Lifetime of Commitment and Responsibility

Although the employment specialist may know more than family members about the mechanics of mental illness, the family members probably know a lot more about the individual, and they are the ones who will continue to be a part of his life for years to come. The strength of a family is very important and the employment specialist must empower family members to rely on their common sense and life experiences to help make employment decisions and arrange support for the individual.

THE EFFECT OF CULTURAL BELIEFS AND TRADITIONS

PROFILE: LEE AND HIS FAMILY

Lee and his mental health case manager went to the state vocational rehabilitation (VR) office to see if Lee could get assistance with transportation to his new job. Lee had an opportunity to work as a baker, but had no way of getting to work from the apartment where he was staying with his cousins.

Lee was 17 years old when he came from Southeast Asia to the United States with his family 3 years ago. Since Lee and his family moved to the United States, Lee has had to overcome many challenges. Lee had struggled with English and other high school classes, been diagnosed as having severe learning disabilities, dropped out of school, became associated loosely with a gang of other refugee boys (where he gained a reputation for being wilder and crazier than anyone else), became estranged from his parents after violent disagreements, experienced depression, and attempted suicide (by taking pills) twice. Lee finally received mental health treatment that stabilized his mood and enabled him to set some vocational goals. Becoming successfully employed was very important to Lee because he came from a family of very hard-working people who were already running a successful business after only a few years in their new community.

Unfortunately, Lee's parents (especially his father) were unwilling to reconcile with him because of what they felt was his disrespectful behavior in the past. The case manager had attempted to get Lee and his parents together and had even talked to the father several times, but felt she had been unsuccessful in developing trust. Lee's father felt that the case manager only saw Lee's side, which put the case manager in a difficult position because she really did feel that representing and advocating for Lee was her primary responsibility, even if it meant disagreeing with other family members. An additional factor was that in the family's culture of origin, mental illness was seen as reflecting shame on a family, and therefore the parents were not really comfortable with acknowledging Lee's illness and providing public support.

Many Factors Influence Recovery

When a person develops a disability through illness or injury, many factors will influence his recovery and rehabilitation. These influences include the severity of the residual disability and the intensity of the rehabilitative services available to him. In addition, the client's own beliefs about disability and his case in particular will affect his level of recovery. These beliefs come partly from the mainstream culture in which we live, and partly from families, ethnic cultures, and communities (Lefley, 1990). Therefore, it is important for the employment specialist to understand and act in accordance with family or cultural influences that are relevant to an individual client and to understand how racial and cultural differences affect the diagnosis and treatment of mental illness. For example, the use of the traditional diagnosis system as summarized in the DSM-IV may lead to misdiagnosis when used with an individual from a non-Western culture.

> Diagnostic assessment can be especially challenging when a clinician from one ethnic or cultural group uses the DSM-IV Classification to evaluate an individual from a different ethnic or cultural group. A clinician who is unfamiliar with the nuances of an individual's cultural frame of reference may incorrectly judge as psychopathology those normal variations in behavior, belief, or experience that are particular to the individual's culture. (American Psychiatric Association, 1994, p. xxiv)

Cultural and Racial Differences

Mental illness diagnoses are made by examining patterns of behavior rather than by administering medical tests. Cultural and racial differences affect the diagnoses because they are directly linked to behavior, even for individuals who originate in the same mainstream communities. For example, Campinha-Bacote (1991) reported that African Americans are more likely to be diagnosed with schizophrenia, and European Americans with the same symptoms are more likely to be diagnosed with a mood disorder. Statistics from Ohio state hospitals from 1984 showed that 63% of the African Americans admitted were diagnosed with schizophrenia, compared to 43% of the Caucasians. Solomon (1988) also found that African Americans were more likely to be diagnosed with schizophrenia; however, African Americans received fewer mental health services than Caucasians.

It is well documented by the National Council on Disability (1993) that people from minority backgrounds (i.e., African American, Hispanic American, Asian American, Native American) who also have disabilities are less likely to receive vocational services than their Caucasian counterparts. This is particularly unfortunate given that having a psychiatric disability and a minority background both cause societal stigma and unique stresses in American culture (Lefley, 1990). Therefore, those who might benefit most from vocational services because of the double challenges they face are the least likely to receive those services.

Recovery Is Higher for People with Schizophrenia in Nonindustrialized Countries

Research studies consistently find that although the incidence of schizophrenia is roughly equivalent around the world, nonindustrialized countries typically report a much higher rate of recovery than industrialized countries—as high as 65% in some studies (Sullivan, 1994) compared to average U.S. recovery rates of 25%. In one study, Sullivan (1994) reported that researchers in India had difficulty scheduling follow-up interviews with people who had been diagnosed with schizophrenia because so many of them were back at work. There are several possible explanations for this striking evidence of the interaction between culture and illness. The primary emphasis on social relationships and group cohesiveness (rather than individual achievement) provides one possible explanation: People with differences, including mental illnesses, are not excluded from nonindustrial societies. People can resume a productive role in a non–wage-based community (e.g., one where farming or herding is the norm) without the skills to search for a job, pursue employers, or work at an average level because no one in the community needs those skills to survive. People are allowed to contribute at whatever level they can, and their contributions are valued by the community. In industrialized countries where extended family structures are not common, the nuclear family alone must provide support to the family member with mental illness. In addition, the Western focus on individual control and responsibility may cause more overt or hidden rejection by families, unlike societies where it is believed that an illness is beyond personal control. This contrast strongly illustrates the power of culture in understanding and providing support to people with mental illness.

The Employment Specialist Must Be Aware of Cultural Differences

When working with a client from a different culture than her own, the employment specialist must know how race and culture affect diagnosis and treatment, as well as have basic information about how the specific culture regards disability issues. In mainstream American culture, mental illness is increasingly being regarded as a treatable, medical issue (National Institute of Mental Health, 1986). In other cultures, mental illness is a curse caused by wrongdoing by the family; a child's mental illness is evidence of the parents' or grandparents' earlier transgressions. Therefore, an individual with mental illness becomes something that causes shame to the family and must be hidden from the community. In still other cultures, hallucinations (e.g., seeing visions) caused by mental illness might be considered as evidence of the individual's great value. In such a situation, the individual and his family may be reluctant to reduce such symptoms aggressively through medication.

Fate versus Personal Control   Another area in which cultural beliefs affect disability and rehabilitation issues is the role of fate versus personal control. Individuals from cultures that believe fate controls each person's destiny will look at their disability very differently than individuals from cultures that believe each individual has control over his future and his own destiny. Similarly, different cultures have different beliefs about patterns of behavior in the community (e.g., competitive versus cooperative), and different beliefs about the role and value of employment (e.g., everyone should work versus it is acceptable to spend time in community or leisure activities). In some cultures and communities, the extended family is expected to take responsibility for the needs of its members, including older people and people with disabilities, which may lead to families not taking advantage of social services even where they are readily available.

Cultural Differences Do Not Necessarily Correlate with Race   Different cultures do not necessarily correlate with race. Two people from the same racial background may have very different cultural beliefs (e.g., a Quaker and a White Supremacist), whereas different racial groups may have similar values. For example, both the Samoan community and members of the mostly White Mormon Church (Church of Latter-day Saints) have a strong belief in the responsibility of the extended family (or church) in supporting its members. Service providers must learn to be sensitive to cultural and family influences of every individual they serve and know how to learn more about these factors.

The Norms and Expectations in the Client's Culture   It is crucial for the employment specialist to understand the social norms and expectations in the client's culture. Understanding respectful behavior (e.g., whether it is appropriate to call someone by his first or last name, whether it is appropriate to ask direct questions to elicit personal information, whether making direct eye contact is acceptable) may make the difference between establishing a relationship of mutual respect or one of distrust.

Understanding the Explanatory Model   It will also be helpful for the employment specialist to understand the explanatory model held by the individual and his family. In other words, how do they understand the disability experienced by the individual? What caused the mental illness? What would be appropriate treatment, and what would be the most desirable results of that treatment? What problems has the illness caused? An understanding of these issues will better enable the employment specialist to help the client and his family develop possible employment options and arrange services and supports that work for them.

Understanding the Power Hierarchy   An employment specialist must understand the power hierarchy in the family and community. Who speaks for the family? Who speaks for the client? The importance of understanding these relationships cannot be overemphasized. People who are from the mainstream culture that values speaking up for oneself and separating from parents in early adulthood may find it difficult to understand a 30-year-old client who still lives with his parents and relies on his father to make important decisions or parents who must speak with another community leader before making decisions. Working in a culture where the parent or another individual has more power over what happens to a person with mental illness than the person himself contradicts the client-centered, empowered model that is one of the defining values of supported employment. In this situation, questions of confidentiality arise, and the employment specialist is often seen as an adversary of the family because what the employment specialist sees as representing the client's interests, the family may see as encouraging disobedience to the family.

Understanding and Accommodating Different Viewpoints   However foreign the views of the family or client may seem, the experienced employment specialist will make every effort to understand and accommodate those views. To do otherwise is often a wasted effort because the job placement will fail through direct action or subtle sabotage. The employment specialist must understand that the client whose family members do not work at regular jobs because they want to be able to take off and go fishing when the mood strikes will probably not do well at an 8 A.M. to 5 P.M., Monday through Friday job. A person whose family regards his mental illness as bad karma and a shame to the family may not be allowed to take a job that would require him to have a job coach, and thus label him as having a disability. Another consideration occurs when a client whose family members all work in white-collar or professional jobs receives little family support for his job as a gas station attendant. The good news is that families who are extremely involved can offer a wealth of support if involved in a respectful and culturally sensitive way.

Ways an Employment Specialist Can Learn

So, how does an employment specialist learn about differences? The best place to start is by getting to know the client and learning how his particular culture and family background might influence the employment process. What culture or community does he consider himself a part of? How would he like to be addressed? What kind of a relationship does he have with his family? Who else is important in his community? Who would he like to have involved in developing and implementing his employment plan? Visiting and talking to the family (when appropriate) will also help the employment specialist begin to identify family dynamics and understand the type of outcome family members find most appropriate and desirable.

There are many other resources that can help the employment specialist learn different cultures. Some agencies have access to language interpreters who can share the social expectations of their culture. Leaders in the community (e.g., ministers, newspaper editors, business owners) may be willing to discuss their culture's attitudes toward disability, family, and employment. (Remember, unless an employment specialist has consent from his clients he cannot divulge any personal information, including the client's name and therefore these discussions must be kept general.) Another good resource is talking with other rehabilitation professionals (e.g., vocational rehabilitation counselors, mental health workers) who are from the same cultural background and are willing to share their insights. The most important resource is keeping an open mind and genuine interest in developing an approach that will be comfortable for all concerned.

CONCLUSION

Although people with mental illness differ in their family involvement and their response to cultural influences, these are factors that can strongly affect the employment process. Providing effective services requires that those services be culturally relevant and sensitive to individual family dynamics.

4

ROLE OF THE EMPLOYMENT SPECIALIST

Since 1985, several studies have addressed the question of what employment specialists (or job coaches) really do on the job (Danley & Mellen, 1987; Kregel & Sale, 1988; Pelissier-Shelton & Wong, 1989; Russell & Associates, 1985; Wehman & Melia, 1985). This question is not as simple as it seems because supported employment services are individualized according to the needs of the client. Therefore, a list of activities typically used by an employment specialist inevitably includes a variety of options, any of which may or may not be used with a particular client.

For example, according to a study of Oregon employment specialists working with clients with mental illness, clients averaged 25.6 hours of jobsite training and supervision per month during the placement phase, which was more than any other single service (Coiner, 1990). However, there were clients placed in jobs who received no jobsite training and supervision from the employment specialist because off-site support was what the client needed or wanted. Somewhere there is a valid exception to every rule about what workers with disabilities need and what employment specialists do.

Another reason why it is difficult to pin down what an employment specialist does is because agencies divide work differently across their staffs. For example, in some agencies an employment specialist is responsible for job development, but in other agencies one person does all the job development and passes along the job leads to an employment specialist for analysis, modification, and matching. In another example, an agency may use the employment specialist in a service coordinator role. The employment specialist then contracts with a skill trainer (who may also be called a job coach) who provides only initial training on the job and then passes the client back to the employment specialist for long-term follow-up. In yet another arrangement, the employment specialist does the job development, placement, and training, and then the mental health counselor takes over to provide long-term support. The possibilities are endless.

By looking at activities across agencies and across clients, it is possible to develop a list that will include most of the services an employment specialist most often provides. Almost all employment specialists provide some of the following:

- Preemployment activities
- Job placement activities
- Job analysis and modification
- On-the-job training and support (including skills instruction)
- Employer and co-worker education and support
- Troubleshooting and problem solving
- Coordination and communication with families and other agencies
- Routine follow-up, advocacy, and documentation

The three categories that seem to be the least predictable are job development, service coordination, and job supervision. As described above, many employment specialists are not responsible for job development. Some act as service coordinators, and others work with a service coordinator who addresses nonwork issues. Job supervision is usually only a part of the employment specialist's role when the clients are involved in a group placement (e.g., crews, enclaves) that includes full-time, ongoing supervision. In individual placements, the expectation usually is that the employer will eventually provide whatever supervision is needed.

PROFILES: TWO EMPLOYMENT SPECIALISTS

Andy is an employment specialist working in a vocational program that is part of a community mental health center. When clients express interest in vocational activity to their case manager, they are referred to the vocational program

"I've found the problem.
But tomorrow let's ask your boss for the manual!"

What do employment specialists really do on the job?

where they attend a group orientation session to learn about the variety of employment (and education) activities available. If the clients choose to participate, they are assigned to an employment specialist who becomes their primary case manager. If appropriate, clients continue to receive therapy and medication management from other staff.

The services Andy provides include the following: career exploration and assessment; job development; referral to vocational rehabilitation (VR); coordination with families, residential providers, and other service providers; job placement, training, and support; development of natural supports and education of employers and co-workers; advocacy; routine follow-up and retraining; and troubleshooting. In short, Andy is responsible for providing and coordinating almost any type of support needed to obtain and maintain employment. His efforts are funded by a combination of vocational rehabilitation and Medicaid.

Jerry is an employment specialist working at a community rehabilitation program that primarily serves individuals with disabilities such as mental retardation and cerebral palsy. Referrals come to him from the VR counselor who works with the local mental health counselors to identify individuals who are interested in employment. Once an individual is referred to Jerry's agency, Jerry meets with the client, the VR counselor, the mental health case manager, and the person in charge of job development to identify the goals and activities for which each will be responsible. The services provided by the agency will be paid for by vocational rehabilitation.

After the job developer has identified potential jobs, Jerry helps the client learn more about the jobs and get through the application process. He then provides the level of job training, advocacy, and development of natural supports necessary for the client to do the job. Once the worker is stable on the job, the mental health case manager resumes responsibility for long-term support (including visits at the jobsite if appropriate and working with the employer), and Jerry moves out of the picture.

Table 1 briefly summarizes the typical activities of the employment specialist during three phases: preemployment, employment and training, and follow-up (after stabilization on a job). Clients may move very quickly between phases, and they may cycle back through preemployment to employment several times as they lose or leave jobs. It is also important to remember that these lists do not describe what the client may be doing during these phases, or exactly how the employment specialist supports the client. For example, the employment specialist's involvement with job development might be contacting employers directly, giving the client leads and teaching her to contact employers, teaching the client to develop leads, or just supporting a client who knows how to develop her own job. Many people believe the employment specialist's role should involve teaching and supporting the client's efforts to become employed, while limiting direct involvement to only those things the client is unable to do.

THE PREEMPLOYMENT PHASE

The preemployment phase includes all the activities that happen between the time the client gets involved in vocational services and the time she moves into a job, whether it is volunteer, transitional, or permanent.

Table 1. Typical employment specialist activities by phase

Activity	Pre-employment	Employment and training	Follow-up
Job development and marketing	X		
Preemployment activities	X		
Outreach	X		
Networking with other agencies	X	X	X
Education and liaison with families	X	X	X
Facilitation of communication	X	X	X
Documentation	X	X	X
Service coordination	X	X	X
Learning of the job		X	
Job placement activities		X	
On-the-job training		X	
Covering the job		X	
Developing and maintaining natural supports		X	X
Individual counseling and problem solving off job		X	X
Advocacy for integration and advancement		X	X
Provision of supervision (groups)		X	X
Education of employer and co-workers		X	X
Routine follow-up and maintenance			X
Troubleshooting and crisis management			X
Retraining (new tasks or decline)			X

Job Development and Marketing

Job development and marketing activities involve both direct and indirect contact with potential employers, including the development of marketing materials, market analyses of opportunities in the community, presentations to community or business groups, networking with other agencies who have job information (e.g., vocational rehabilitation or employment security), meeting personally with employers, and touring possible jobsites.

Preemployment Activities

Preemployment activities attempt to prepare a client for employment and determine what type of job the client desires and is able to do. Different preemployment activities and their characteristics follow.

Assessment Assessment of a client includes activities such as the review of referral materials, testing, functional analyses, and interviews.

Career Counseling Career counseling includes exploring previous work experience, examining job values and work resources, and practicing decision making. It may be provided to clarify employment goals and timetables.

Job Sampling or Shadowing Job sampling (i.e., trying a job on a short-term basis, paid or unpaid) and job shadowing (i.e., following a person in a given job as she goes about her day) may be provided to increase the client's knowledge about the world of work and the requirements of specific jobs.

Skills Training Training may be offered across several different areas, including jobseeking (e.g., interviewing, résumé writing, developing job leads), work readiness (e.g., attendance, following instructions, grooming), social skills (e.g., greetings, conversations, understanding the intent of humor), and specific job skills (e.g., filing, answering telephones, using particular tools).

Outreach

An important part of the preemployment phase is outreach, which includes identifying potential clients, contacting current clients who may be temporarily out of vocational services, and encouraging program attendance and participation. Outreach is often part of preemployment activities because of the difficulty involved in engaging people with mental illness in services.

Networking with Other Agencies

Whether or not an employment specialist has any responsibility for service coordination, networking with other agencies is an important part of the employment specialist's job. People with long-term mental illness often are involved in complicated service arrangements with mental health centers, doctors, residential providers, public assistance, and Social Security before they get involved in vocational services. By adding the employment specialist and VR counselor into the equation, good communication and agreement on goals become even more crucial to the rehabilitation of the client, even in the preemployment phase.

Education and Liaison with Families

The importance of educating and coordinating with family members varies across clients. Although some people with long-term mental illness have no family support available, many others live with or have frequent contact with family members. Family support can be a critical variable in sustaining employment, and family members may need information and encouragement from the employment specialist to give that support.

Facilitating Communication

The employment specialist may need to facilitate communication among the client, the family, the employer, and the mental health agency because once the client moves into a job, many of her life support systems will be affected and need adjustment. The employment specialist often takes on the responsibility of making sure everyone involved is up-to-date. This includes attending and participating in case review meetings.

Documentation

Documentation is a necessary part of any service provider's routine. The types of services provided, the plans developed, and the outcomes of activities are examples of things that are usually documented in reports or hard data.

Other Service Coordination Activities

Although some clients are able to manage most aspects of their lives, other clients need assistance and support across the board—vocationally, residentially, medically, recreationally, and socially. Moving into employment means that good service coordination support will be needed to help the client adjust to her new role and the new demands being placed on her.

EMPLOYMENT AND TRAINING PHASE

The employment and training phase adds new roles to the employment specialist's repertoire. This phase begins when the client accepts a job and ends when she has learned all the requirements of the job and is performing them in a stable fashion. This phase may last for only a few days or it may last for many weeks, depending on the client's level of independence and need for support.

Learning the Job Prior to Placement

Learning the job prior to placement may be important for job matching, and is critical when the employment specialist must provide on-the-job training once the client starts work. A thorough knowledge of the job is also useful for an employment specialist to have in case problems arise during the follow-up phase.

Job Placement Activities

Job placement activities include applications, interviews, orientation, and making transportation arrangements, and may be done by the client (with or without support) or by the employment specialist.

On-the-Job Training

On-the-job training is the biggest single category of service in terms of time spent, although as stated previously, not all clients receive it. This category consists of several possible activities.

"I have your plan here somewhere!"

Documentation is a necessary part of any service provider's routine.

Job Analysis and Restructuring   Analysis and restructuring often begin before the client starts working, but may continue as the client and employment specialist assess performance levels. Building structure and analysis into the job allows the employment specialist to catch potential problem areas early and intervene before things become out of hand.

Negotiation with the Employer   Working with the employer may include negotiating job duties, schedules, approaches or techniques used for specific tasks, or any other areas where the job may need to be restructured (or structured for the first time). Negotiations also set a stage for developing a relationship with the employer that will eventually serve as an early warning system for future problems.

Teaching Vocational Skills, Social Skills, and Job-Related Skills   It is essential that an employment specialist teach and help the client apply the following three levels of skills: 1) vocational skills in different work situations and production levels; 2) social skills in the work environment; and 3) job-related skills (e.g., getting to work, grooming, lunch breaks, learning where to pick up informal information about the workplace).

Data Collection   Data collection of all types is an important part of the employment specialist's job. This collection may be formal (e.g., production rates, use of social skills, attendance, written evaluations) or informal (e.g., comments from the supervisor, self-assessment ratings by client), and is used to assess the effectiveness of the interventions or approaches being used by the employment specialist and the need for continued or increased activity.

Cues and Reinforcers   Identifying, strengthening, or building in cues and reinforcers is often a keystone of on-the-job training because existing cues and reinforcers are often too weak or inconsistent to maintain performance.

Covering the Job

Covering the job (i.e., doing the job when the client cannot) is a controversial part of the employment specialist's repertoire. Covering is often done only during the initial training period. For example, during the first few days or weeks on the job the employment specialist takes over some of the tasks to lessen the stress on the client, or the employment specialist may complete work the client is unable to do.

In some cases, the agency guarantees that a job will be done whether the client does it on an ongoing basis or not. Therefore, if the client needs to take a week off after working for 6 months, the agency is responsible for filling that position with another client or the employment specialist. Some agencies offer this service as a marketing strategy, hoping to assuage employer fears about the worker's potential instability by guaranteeing that the work will get done when placements are set up as transitional employment sites (i.e., each worker is there for a specific, time-limited period, and the agency is given free rein regarding which workers have access to the job).

Guaranteed coverage beyond the initial training period can be an expensive promise for an agency to keep, especially as the number of people getting support begins to increase. For this reason and to lessen the stigma associated with special treatment, most agencies believe that client–worker absences should be covered by the employer exactly as absences by other workers are. No matter what policy the agency has about covering the job, it is important that the employer, the client, and the employment specialist understand beforehand how such situations will be handled.

Development of Natural Supports

The development of natural supports on and off the job is becoming recognized as a significant part of the employment specialist's responsibilities. In most cases, the employment specialist will fade out of intensive involvement in the employment situation when the client becomes stable in her employment, and the support will be provided by the employer, co-workers, family, and friends. However, natural supports must often be carefully cultured and maintained by the employment specialist if they are to function consistently and effectively (Griffin, 1992).

Individual Counseling, Support, and Problem Solving

Off-site counseling, support, and problem solving are provided by employment specialists in situations where the client needs very limited or no training in the skills needed on the job. Counseling and problem-solving support are provided by meeting with the client away from the worksite and outside of work hours.

Advocacy with Employers

Advocacy with employers (e.g., for integration or advancement) may be provided in situations where the employment specialist has been involved in the job development, analysis, modification, or training and therefore is known to those in the worksite.

Providing Ongoing Supervision

The employment specialist is usually responsible for providing ongoing supervision in group employment situations (e.g., crews, enclaves, small businesses).

Education of Employer and/or Co-workers

An employment specialist may be responsible for educating employers and co-workers either formally (by meeting with others in the workplace) or informally (by modeling interactions and support). Many employers and co-workers have never had a relationship with a person with a mental illness and have concerns that can be addressed through education and experience. The relationships established with the employer and co-workers become a valuable early warning system when the employment situation changes over time.

Additional Responsibilities

Education and liaison with families, facilitating communication, service coordination, networking, and documentation all continue to be important responsibilities as clients move into the employment and training phase.

FOLLOW-UP PHASE

The follow-up phase begins when the client becomes stable on the job and it continues for as long as she is employed. The employment specialist usually spends very little time at the jobsite during this phase and his major responsibilities include routine follow-up, troubleshooting, crisis intervention, and any needed retraining, as well as continuing his advocacy, education, and coordination efforts.

Routine Follow-Up

Routine follow-up involves regular visits with the client, and sometimes with the employer, family, or residential providers, to assess maintenance of the client's performance and adequacy of the support systems. These visits may occur at the job-site, at a restaurant in the community, at a mental health center, at a support group meeting, or in any other setting that meets the needs of the client. Written employer evaluations are often used to facilitate ongoing communication.

Regardless of how it is implemented, routine follow-up is one of the most crucial responsibilities of the employment specialist. One of the keystones of supported employment is that routine support, albeit sometimes minimal, assists people with disabilities in dealing with minor issues as they arise and, therefore, avoids crises of all kinds. This can *only* be done with an effective early warning system and the flexibility to provide preventive support and minor repairs as they are needed.

Troubleshooting and Crisis Management

Troubleshooting and crisis management involve responding to concerns of the employer, the client, or others involved with the client (e.g., her family). Troubleshooting may lead to retraining the client or clarifying of issues that need to be dealt with by others involved. Crisis management may involve direct intervention or assisting the client in obtaining mental health or other services.

Retraining

Retraining may be required by the addition of new tasks, new social situations, or a decline in performance.

Individual Counseling, Problem Solving, and Support

Off-the-job counseling, problem solving, and support may become a larger part of the employment specialist's responsibilities during this phase, because he is no longer needed on the jobsite for skills training.

Advocacy

Although advocacy continues during this phase, the focus may shift from integration and job modification to opportunities for advancement and continued employment.

Ongoing Responsibilities

Providing supervision continues as an ongoing responsibility for employment specialists involved in group employment models, and educating employers and co-workers continues as new issues arise and/or turnover among co-workers and supervisors occurs. Facilitating communication among the client, her family, the mental health provider, and the vocational rehabilitation counselor becomes even more critical in the follow-up phase because the novelty of the situation wears off and the support systems originally established begin to erode. Education and liaison with families, service coordination, networking, and documentation continue as in earlier phases.

Because of the variability in employment specialist's job descriptions, it is difficult to pin down which tasks are done most often and which responsibilities have the highest priority. A study by Pelissier-Shelton and Wong (1989) examined job coaching roles in the 27 states that were involved in federally financed grant projects to provide for the statewide development of supported employment services. Although the individuals surveyed had a range of disabilities and, therefore, the results are not 100% applicable to employment specialists serving only people with long-term mental illness, the studies reported interesting information on what is actually done.

The services most often provided in order from most often to least often are on-site training after placement, preplacement activities, follow-up activities, assessment activities, rehabilitation plan development, job development, and preparation of reports. Similarly, Coiner's 1990 study of Oregon job coaches serving people with long-term mental illness reported that the service provided for the most hours was job training and supervision. However, the second most time-consuming service was job development, followed by learning the client's job, placement activities, counseling off the job, follow-up visits, and retraining. Coiner also reported that clients in the preemployment phase received an average of 25.7 staff hours per month (and were in that phase for 1.9 months); clients in the job-training phase received an average of 27.5 staff hours per month (and were in that phase for 1.9 months); and clients in the follow-up phase received an average of 14.7 staff hours per month (and were in this phase anywhere from 1 to 20 months). The average hours worked per week was 24.3.

CONCLUSION

It is clear from the above descriptions that employment specialists must be skilled in many areas. This is especially true for employment specialists serving people with mental illness because they must have a working knowledge of psychiatric rehabilitation, as well as an understanding of vocational services. They also must be ready to provide services in a very flexible manner, responding to the needs of the worker and the employer.

II
THE SYSTEMS

5

SUPPORTED EMPLOYMENT
AND PEOPLE WITH
LONG-TERM MENTAL ILLNESS

Employment programs for people with long-term mental illness are the results of a long history of efforts. Pilot employment models developed in the 1940s and 1950s for people with mental illness preceded the current national supported employment movement by 20–30 years.

This chapter examines the roots of employment programs for people with mental illness, the development and major characteristics of supported employment, and the ongoing synthesis of these movements and their effect on the delivery of services.

THE DEVELOPMENT OF COMMUNITY-BASED
EMPLOYMENT PROGRAMS FOR PEOPLE WITH LONG-TERM MENTAL ILLNESS

Early approaches to vocational rehabilitation for people with disabilities were based on the assumption that there were two types of employment: competitive (i.e., unsupported) and sheltered. Because many people with long-term illness were unable to maintain competitive jobs with no support and were not interested in the typically low-paying and repetitive jobs provided by sheltered workshops, neither of these options met their needs, which prevented them for the most part from obtaining employment. According to Anthony and Blanch (1987),

> The development of interest in supported employment [for people who were mentally retarded] reflected dissatisfaction with a mental retardation service system that prepared people endlessly for jobs that never materialized. The problem for people with mental illness was more a complete lack of access to any kind of appropriate vocational services. (p. 8)

Mental illness treatment involved treating the symptoms and fighting the disease; work was not seen as an important activity. Along these lines, Campbell (1989)

63

pointed out that traditional treatment programs usually believed that wellness and social independence should precede most employment efforts. For most individuals with long-term mental illness, this meant that they never had access to vocational services because they still had a mental illness.

Community-based employment for people with mental illness started on a formal basis in the 1940s and 1950s with the development of two new treatment and support approaches: the Fountain House in New York and the Fairweather Lodge in California. The Fountain House grew out of the deinstitutionalization movement, starting as a social club founded by a group of former patients for the purpose of providing and receiving aid and support. This early program developed into a comprehensive, multiservice approach that gave birth to two very significant models: the clubhouse model and the transitional employment model. Many of the principles currently regarded as critical to supported employment (i.e., working in a real job setting, ongoing support, believing in the right of people with disabilities to be employed) were also basic values of the early clubhouses such as the Fountain House (Anthony & Blanch, 1987) (see Chapter 6 for more information).

The Fairweather Lodge began in the late 1950s as a group residence and working environment for people leaving the hospital. While in the hospital, people with mental illness participated in work groups to build vocational skills and establish relationships. After discharge, group members continued to live and work together as they moved back into the community. Subsequent research showed that people who participated in lodges were less likely to return to the hospital, and that the model has been widely replicated (Fifteenth Institute on Rehabilitation Issues,

Early approaches to vocational rehabilitation for people with disabilities assumed there were two types of employment—competitive (unsupported) and sheltered.

1988). Lodges operate without live-in staff members, and the 5–15 people who participate manage their own households and businesses with access to professional assistance on request.

The Fountain House and Fairweather Lodge movements were radical approaches that differed from existing services because they emphasized both the value of work and client self-help and control. With the medical model reigning supreme, the idea of letting clients have some control and responsibility over their treatment was as novel to mental health professionals as the corresponding notion that people with mental illness could work. During this same period, the increased use of antipsychotic medication to control symptoms, the tremendous overcrowding in institutions, and the philosophical principle referred to as *normalization* (now known as *social role valorization*) led to the passage of PL 88-164, the Mental Retardation Facilities and Community Mental Health Centers (CMHC) Construction Act of 1963 (Barker, 1988). The principles of normalization are based on the idea that people with disabilities should be given access to patterns of everyday life that are as close as possible to those experienced by people without disabilities and that fears and myths about people with disabilities are reduced by shared participation in the life of the community (Blatt, 1987). The purpose of the CMHC Act was to provide community-based services to individuals leaving the hospitals so that they might live in the least restrictive setting. In many states, the presence of a full- or part-time VR counselor within the CMHC became standard practice. In retrospect, this may have encouraged the mental health system to take less responsibility for the clients' vocational development support.

Since these early efforts, the continued movement toward deinstitutionalization, briefer hospital stays, and community support systems has encouraged the increased development of vocational programs in mental health centers. Although the quality of these programs varies, they do provide fertile ground for the adaptation of supported employment principles and procedures developed mainly for individuals with developmental disabilities.

THE DEVELOPMENT OF SUPPORTED EMPLOYMENT

Bellamy et al. (1988) attributed the development of supported employment to three influential trends. First, there was growing evidence from research projects in the 1970s that people with severe disabilities were able and willing to work. Landmark work by Bellamy, O'Connor, and Karan (1979), Gold (1976), and others documented that even people with severe disabilities were able to learn complex tasks when a task analytic teaching approach was used. This approach, combined with the concurrent development and refinement of applied behavior analysis techniques, enabled service providers to work effectively with individuals previously believed to have been unteachable because of their disruptive behavior. Techniques developed by research and training centers at Virginia Commonwealth University and the Universities of Kansas, Illinois, Oregon, and Washington were increasingly being used by independent (i.e., non–facility-based) placement and training programs to assist individuals in finding competitive jobs in the community (Rusch, 1986).

After the passage of PL 94-142, the Education for All Handicapped Children Act of 1975, when people with disabilities began to emerge from the public school system, they and their parents began to express intense dissatisfaction with a vocational service system that offered primarily segregated, poorly paid work. The traditional continuum of employment services for an individual with a disability (i.e., before being ready for employment they had to first participate in prevocational education, then in a work activity center, and then in sheltered employment before earning a chance at outside employment) was recognized as ineffective for people with severe disabilities. Bellamy et al. (1988) wrote:

> If an individual with a severe disability entered the continuum in a day-activity program and progressed through the continuum at the estimated average rate, he or she would spend 37 years preparing for a work-activity center, another 10 years in such a center before moving to a workshop or job, and 9 more years in a regular program workshop. In other words, an individual who entered this continuum upon completing school at age 21 would begin his or her first job at age 77. (p. 5)

People who had participated in integrated education and community-based prevocational programs were not enthusiastic about getting involved in anything less than integrated and community-based employment.

The third trend grew out of the experiences of the programs that were placing individuals with severe disabilities in community-based, competitive jobs. The assumption was that if people were taught the vocational skills needed for a job and then carefully matched with competitive jobs, they would quickly stabilize and stay employed for a long time without much agency attention. However, what actually happened was that people continued to need support on the job for periods that were much longer than those typically provided by vocational rehabilitation services (Ford, Dineen, & Hall, 1985). Many clients would stay in their jobs (usually entry-level service jobs) for about 2 years but then want or need access to another job placement, which required another round of training, support, and advocacy on the job. There were also potential clients (or the parents of potential clients) who were reluctant to get involved in community-based employment because there was no guarantee of ongoing support after placement. Because of their reluctance, ongoing but nonvocational service options (e.g., day activity programs) were being chosen in preference to time-limited vocational programs.

Supported employment integrated these three trends by specifying paid employment in an integrated work setting where the worker receives ongoing support. Over time, the supported employment movement has grown to be as much about the civil rights and inclusion of people with disabilities as it is about the most effective way to deliver services (Marrone, 1993).

On the federal level, supported employment was initially defined in the regulations of the Office of Special Education and Rehabilitative Services (OSERS) in 1984. Since then, agency initiatives in both the U.S. Department of Education and the U.S. Department of Health and Human Services have provided state and local agencies with funds to build supported employment services. In 1986 and 1987, 27 states were awarded systems change model demonstration funds from the Rehabilitation Services Administration (RSA), a branch of OSERS, with the goal of modifying existing adult day programs for people with severe disabilities, including mental illness (Wehman, 1989). PL 99-506, the Rehabilitation Act Amendments of 1986, specifically included people with long-term mental illness in supported employment services. In 1993, about 15% of the 125,000 participants in supported employment had mental illness as their primary diagnosis (Wehman,

1993). In addition, a certain amount of VR funds was designated for supported employment placements (Title VI-C). Although these funds were administered a bit differently in each state, the general intent was to ensure that workers with severe disabilities, who needed supported employment services, would have access to VR funds and services.

RESEARCH FINDINGS:
VOCATIONAL OUTCOMES FOR PEOPLE WITH LONG-TERM MENTAL ILLNESS

Although widely known and successful vocational programs do exist, most people with long-term mental illness are not employed at any level. Anthony (1994b) reviewed four studies (Anthony, Buell, Shannatt, & Althoff, 1972; Anthony, Cohen, & Danley, 1988; Anthony, Cohen, & Vitalo, 1978; Anthony & Jansen, 1984) conducted between 1972 and 1988 on employment outcomes for people who were discharged from psychiatric hospitals and cited employment figures of 20%–30%, with the most recent studies showing a 10%–15% employment figure.

Bond and Boyer (1988) reported on 21 studies that examined outcomes associated with different vocational programs for people with mental illness. Although many of the studies were not rigorously designed and had a limited experimental focus, the authors were able to draw some interesting conclusions. Bond and Boyer found that involvement in some type of vocational program (e.g., supported employment, hospital-based work, job clubs, occupational training) increased the likelihood of eventual paid employment, whether it be competitive, transitional, or sheltered. In fact, 51% of the individuals with mental illness involved in vocational programs eventually became employed, while only 27% of those not involved in vocational programs returned to paid employment. They also found that individuals who moved quickly into community employment (especially those who had prior work histories) did not have more problems in employment than those who spent more time in preemployment activities. In fact, sheltered settings (e.g., hospitals, sheltered workshops, prevocational training) were self-perpetuating and tended to create dependency in the clients involved with them. Bond and Boyer also found that clients who participated in vocational programs with high expectations (e.g., transitional or supported employment) were not at a higher risk for rehospitalization than those who were in less demanding programs or not involved with vocational programs at all.

Shultheis and Bond (1993) examined the relationships between client performance and paid work by measuring the work behaviors (e.g., work readiness, work attitudes, interpersonal relations, work quality) of clients who were randomly assigned to either paid transitional employment or unpaid prevocational crews. Not only did the group of individuals assigned to paid work score higher on the work behavior measures than the group assigned to unpaid work, but individual workers consistently scored higher when assessed in a paid job than when assessed in an unpaid job. Bell, Milstein, and Lysaker (1993) pointed out in another study that clients who perform poorly in unpaid prevocational programs are often considered too ill or unmotivated for a paid job. Their study hypothesized that clients with schizophrenia did not perform as well because of the lack of pay, not because of their disability. Although participation in both paid and unpaid work reduced positive and negative symptoms, clients assigned to the paid group participated for a much longer period than those assigned to the unpaid group and experienced a greater reduction in symptoms.

Other studies have consistently shown the importance of ongoing, long-term treatment to the rehabilitation of people with mental illness. Bond and Boyer (1988) found a direct correlation between the length of time a person participated in a vocational program and the person's eventual success in employment, concluding that people who remain engaged in vocational services have better outcomes than those who drop out. They also reported that people tend to regress once they end a time-limited program. Similarly, Anthony et al. (1990) reported that time-limited community-based treatment did not produce better rehabilitation outcomes than time-limited hospital treatment, indicating that the ongoing nature of services is perhaps the most crucial variable.

Unfortunately, it is often difficult to engage and retain people with mental illness in vocational programs. Even when such programs are available clients do not readily participate. Studies have shown that one fourth to one third of people discharged from psychiatric hospitalizations do not follow up on referrals for services and that a substantial percentage who do enroll quickly drop out of treatment (Solomon, Gordon, & Davis, 1986; Sue, McKinney, & Allen, 1976). Stanton et al. (1984) reported that 42% of people involved in state-of-the-art psychotherapy and medication management dropped out by 6 months, 56% dropped out by the first year, and 69% by the second year.

FEATURES OF SUPPORTED EMPLOYMENT

The federal definition of supported employment specifies three requirements. First, the individual who is working must be paid for that work. This standard attempts to shift employment programs for people with disabilities away from the work-readiness, skill-developing model, toward regular, paid employment. This requirement does not exclude individuals who are unable to work at competitive rates of production or quality. Although seldom used for workers with mental illness, subminimum wages are acceptable in supported employment if properly negotiated and documented according to Department of Labor standards. The U.S. Department of Education changed the standard of a minimum of 20 hours of paid work per week to the requirement of an individualized written rehabilitation plan (IWRP) that determines the appropriate number of hours for each person.

Second, the employment must be in settings where individuals without disabilities are also employed. This requirement attempts to increase the integration of workers with disabilities in the work force. The federal standard specifies that eight or fewer people with disabilities work together, and that the location is not adjacent to another disability program. In other words, an entrepreneurial business located next to the sheltered workshop that sponsored it would not qualify. In addition, job interaction with co-workers and other individuals, including the general public, without disabilities is required.

Third, the individual must require, and be provided with, ongoing and long-term support in the work setting. This standard attempts to include individuals with more severe disabilities by requiring that supported employment agencies provide ongoing support, while attempting to exclude individuals who are capable of independent employment by specifying that ongoing support must be necessary in order for the person to maintain employment. PL 102-569, the Rehabilitation

Act Amendments of 1992, says that ongoing support (including skills training) must be provided at least twice a month. This support may be provided away from the job if authorized by the vocational rehabilitation counselor, and does not necessarily need to include job-skills training.

The basic tenet of supported employment is that anyone who is capable of work can do so in an integrated setting if given the appropriate support. This represents quite a shift from the previous job-readiness continuum model, and radically increases the number of individuals with disabilities who are now seen as appropriate for community-based employment. The philosophy behind supported employment is that people with special support needs are best served by providing support in the same environment where people without disabilities work, rather than by building special environments that compensate for their needs. Another aspect of supported employment that is particularly salient for people with mental illness is that success in employment cannot be isolated from other areas of the individual's life. A great deal of what a supported employment specialist does falls into the category of service coordinator (e.g., advocacy, nonvocational skill training). Many people with mental illness need support in nonwork areas in order for them to continue working, and the supported employment model recognizes this as a legitimate contributing factor in vocational success.

The strength of supported employment lies in its capability to provide individualized support that is appropriate for the specific worker being served. Although it may be more convenient for funding agencies and employment specialists to insti-

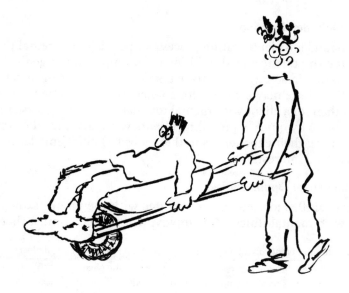

"Now, that was one tough first day!"

The strength of supported employment lies in its capability to provide individualized support as needed.

tutionalize employment models and standard procedures, to do so is to deny the client-centered values that inspired supported employment in the first place. An employment specialist must focus less on how the client fits into the sheltered or competitive jobs available, and more on the kind of support this client needs to work successfully in the community. Flexibility and adaptation are not the responsibility of the client, but rather the responsibility of the employment specialist.

SPECIAL FEATURES OF
EMPLOYMENT PROGRAMS FOR PEOPLE WITH LONG-TERM MENTAL ILLNESS

There are inherent dangers in generalizing groups of people who share only one characteristic. To say "All people with mental illness need the following services" is too general because mental illness is only one aspect of who those people are.

The basic values and principles of supported employment remain constant across disability groups, with an emphasis on individualized support and the other values listed above. However, Anthony and Blanch (1987) and others suggested that the way supported employment is implemented for people with long-term mental illness differs (e.g., wider range, greater stigma) from the way it is implemented for people with mental retardation (i.e., those who represent the majority of supported employment participants). They also emphasized that many of the points listed in Table 1 are also important for participants who have mental retardation, but have not traditionally been emphasized in supported employment programs serving that population.

Assessment and Job Identification

The assessment and job identification process for people with mental illness must actively involve the client and should focus on employment goals, vocational interests, and skills. In some cases, this is taken to mean that the assessment and career counseling phase may continue for a longer period of time for a client with mental illness than for a client with mental retardation. Some successful programs approach this issue by quickly providing clients with entry-level or transitional jobs, and then using their experiences in these jobs to help them clarify long-term vocational goals and interests.

A Range of Employment Opportunities

Entry-level or unskilled jobs are not compatible with the interests and abilities of many people with mental illness. An employment specialist must therefore offer

Table 1.   Special features of employment programs for people with long-term mental illness

The assessment and job identification process must actively involve the client.
Clients need to have access to a range of employment opportunities.
Stigma against people with mental illness is greater than for any other disability group.
Clients may prefer only off-site support.
Clients need to sustain performance.
Clients have different individual characteristics from people with mental retardation, including the following:
    Disability happens later in life.
    Illness is episodic in nature.
    Society blames the clients and their families.
    Functioning level is generally higher.
Clients are involved with many service providers.

Source: Anthony & Blanch (1987).

clients access to a range of employment opportunities. It is also true, however, that many people with mental illness have only worked in entry-level, unskilled jobs or have no work history at all (Ford, Dineen, & Codd, 1993). People with mental illness may feel most comfortable by first trying an unskilled job or furthering their education (remedial or otherwise) before moving into more demanding employment. Clients should have access to a range of career opportunities that are commensurate with their individual needs, wants, and capabilities.

Greater Stigma

There is a greater stigma against people with mental illness than there is for any other disability group (National Institute of Mental Health, 1986). The media images society sees of people "going crazy" and becoming violent are powerful and pervade our culture, although it is well known that only a small percent of this population displays dangerous or criminal behavior (Barker, 1988). Because mental illness can be hidden from society, people who handle their illness gracefully and are skilled at completing typical daily activities are not identified as having a mental illness. People who obviously have a mental illness generally stand out in society because their behavior is bizarre or unusual. For employment specialists, as well as for the general public, it is difficult to go beyond that first impression of a person with a mental illness and focus on skills and capabilities. Many employment specialists must face and challenge their own assumptions about people with mental illness before effectively providing support to clients with mental illness.

Off-Site Support

Some people with mental illness prefer not to be identified on their jobs as having a disability, and therefore support must be provided discreetly and possibly completely off-site. Another issue is that clients often need support for nonwork areas of their lives in order to be able to continue working. The employment specialist is challenged to provide flexible support outside of work hours and away from the worksite, rather than always addressing problems directly.

Sustaining Performance

Many people with mental illness learn skills quickly, but have trouble putting them into practice and sustaining performance. Therefore, the support provided to these individuals must focus on performing skills effectively and consistently rather than on initial skills training. Sustaining performance is as important for social and interpersonal skills as it is for vocational skills.

Differences in Client Characteristics

There are some significant differences in client characteristics between people with long-term mental illness and people with mental retardation.

Disability Happens Later in Life   People with mental illness develop disabilities later in life than people with mental retardation and other developmental disabilities. Therefore, individuals with mental illness and their families often must work through their grief for the loss of potential that the illness represents, as well as deal with the long-term consequences.

Illness Is Episodic in Nature   Because mental illness tends to be episodic, there is generally greater variability in performance than for individuals with mental retardation.

Society Blames the Clients and Their Families   Many people with mental illness are blamed for their failure to improve with treatment or for their illness. People with mental retardation are blamed significantly less than those individuals with mental illness (Anthony & Blanch, 1987).

Functioning Level Is Generally Higher   As a group, people with mental illness generally function at a higher intellectual level and are more adept in gross physical activities than people who have mental retardation. However, people with mental illness do usually experience some impairment compared to people without mental disabilities.

Many Service Providers

People with long-term mental illness are typically involved with many service providers in addition to employment specialists. These may include medical personnel, residential service providers, mental health counselors and caseworkers, peer support groups, and VR counselors. Because employment is only one component of the rehabilitation program, the employment specialist must emphasize coordination with other community support services. The client's continued employment may eventually depend on the skill and support of people other than the employment specialist.

SYSTEMS BARRIERS TO SUPPORTED EMPLOYMENT

Anthony and Blanch (1987) and Noble and Collignon (1987) identified several systems barriers that have made it difficult for people with long-term mental illness to gain full access to the vocational rehabilitation system and a range of employment opportunities. Table 2 highlights these barriers.

Dissimilar Systems Jointly Serving the Same Client

It is very difficult to serve a client effectively when dissimilar systems are involved. The vocational rehabilitation system is time limited, emphasizes and values employment, sets specific goals, and deals primarily with the vocational aspects of the client's life, whereas the mental health system is process oriented, emphasizes treatment that may not involve employment, provides open-ended services for as long as the client needs and wants them, and deals with all aspects of the client's life. In fact, open-ended and comprehensive qualities of the mental health service system may promote feelings of dependency that become a barrier to independent employment (Rutman, 1994).

The Medical Model and Mental Illness

The medical model traditionally used by mental health focuses on symptoms and sees people with mental illness as "patients" who need to have things done

Table 2.   Systems barriers to supported employment for people with long-term mental illness

Dissimilar systems jointly serving the same client
The medical model and mental illness
Mental health practitioners and community-based services
Vocational rehabilitation counselors
Work disincentives
Societal stereotyping and misconceptions

Sources: Anthony & Blanch (1987); Noble & Collignon (1987).

for and to them. Fisher (1994) characterized the medical model as including a hierarchical arrangement of power, a mechanistic view of the mind, a belief in causality outside the person, and a commitment to treatment relying on external technology, and described the medical model as antithetical to a consumer-centered service system. Although many mental health practitioners have adopted a more strength-oriented approach, there are still many mental health centers that continue to provide treatment and services based on the medical model. In contrast, the rehabilitation approach focuses on maximizing the skills and resources the person does have in order to achieve specific vocational goals, and supported employment focuses on the idea that people do not have to prove they can work before they can have a chance to work. People with mental illness have been served by vocational rehabilitation programs since 1954, and mental health centers and vocational rehabilitation have been working together since 1978, but many coordination problems continue to exist at the state and local levels (Bond, 1987; see Chapter 8 for additional vocational rehabilitation/mental health comparisons).

Mental Health Practitioners and Community-Based Services

Most mental health practitioners are educated and prepared for private practice, which is typically more lucrative and involves working with individuals whose disabilities are less severe than those treated in public clinics. Many mental health counselors and case managers are not enthusiastic about working with people with long-term mental illness or providing community-based services to their clients. Of those who find themselves working in this situation, many are worried about the effect this change will have on their own jobs. A common comment is "I didn't get a master's degree in order to teach someone to be a dishwasher or scrub floors."

Vocational Rehabilitation Counselors

Vocational rehabilitation personnel generally know very little about people with mental illness and share common misconceptions about them. A 1988 national study asked VR counselors to rank the importance of selected client characteristics in determining vocational rehabilitation eligibility for people with mental illness (Tashjian et al., 1989). The characteristic ranked most important was client symptomatology (i.e., symptoms experienced by the client) even though research showed that symptomatology was not correlated with vocational success. Good joint service can be provided only when the professionals from both agencies can agree on the same goals and approaches, without fighting about who ultimately is making the decisions and controlling the process. In my experience, whether this happens has less to do with the presence of a formal interagency agreement than with the attitudes and flexibility of the individuals who work for the agencies. Professionals who value employment as a client choice somehow find ways the systems can work together to support that choice, while professionals who are more concerned about their own status and control somehow find ways to make the same systems into barriers.

Work Disincentives

Other major service systems present their own barriers to moving into employment. Work disincentives (e.g., those involved in Social Security Disability Insurance [SSDI]) and the fear of losing benefits such as Supplemental Security Income (SSI) are very important issues for people with mental illness. In fact, the fear of losing unearned benefits is one of the few things that does correlate with vocational success (Anthony & Jansen, 1984). Although the Social Security system has made some changes in order to encourage their recipients to return to work (e.g., allowing prorating of SSI benefits and reentry into the SSDI system without a new waiting period), much more must be done. Also, there is very little information about whether supported employment services for people with mental illness are cost-effective or at least comparable in cost to the traditional day treatment services. Anticipated changes in federally funded health insurance programs (e.g., Medicaid) will present further challenges as operational details are determined.

Societal Stereotyping and Misconceptions

As mentioned previously, societal stereotyping regarding people with long-term mental illness causes a significant employment barrier for people with mental illness. The following are common myths about people with mental illness:

1. Mental illness is always a chronic, static condition from which people never recover.
2. People with mental illness cannot live independently or produce real work.
3. Dangerousness is always associated with mental illness.
4. People who have mental illness will quickly decompensate without warning if they move into a stressful situation such as employment.
5. People with mental illness are fragile.
6. People with mental illness cannot distinguish right from wrong, reality from hallucinations, and so forth.

Employers, co-workers, family members, neighbors, and vocational service providers may all have these assumptions, which are fanned by the media and represent significant barriers to integration and employment success.

WHY SUPPORTED EMPLOYMENT?

Although there are barriers and challenges, many people believe that supported employment is a viable and valuable service for people with severe disabilities, including those with long-term mental illness (Wehman, 1988). Most people with severe disabilities are unable to obtain a job without professional assistance in locating a valued and appropriate position, as well as in dealing with such issues as transportation planning, parental concerns, and employer skepticism. Many people with disabilities are unable to maintain employment without professional support, although the nature and delivery of the support will vary from person to person and is influenced by the nature of the disability involved. Many people with disabilities have difficulty transferring skills across settings and need training and support on each new job to be successful. Although no information is available on the cost-effectiveness of supported employment, it does not seem to be more expensive than traditional day treatment programs.

Supported employment is important because people with severe disabilities generally do not otherwise have a chance to be employed in the community, and people with long-term mental illness clearly want to have access to employment.

Supported employment provides a new definition of success; people can be successful and stable in their employment, albeit with ongoing support, and have that recognized as a successful outcome. Supported employment allows an employment specialist to assist clients to accomplish an important goal.

CONCLUSION

To conclude this chapter's discussion of supported employment for people with long-term mental illness, it is necessary to comment on the application of the approaches and guidelines described in this book. Employment specialists should deliberately separate federally defined and funded "supported employment" from the activity of providing support to people with disabilities as they move into employment. Mental health center staff often say, "We cannot do supported employment with our clients because we do not have any vocational rehabilitation funding." By limiting the kinds of employment support mental health centers provide their clients to only those that are funded by vocational rehabilitation, agencies are unnecessarily limiting their clients' access to employment opportunities. There is a range of community-based, vocational outcomes (e.g., supported education, unpaid volunteer work) that might interest people with long-term mental illness and be appropriately supported by employment specialists, even though these outcomes might not meet all of the federal guidelines or qualify for Title VI-C funding. For example, the client who prefers to work in a volunteer job at this time in his life may not meet federal supported employment guidelines but nonetheless needs employment support; the employment specialist who provides the needed support may be providing very useful services despite not meeting federal guidelines.

In short, an employment specialist must separate the services needed by a given client to reach a desired goal from the usual funding mechanisms used to pay for those services. It may be possible to provide job coaching and off-site support through a funding source other than Title VI-C vocational rehabilitation (e.g., Title XIX Medicaid, Social Security work incentive programs such as a Plan for Achieving Self Support [PASS]). For some clients, employment specialists may not need to officially participate in "supported employment" as federally defined and funded.

6

EMPLOYMENT MODELS
AND SUPPORTED EDUCATION

As mentioned previously, one of the strengths of supported employment is its emphasis on individualized services. Therefore, ideally there would be no need to discuss service models because each client would be provided with the individualized service needed for success. Realistically, however, model descriptions help employment specialists understand the kinds of supported employment services that are provided for people with long-term mental illness, better enabling them to design services for the particular clients employment specialists are trying to serve. This chapter looks at service models across two variables: 1) who is providing the services, and 2) what the jobs look like. This chapter also looks at two specific approaches that have become widely known: the Choose-Get-Keep model and the Clubhouse model. The extension of supported employment approaches and activities into the academic setting (i.e., supported education) is also considered.

WHO IS PROVIDING SERVICES?

People with mental retardation are almost always provided with employment services by community rehabilitation programs or independent vocational placement agencies, whereas people with mental illness are served by both vocational programs and mental health agencies. A brief description of the common players and their roles follows.

Community Rehabilitation Programs

Facility-based community rehabilitation programs typically serve people with a range of disabilities and provide vocational or employment-related services. These services may include sheltered employment; vocational assessment; preemployment services such as work hardening (a gradual exposure to work) or work adjustment; peer support groups; community job development, placement, and replacement into individual or group employment; job coaching; advocacy; coordination with other agencies; and long-term follow-up.

Independent Placement and Supported Employment Agencies

Supported employment agencies are sometimes grouped with other rehabilitation facilities in being considered community rehabilitation programs, but they differ in that almost all of their services are provided in the community. These agencies may work with clients who have a variety of disabilities, or they may specialize in clients who have a particular disability. They do not offer in-house sheltered employment, although they may develop and support group community placements. Preemployment activity is usually limited because the emphasis is on supporting clients in jobs in the community. In some communities, independent agencies may be stronger advocates for supported employment than the agencies that maintain large in-house programs. In other cases, the traditional facility offers a strong supported employment program in addition to more sheltered work settings. A 1993 study reported that 73% of supported employment services nationally were being provided by agencies that also provided more traditional services (Human Services Research Institute, 1994).

Sometimes supported employment programs and more traditional facilities work closely with a mental health center that provides long-term support, and other times they serve people with mental illness more independently and provide long-term support through their own vocational staff.

Mental Health Agencies

Mental health agencies usually work only with people who have mental illness, but in some smaller communities mental health services are combined with services for people with developmental and other disabilities. Mental health agencies usually provide services across a range of functioning areas, addressing such issues as residential support, daily life skills, psychotherapy, medication management, social and recreational activities, and vocational rehabilitation.

Mental health agencies generally have three different approaches to handling supported employment. In the first approach, case managers or counselors are responsible for providing employment support directly as part of the client's general treatment. In many cases this approach is difficult to implement because of the large numbers of clients with whom most case managers and counselors are expected to work, and because most mental health professionals feel that they lack the skills needed for job development, training, and support. However, this approach is attractive to some agencies because it limits the number of professionals involved with the client and gives the mental health agency more control over employment efforts.

In the second approach, case managers arrange supported employment services for their clients and work closely with a rehabilitation facility or supported employment program that provides the actual job development and job coaching. The case manager or counselor provides ongoing mental health support during the initial period of employment, while coordinating with the employment specialist, and then provides long-term support (direct or indirect involvement at the jobsite) to the client after the job coach is no longer needed.

In the third approach, the mental health agency develops and maintains a vocational unit similar to an independent supported employment agency, which provides vocational services to clients who are receiving mental health services from other agency staff. The vocational services provided may include sheltered employment, transitional employment, preemployment activities, volunteer work, job placement and coaching, and long-term support. The vocational rehabilitation staff work closely with the counselors and case managers, who also continue to provide services. The status of the vocational unit varies across agencies using this approach. In some cases, vocational rehabilitation is seen as a valued and integral part of overall treatment, but in other cases it is seen as peripheral and the vocational staff seem to have less status than the mental health staff.

WHAT DO THE JOBS LOOK LIKE?

The jobs involved in employment programs differ across several variables, including the number of clients involved, the wages paid, for whom the client works, the presence or absence of a job coach or special supervisor, and the location of the work. Following are brief descriptions of common arrangements.

Individual Placements

Individual job placements involve a single worker being supported in a job. The client is usually hired as a regular employee by the employer and earns the same wages and benefits paid to a worker without disabilities, but the job may be modified through negotiations before placement. In some cases where production rates are very low, a special wage rate (below minimum wage) may be negotiated with the employer and approved by the U.S. Department of Labor. An employment specialist usually provides job analysis, training, advocacy, and support on the job, fading out over time as the worker becomes proficient. The level of support provided is determined by the needs of the worker and the demands of the job. Usually in this type of arrangement, others in the work environment know that the individual has a disability because of the need for job coaching or other special support, but they may not know what the disability is.

Some workers with mental illness are capable of, and prefer, learning the job without the employment specialist's direct assistance. In these situations support is provided away from the job and the employer and co-workers may not know that the worker has a disability. Individual placements are used when the worker is capable of working at typical production rates and with typical levels of supervision and reinforcement from the work environment. They are the only option for individuals who choose not to disclose their disability and also for those who seek highly skilled jobs.

A 1988 national study showed 64.5% of all the individuals working in supported employment were in individual jobs (Wehman, Kregel, Shafer, & West, 1989), making the individual job approach the most common one used in supported employment. Individual placements are arguably the least stigmatizing approach to employment for people with disabilities, because they do not require special groupings, buildings, or other potentially stigmatizing arrangements. This approach also allows for the development and selection of job opportunities that closely match an individual's needs. However, this approach is more difficult to maintain for clients whose behavior patterns or production rates do not match job requirements, because the expectation is that the employment specialist will fade out over time and go on to place more workers.

Group Employment Approaches (Enclaves in Industry and Work Crews)

Group models differ from individual models in that a group of individuals with disabilities work closely enough together that a job coach or special supervisor can be available full time without any expectation of fading. Therefore, this approach is appropriate for individuals whose ongoing support needs are too high for independent work. For people with long-term mental illness, these support needs may relate to low production rates, intensive behavioral issues, instability in performance or attendance, or just very low confidence about working independently. Some people choose group employment because they feel more secure working in an environment where other people with disabilities are working, and under the direction of a supervisor they know and trust.

The risk involved in placing a worker into group employment is less than in individual placement where the worker is eventually expected to work under typical levels of supervision and support, because the support agency usually has far more control over the job environment in group placements. Group employment may provide clients with a transitional step toward independent employment or may be considered a long-term employment option. In some cases, an individual may become accustomed to levels of group support that are difficult to duplicate in

"I can do this!"

Some workers with mental illness are capable of and prefer learning the job without the employment specialist's direct assistance.

individual placements and may have difficulty moving on to independent employment. In addition, the support agency must consider issues of segregation and access to consistent work before designing group employment opportunities. These models are often used with clients who work slowly, are unable to maintain quality without supervision, or have disruptive behaviors. They can also be good options for individuals whose illness is not stable and who may not be able to attend work consistently enough for a competitive job, or for people who have very limited confidence in their own ability to be successfully employed on their own.

Enclaves   Enclaves involve groups of up to eight workers with disabilities who work alongside workers without disabilities in a business, but who are provided with full-time supervision and support by a special supervisor. A 1988 national study showed that enclaves were the second most common model of supported employment, serving 20% of those participating (Wehman et al., 1989). In this type of model, the enclave supervisor is responsible for securing and organizing work assignments from the company, training the workers, and supporting integration (Bellamy et al., 1988). The enclave supervisor may be paid by the supported employment agency or by the business, and the workers may be hired directly by the business (at the going rate or a specially negotiated wage), or by the supported employment agency who contracts with the company to accomplish a certain amount of work and then pays the workers. Once an enclave worker meets production standards and is oriented to the business, she may have the opportunity to become a regular (i.e., non-enclave) employee.

Workers in enclaves do not need to be working at the same table or in the same work unit to be considered an enclave, and in many cases deliberate attempts are made to spread enclave workers throughout the business in order to increase opportunities for integration. These enclaves are sometimes called cluster placements because they look more like individual workers than an enclave, with the exception that the enclave supervisor is available somewhere in the business on an ongoing basis.

Work Crews   Sometimes called mobile crews, work crews are small businesses that work for customers on a contract basis at the customer's regular workplace. The type of work done by crew members varies, but most commonly includes janitorial, shelf stocking, groundskeeping, or similar jobs. Integration is achieved by having workers without disabilities participate on crews, or by having the crews do their jobs during regular business hours. Ideally, work crews (e.g., janitorial) would work during regular business hours in order to have contact with others who use the office, but many crews work at night and have difficulty maintaining integration opportunities in the context of employment.

The crew supervisor is responsible for training and supporting crew members as well as ensuring that production and quality standards are maintained. The supervisor also controls the flow and pace of work, so that even individuals with low productivity can participate. The supervisor and crew members are paid by the community rehabilitation program from contract revenue and fees-for-service dollars. The responsibilities of the staff involved in managing crews include all of the training and supervision involved in enclaves, plus the tasks involved in managing and marketing a small business. The possibility of combining a number of smaller, dispersed contracts into a part- or full-time employment opportunity makes the crew approach worth considering in rural areas with few jobs (Bellamy et al., 1988).

Wehman et al. (1989) reported that 6% of all the individuals working in supported employment nationwide were in work crews. Some mental health programs use in-house crews to provide paid employment experience to clients, who do janitorial and groundskeeping chores at the mental health center.

Small Business or Entrepreneurial Approaches

The small business or entrepreneurial approach is described by Bellamy et al. (1988) as one in which organizations provide supported employment to people with disabilities by selling products or services. These businesses must generate enough work to guarantee paid employment, provide training and ongoing support to workers with disabilities, and employ a maximum of eight people with disabilities at one place of employment. The small business may either subcontract to produce goods or services or manufacture its own product for sale in a retail or wholesale market (e.g., a deli producing and selling sandwiches). Workers are paid by the agency from the business income, although some of the cost of providing ongoing support, training, and supervision is usually covered by public funds. As with work crews, the small business approach is often recommended for communities with limited employment opportunities because it is not dependent on access to jobs that already exist in the community. This model is also good for individuals with strong business skills and experience and, because of the opportunity to provide flexible, ongoing support for individuals whose behavior or instability makes independent employment difficult.

An uncommon variation of the small business approach involves clients with mental illness starting their own business as a cooperative venture by using capital borrowed from family, public sources, or saved through a Plan for Achieving Self Support (PASS). (See Chapter 9 for more information on PASS plans.) In these situations the clients are self-employed but still receive support as needed from the employment specialist.

Bellamy et al. (1988) suggested that supported employment models should be divided into two categories: personnel and entrepreneurial models. *Personnel models* help people with disabilities find and perform in jobs as employees in companies. Individual jobs and most enclaves fall into the personnel model. In *entrepreneurial models*, the support organization is also the employer. Entrepreneurial models include work crews, small businesses, and enclaves where the agencies pay the worker directly. The added responsibilities of running a business in addition to providing rehabilitative services make entrepreneurial models complex and difficult to operate effectively (Bellamy et al., 1988).

Several employment programs across the United States have been successful in setting up temporary employment service agencies as an entrepreneurial venture. Some of the agencies place only individuals with disabilities, providing job training and support as needed. Others serve people without disabilities as well. Employers are charged a fee if they hire a worker without disabilities through the agency (standard practice for temporary employment agencies), but have the fee waived if a permanent job offer is made to a worker with a disability. The cost of job training and support is covered by government fees-for-service dollars. In situations where a strong state-use law requires state agencies to purchase services from rehabilitation programs when available, the community rehabilitation program can offer clients an excellent array of temporary opportunities to develop skills and build résumés.

Transitional Employment (TE)

Transitional employment (TE) is a supported employment variation that was originally developed for people with mental illness involved in clubhouse programs. In this type of approach, the agency openly negotiates access to jobs in community businesses and then guarantees completion of the work. Clients are then given an opportunity to work in the job and are paid by the employer for their work. By definition, transitional employment is intended to be temporary, usually 6 months or less. Transitional employment offers the client the opportunity to try various jobs and learn work skills rather than work in a stable, permanent job. The employment specialist typically provides initial training and support to a client in transitional employment, just as he would for a client in permanent employment, with the expectation that he will fade and the client will be able to work independently. In some cases, group transitional employment jobs (similar to enclaves) are developed and the employment specialist may be a permanent fixture. In transitional employment, the employer and co-workers are aware that the workers have disabilities, and if a particular worker is unable to do a job for a period of time, the job will usually be filled by another client or by the employment specialist. Transitional jobs are generally part-time, and sometimes a full-time job is split to provide two transitional slots. For many people, transitional employment offers a desirable step toward permanent employment. TE also provides employers an opportunity to work with individuals with long-term mental illness in a way that gives employers support and control over the situation.

There are, however, some concerns about transitional employment. First, clients sometimes get very comfortable with transitional employment and are reluctant to move into permanent jobs. Second, program staff may spend too much time developing and supporting transitional jobs, and not enough time developing and negotiating permanent ones. Third, people with long-term mental illness may not transfer skills well across settings, and therefore time spent learning vocational or social skills on one job may have to be repeated on the next job. Fourth, because of the need to move workers into and out of TE positions rapidly, TE positions are rarely developed in white-collar or skilled jobs.

Marrone (1993) recommended that transitional employment approaches work best for people without much work experience, who have not worked in a long time, or who are unsure about pursuing paid work. He also found that transitional employment works better in an urban or suburban setting, and in a service rather than a manufacturing economy, because it requires access to multiple jobs that can be taught fairly quickly and access to a steady flow of new workers.

There is quite a bit of overlap among transitional employment and other types of supported employment. Transitional employment sometimes turns into permanent employment, and many jobs that are intended to be permanent turn out to be transitional because the client loses or leaves the job after a brief period of time. Vocational rehabilitation can fund transitional employment under their supported employment program, as long as the employment specialist promises continuous transitional employment over an 18-month period.

WHICH MODEL IS BEST?

It is important to remember that support models have been developed and are selected in response to the needs of individual clients and should be only a guide to describing the support that is being provided. Unfortunately, the model offered sometimes has more to do with easily obtained jobs, the convenience of the agency and its staff, or a lack of confidence in the clients' capabilities than with the needs of the individual workers. However, some approaches are considered to be a better match with certain types of clients (see Table 1 for a summary of the models).

All these approaches, with the exception of the entrepreneurial model, can be used with unpaid volunteer jobs as well as paid jobs. Individuals who are extremely fearful about jeopardizing their unearned benefits, who lack the self-confidence to pursue paid employment, or who have other reasons for preferring unpaid work, may choose to take a position in a setting that utilizes other volunteers (typically a nonprofit organization such as a hospital). These may be individual (with or without a job coach) or group placements, and may or may not be transitional by design.

TWO WIDELY KNOWN MODELS: CHOOSE-GET-KEEP AND CLUBHOUSES

Choose-Get-Keep

The *Choose-Get-Keep model* was developed by William Anthony and Karen Danley and their colleagues at Boston University, and was first described by Anthony, Howell, and Danley in 1984. This model departed from the traditional supported employment labels of preemployment, placement, training, and follow-up by using words describing the client's role in each phase (Anthony, 1994b). Therefore, choosing, getting, and keeping were used instead of talking about being placed and trained. The choose-get-keep approach attempts to involve the client actively in her rehabilitation and in doing so have her share responsibility for the ultimate outcome with the employment specialist.

The Choose Phase The choose phase focuses on the client's choice of whether or not she wishes to work. If work is chosen, the client and employment specialist work together to clarify the personal values, experiences, and preferences that need to be considered in job identification. Personal values and interests are translated into criteria that can be compared with possible employment opportunities. The choose phase involves setting employment goals, developing a job, and decision making (MacDonald-Wilson, Mancuso, Danley, & Anthony, 1989). Because of the time involved in developing a trusting relationship between the client and the employment specialist and establishing values and goals, the choose phase takes longer than is typically devoted to preemployment phases (Anthony & Blanch, 1987).

Table 1. Summary of employment model features

Feature	Individual	Enclaves	Crews	Entrepreneurial	Transitional
Number of workers involved	1	Up to 8	Up to 8	1 or more	1 or more
Wages	Hourly or salaried	Hourly or production	Hourly or production	Hourly or salaried	Hourly
For whom do workers work?	Employer	Employer or agency	Agency	Themselves or agency	Employer
Permanent job coach?	No	Yes	Yes	Sometimes	Sometimes
Location of work	Business	Business	Business	Agency or business	Business

The Get Phase   The goal of the get phase is to assist the client to secure a position with a preferred employer. This phase includes such activities as employment planning (e.g., identifying tasks needed for the job, assessing the client's abilities and resources, selecting skill and resource interventions, assigning responsibilities, scheduling tasks), direct placement (i.e., the employment specialist presents the client, as well as the service to potential employers), and employment support (e.g., teaching job-seeking skills, securing resources for the client so that she can obtain the job independently). Attention is also given during this phase to overcoming liabilities by identifying assets that offset them, developing alternate approaches and supports to compensate for them, or clarifying whether they are critical to performing the job (MacDonald-Wilson et al., 1989).

The Keep Phase   The keep phase addresses assisting workers in sustaining employment. During the keep phase, the employment specialist focuses less on helping the worker learn the skills needed on the job and more on helping the person use the skills at the level required. This phase includes assessing the skills and supports needed, planning the interventions needed to address skill and resource limitations, and planning for continued skill development, service coordination, and environmental modification (MacDonald-Wilson et al., 1989).

The Choose-Get-Keep model is in many ways less a separate approach than it is a different way of organizing and describing possible services in a way that emphasizes client control, activities, and choices (Anthony, 1994b). As in all effective employment approaches, the actual services provided to an individual client are dependent on the needs and preferences of the client rather than on a particular model.

Clubhouses

The *Clubhouse model*, with its associated transitional employment approach, is probably the most widely known and best researched of all vocational service approaches for people with mental illness. It has been said that the Clubhouse model "cannot be described as a structure, program, or system but must be perceived as a culture and experienced through individual journey and discovery" (Fifteenth Institute on Rehabilitation Issues [IRI], 1988, p. 47). The clubhouse approach, which originated and was refined by the Fountain House in New York, provides broad-based support to clients across areas of functioning and recognizes work as an integral part of treatment. The Fifteenth IRI (1988) described the clubhouse approach; a summary is provided below. *Enhancing the Rehabilitation of Persons with Long-Term Mental Illness* (Fifteenth IRI, 1988) offers the following descriptors.

The clubhouse is not time-limited; members may use and contribute to the clubhouse indefinitely. Clubhouse services and activities are not tracked, in the sense that there are no set program steps or prerequisites. Members gain access to activities (including employment) in a nonlinear fashion and may drop out of, and subsequently reenter, as needed.

The clubhouse is not disability based; the needs of the clubhouse form the center to which member abilities are drawn. Clubhouses do not provide individual or group therapy, activities of daily living (ADL) training, or in-house sheltered employment. Transitional employment is considered a right of membership, and job failures are viewed as experiences that members must usually undergo to eventually achieve employment success.

Fully developed clubhouses provide day program activities (e.g., clerical, food service, tutoring, intake and orientation, housekeeping, maintenance, reception, touring of visitors, newspaper) that provide a work-ordered day for all members who choose to participate; housing or housing support services; transitional employment for 40% of the members at any time; social recreational programming 1 or 2 evenings per week and on weekends; and operate 7 days per week.

There is a clear commitment to member leadership in all clubhouse activities. Both the members and staff of clubhouses perform service coordination (case management) functions, and there is a daily outreach function to members who do not attend. An important aspect of the clubhouse approach is mutual help. "When members understand that they have the capacity to be helpful, to powerfully affect another member's life, they gain a sense of wholeness and independence that is the goal of rehabilitation" (Fifteenth IRI, 1988, p. 51). Clubhouses should have an independent board of directors or advisory board, their own budgets, their own physical space, and their own staff.

In practice, clubhouses that are associated with community mental health centers (more than 50%) must compete with the other mental health programs for both financial and personnel resources, and are not always seen as a valued part of the center (Mastboom, 1992). Staff assigned to a clubhouse may be expected to do other activities such as training in ADL, as well as performing their roles in the clubhouse framework.

As the clubhouse model has become widely known, the clubhouse label has been borrowed to describe programs that do not meet many of the characteristics common to the clubhouse model despite the fact that formal training and support are available to agencies wishing to adopt a clubhouse model. Mental health centers have been known to clean out a room, add some day activities, start calling their clients "members," and declare themselves a clubhouse although the values of the agency and the services provided have not really changed. Therefore, caution is advised in assuming that a clubhouse actually has the crucial elements incorporated into the program. There is also concern that clients become very comfortable with clubhouse routines and are reluctant to move further out into the community. However, the clubhouse movement has been influential and its vocational emphasis is consistent with supported employment efforts.

SUPPORTED EDUCATION

Mental illness typically is diagnosed during an individual's teenage years or early 20s, interrupting the educational and career development activities most people experience during that time. The lack of formal education increases the challenges already experienced by people with mental illness. For example, Unger (1994) reported that people with less than 8 years of schooling were over eight times more likely to have a work disability than were college graduates. The lack of education experienced by people with mental illness is an additional barrier to employment.

As more attention has been given to providing employment support to people with mental illness, there has been a parallel interest in providing support for educational goals and activities. A person who did not finish high school may want to work on a general equivalency diploma (GED), another may want vocational instruction and training from the local community college, and a third may want to start or finish working toward a college degree. A 1991 study showed that 62% of adults with mental illness wanted more education, and participation in supported education increased the participant's self-esteem, which is positively associated with employability (Unger, 1994).

The obstacles faced by a person with mental illness who is considering schooling are similar to those faced when going to work: a reduced level of expectations by herself and others, decreased self-confidence and self-esteem, a lack of needed work and study skills, difficulty in identifying and gaining access to educational opportunities, and insufficient social supports (Dougherty, Hastie, Bernard, Broadhurst, & Marcus, 1992).

Supported education is provided through three different approaches: 1) within a self-contained classroom where all the students experience disabilities; 2) through the resources of a particular school (e.g., Disabled Student Services); and 3) by mental health agency staff in a mobile support program (Unger, 1990). In some cases, the support agency works in partnership with a specific educational institution to identify and develop appropriate programs and supports needed, and in others the support agency negotiates individually with the institution that best meets an individual client's educational needs. The provision of services on postsecondary campuses promotes community integration in a typical, nonstigmatizing environment (Unger, Anthony, Sciarappa, & Rogers, 1991).

Supported education services vary across agencies and participants, but typically include assessing educational strengths and support needs, assisting in the development of educational and career choices, assisting in the identification of educational resources in the community, instructing the client in study skills and other areas (e.g., making the transition back to school), coordinating services on and off campus, and advocating on the client's behalf. Additional accommodations may be provided by the school in areas such as assistance with registration or financial aid, extended time or changed locations for exams, permission to tape lectures and discussions, priority parking, modified seat assignments, permission to bring beverages to class, and extended time to complete course work if the illness interferes.

Similar to an employment specialist, the supported education provider arranges or offers the support needed by the client in order to be successful, whether that be wake-up calls, help with homework, or advocacy with an instruc-

Supported education services vary across agencies and participants.

tor to arrange to have exams postponed when the student has been temporarily hospitalized. Some agencies may sponsor peer support groups, or establish a location on campus where participants may relax or seek assistance before and after class.

A 1991 research study showed that the 52 individuals with long-term mental illness who voluntarily participated in a supported education program significantly increased their rate of competitive employment, decreased their number of hospitalizations, and increased their self-esteem (Unger et al., 1991).

CONCLUSION

The area of supported education will undoubtedly continue to grow as consumers express their interest, and the links between education and employment for people with disabilities become clearer. There is increasing evidence that many people with mental illness can successfully enroll in and complete academic courses, and that participating in supported education programs allows people to assume a valued role (student) and to continue their recovery from mental illness (Unger, 1993).

7

QUALITY INDICATORS
IN EMPLOYMENT PROGRAMS

The quality of employment programs is measured by many indicators. Some quality indicators are program management issues (e.g., the experience of the staff, the composition of the board of directors), some are process measures (e.g., the type of services offered to program participants), and some are outcome measures (e.g., the wages earned, hours worked per week). All the different indicators attempt to provide a way to assess if the services provided to clients are as good as they can be.

Having staff members with the skills and experience needed to provide good services is only part of the picture; the structure and characteristics of the program that employs the staff also is an important factor. Linda Toms Barker (1994) examined common characteristics of successful vocational programs serving people with mental illness and identified the following as crucial attributes:

1. A clear mission emphasizing employment outcomes, independence, and full consumer participation.
2. Strong leadership by the program director.
3. Strong support from the umbrella agency.
4. A dedication to consumer empowerment and involvement.
5. The ability to think like a business and respond to all the customer groups (i.e. clients, families, funding agencies).
6. The ability to develop effective working relationships with others in the community.
7. A strong commitment to achieving outcomes, not just providing services.
8. A strong commitment to continuing to change and improve.
9. A willingness to do whatever it takes to provide support in a creative and flexible manner. (p. 61)

Likewise, Powell et al. (1991) recommended that employment programs develop a creed (mission statement) and principles to guide the development and implementation of services, including statements such as "People with disabilities are entitled to full participation in all aspects of life within their communities" and

"No person should be denied access to supported employment because of the severity of that person's disability, behavioral deficits, or behavioral excesses" (p. 16).

The federal definition of supported employment specifies only the basic requirements: The client must be in paid employment, in an integrated setting with ongoing support, and must have a severe disability. The implementation of these basic elements is up to the individual programs and service providers because individualized service is a cornerstone of supported employment. However, there are some quality indicators that are generally recognized as significant for all supported employment programs.

These quality indicators are universal for programs providing vocational services to people with disabilities, although some issues may affect people with some disabilities more than people with other disabilities. For example, although providing nonstigmatizing support on the job is always desirable, it is even more of an issue when working with a client whose disability is not immediately obvious and who does not need assistance in learning the basic job tasks. Quality indicators for supported employment are really descriptors of the kinds of jobs and support everyone would like to have, whether or not they have a disability. Everyone wants an interesting job that matches his skills and interests, pays well, and offers a chance for advancement. Everyone would also like to have support that is gracious and subtle but gives him what he needs to stay employed, as well as relationships with people that respect individuality and value the right to employment.

"Psst! Job coach!"

An employment specialist must be willing to provide support in a creative and flexible manner.

Quality indicators for employment programs are divided into five categories: the basic principles; client eligibility issues; assessment, preemployment, and planning; job development and selection issues; and placement, training, and support issues. These indicators represent the ideal in potential vocational services. Systems barriers or lack of resources (including knowledge and experience) may prevent even the best-intended and purest-valued providers from meeting all criteria, but understanding the quality indicators helps employment specialists be more prepared to meet the needs of their clients. Table 1 provides a listing of the 27 quality indicators discussed in this chapter.

THE BASIC PRINCIPLES

The Agency and Staff Actively Involve the Client and Significant Others

The keystone to good vocational services is the active involvement of the client and significant others. This is often one of the most difficult values to implement, particularly when working with people who have long-term mental illness. The medical model traditionally used in mental health services focused on the profes-

---

Table 1.　The quality indicators in employment programs

The basic principles
 1. The agency and staff actively involve the client and significant others.
 2. The agency and staff value the right to employment.
 3. The agency and the staff believe in their clients' competence.

Client eligibility issues
 4. Client limitations are not reasons for rejection.
 5. Cost and intensity of needed support are not used to reject applicants.
 6. Services are provided with little or no waiting.
 7. Flexible programming allows multiple entries and exits.

Assessment, preemployment, and planning issues
 8. Rehabilitation planning is comprehensive.
 9. A range of employment opportunities is provided.
10. Opportunities to opt out of the fast track are offered.
11. A variety of prevocational services is available.
12. Assessment takes place in the natural environment and relates to real, desired jobs.
13. There is financial coordination in maximizing the positive affect of employment.
14. Family and residential providers are involved and informed.

Job development and selection issues
15. Client and family and friends are involved in job development and matching.
16. Job development efforts are client specific.
17. Paid jobs are valued and desirable.
18. Volunteer jobs are valued and integrated.
19. Potential jobsites are analyzed for possible modification.
20. Care is taken to ensure that jobs are actually integrated.

Placement, training, and support issues
21. Job training is based on data and relates directly to real work requirements.
22. The amount and intensity of support vary.
23. Nonprofessionals are enlisted to provide long-term support.
24. Job modification or reemployment services are available as desired.
25. Support is proactive and emphasizes prevention.
26. Support is personal and caring, not just technical.
27. Interagency cooperation focuses on client concerns and choices.

sional's responsibility for making decisions that were best for the "patient," instead of on client-centered activity and choices (Fisher, 1994). Many employment specialists have remnants of that expert professional role still hanging around and at heart really believe they do know what is best for their clients. The clients often also believe that the professional knows what is best because they are conditioned to be good patients and recipients of services. Therefore, service providers must work hard to ensure that their clients are actively involved in planning, decision making, implementing, evaluating, and learning the skills needed to be full participants in every part of the rehabilitation process.

People with Mental Illness Are Competent and Have a Right to Community-Based Employment

The agency and its staff must be committed to the belief that people with mental illness are competent and have a right to community-based employment. Clients and employers may be doubtful about whether people with long-term mental illness can or should be employed. The agency and its staff must have a strong, public commitment to believing that employment is the right of all people, with or without disabilities, and that people with long-term mental illness can be valuable employees. It is crucial that not only employment specialists, but all other agency staff (from the job developer to the receptionist) represent the agency's clients as capable and competent rather than as recipients of charity, because if employment support providers do not believe in their clients, the employers will not believe in them either.

Some vocational units may be part of a larger mental health agency where the policies and procedures do not support this type of commitment. In this type of situation it is not impossible for the employment specialist to provide excellent vocational services and assist clients in meeting vocational goals, but it is very difficult. The employment program staff, as well as the clients who participate in and benefit from employment services, should consider two different approaches when in this type of system: 1) trying to establish a separate identity in the community through the use of a different name and location, and 2) using their best team-building skills to educate the other mental health staff about the competencies and rights of people with mental illness.

CLIENT ELIGIBILITY ISSUES

Client Limitations Are Not Reasons for Rejection

Because supported employment does not subscribe to the work readiness model for eligibility, potential clients are not excluded from good programs because of their behavior problems, poor social skills, communication ability, symptom activity, motivational issues, or degree of intellectual disability. The assumption is that the program should provide the training and support that each individual needs.

Cost and Intensity of Needed Support Is Not Used to Reject Applicants

The projected cost and intensity of needed support should never be used to reject applicants. Ideally, any person with a disability should be given full access to any type of employment service regardless of the amount of support needed. Realistically, few programs can afford to provide full-time, one-to-one support to a client forever because of the funding available. Many programs deal with this problem by providing group employment opportunities to clients who need full-time support.

Services Are Provided with Little or No Waiting

Vocational services should be available with little or no waiting for all individuals who wish to use them. Again, here is an area where reality may also clash with idealism because funding or staffing limitations may impose waiting periods before clients can have access to services. Referrals to other services should also be provided to individuals wanting services not available from the agency. For example, if an employment specialist determines during the intake process that an individual has educational needs and interests that cannot be met by her agency, she should help the client gain access to those services elsewhere rather than convincing him to participate in a service the agency does provide.

Flexible Programming Allows Multiple Entries and Exits

A flexible program is important because it allows the client multiple entries and exits. The rehabilitation process for mental illness is usually lengthy and not particularly linear. Therefore, to expect every client to start at point A and proceed through a structured program to point Z without many detours is unrealistic. In an individualized approach, clients are able to enter programs at different levels, drop out of services temporarily, and reenter them as needed. In other words, a client with a clear vocational goal might skip preemployment and assessment activities and move right into employment. Another client with little interest in formal assessment might choose to start by trying several transitional employment placements before settling on a more permanent goal. Still another client might sample some transitional jobs, drop out of services for a few months, and then reenter the program in a volunteer work crew.

ASSESSMENT, PREEMPLOYMENT, AND PLANNING ISSUES

Rehabilitation Planning Is Comprehensive

Rehabilitation planning must be comprehensive in nature because it is impossible to completely separate work and nonwork issues. No one works in a vacuum. People with long-term mental illness are unlikely to be successful in employment unless they have the support they need in other areas of their lives (e.g., residential, recreational, interpersonal relationships, health). This support may already exist in the client's environment or it may need to be provided by paid providers (e.g., residential, case manager), but it needs to be considered when planning ongoing activities.

A Range of Employment Opportunities Is Provided

Employment programs should be able to help their clients gain access to a range of employment opportunities, whether they are paid or unpaid, part- or full-time, transitional or permanent, or entry or advanced level. It is important to recognize that client preference may conflict with federal legislation defining supported employment. As discussed in Chapter 5, a good program must separate the services needed and wanted by their clients from the available programs (e.g., VR, Medicaid) used to fund the services.

Opportunities to Opt Out of the Fast Track

There should be the opportunity to get out of the fast track by working in a job that does not necessarily represent the most ambitious choice for that individual. Because many people with long-term mental illness have not made many life decisions that turned out well for them, employment specialists may need to repeatedly encourage clients to give vocational opportunities a try. However, clients must not be made to feel guilty for making decisions that prioritize other values (e.g., security, family, time for recreation) over a chance to operate at their highest level of vocational functioning. A worker who is capable of competitive, full-time employment might still choose to continue working in his current, part-time job because he has friends at work and feels comfortable. Although this choice may not maximize his vocational potential (at least in the opinion of the employment specialist), it should be respected and supported.

A Variety of Prevocational Services

A range of prevocational services should be available in all employment programs. These services should include vocational assessment, career counseling and planning, training in basic work skills, and job-seeking skills. Activities such as internships, volunteer work, transitional employment, job clubs, or job shadowing should be available for people who want to use them to clarify vocational goals or practice skills, but no one should be required to participate in prevocational activities if they prefer to go directly into paid employment. Prevocational activities have not been shown to increase the likelihood of eventual employment success.

Assessment Takes Place in the Natural Environment and Relates to Real, Desired Jobs

Assessment activities should take place in the natural environment and relate to real, desired jobs. Environments significantly affect behavior, and therefore assessment activities should take place in the natural environment or in an environment that best approximates the natural environment. A person who has no difficulty with a filing task done in an empty, quiet room might have many problems trying to work in a noisy basement with nine other filing clerks. Assessment should also relate to real, desired jobs. For many years, standard assessments were used to keep people with disabilities out of employment programs. This approach was based on people without severe disabilities, and the measures used assumed a narrow view of work as a skills-only issue. If a person walked slowly, had limited academic or communication skills, or showed poor decision-making skills, he was considered unemployable.

A good approach includes assessing only those characteristics that are necessary for a particular job and using the information to identify the training and support needed, instead of to screen people out of programs. Walking speed is irrelevant for a person who wants to be a computer operator, but the question of whether the client can groom himself appropriately for work each day is important and may indicate that he needs additional training or support in order to be successful.

Financial Coordination

Financial coordination is a vital part of the employment support process. The loss of unearned benefits such as Supplemental Security Income (SSI), Social Security Disability Insurance (SSDI), and medical insurance is a major concern to many individuals with disabilities. Good service providers make sure that clients have detailed information about the effect working will have on their financial situation and help clients work within the benefit system to maximize income and financial stability.

Families and Residential Providers Are Involved

As discussed in Chapter 3, family members and residential providers should be involved and informed. Although many people with long-term mental illness have no contact with their families, many do continue to be involved with and receive support from family members. Other clients may be involved in some type of residential services, (e.g., group homes, supervised apartments) as well as supported employment. The employment specialist must implement strategies (when appropriate) to ensure that family members and residential providers are involved and able to support the client's goal of employment. Although this is not always easy, it usually is crucial because these people often have the power to support or obstruct rehabilitation efforts. Besides, an employment specialist spends no more than 40 hours per week with the client over a limited period of time (months or years), while a client may be with his family or residential providers twice that much time per week and still live with them long after he is stable in a job or has dropped out of vocational services.

JOB DEVELOPMENT AND SELECTION ISSUES

Clients and Their Families and Friends Should Be Involved

Actively involving the client and his family and friends in job development and selection ensures that the client's preferences and interests will be considered and also gives him more control of the process and increases the likelihood of job success. Friends and family may also be valuable resources for job leads that match the client's skills and interest.

Job Development Efforts Are Client Specific

This standard reflects the value of client choice and control in finding a job. The person responsible for job development must have in-depth knowledge of the client being served, as well as the services offered by the agency. People with severe disabilities often have limited work skills that make specialized job development necessary to ensure success. When programs provide only general job development, clients with limited work skills tend to be passed over as job opportunities are filled.

Paid Jobs Are Valued and Desirable

Ideally, employment specialists should be helping their clients succeed in paid jobs that they themselves would feel comfortable in or that they would choose for their children or siblings. Realistically, many people with disabilities begin working in entry-level service jobs that are easy to obtain, easy to learn, repetitive, and often tolerant of different behaviors. The employment specialist should at least attempt to find jobs that meet basic quality criteria including the following:

- Hours of employment that are typical of those worked by others in the community (unless the client strongly prefers otherwise)

- A work environment that is safe, friendly, and comfortable
- Jobs that are permanent
- Jobs that have low turnover of supervisors and co-workers and have opportunities for advancement
- Jobs that pay workers commensurate wages
- An integrated workplace

The employment specialist must also ensure that clients have choices beyond entry-level service jobs and that low expectations of their clients' capabilities do not interfere with their right to choose. It is wrong to assume that all people with long-term mental illness would choose a service job or that they need to succeed in an entry-level job before moving on to more advanced positions. Individual planning and client choice are two very important issues in identifying jobs.

Volunteer Jobs Are Valued and Integrated

Volunteer jobs should also be in valued and integrated positions. Employment programs should make volunteer jobs available to clients who want to work but prefer unpaid employment for any of a variety of reasons. Clients may feel unprepared to make a commitment to paid employment, they may want to protect their access to unearned income (e.g., SSDI), or they may feel more confident of their success in a volunteer position. Volunteer jobs should be in valued and integrated sites where people without disabilities also work as volunteers.

Potential Jobsites Are Analyzed for Possible Modification

The employment specialist should analyze potential jobsites and job descriptions for adaptation and modification. It is common that no available job opportunity exactly meets the identified needs of a given client, so the employment specialist must be alert for possible ways of modifying the jobsite or adapting the existing job description. This may involve trying to narrow or combine existing job responsibilities to suit individual needs, negotiating different work schedules, or modifying work procedures to make them more routine.

Care Is Taken to Ensure that Jobs Are Actually Integrated

Jobs that seem to offer integrated employment may in fact be quite segregated. For example, a dishwasher who works in a cafeteria with workers without disabilities may be in an integrated environment, but if he is the only worker in the dishwashing area and takes his breaks alone, then he really has limited contact with others on the job. In addition, clients may be excluded from typical workplace routines because of their disabilities. Providing support for inclusion may mean that the employment specialist must deal directly with the stigma associated with mental illness or develop routines that compensate for inadequate social skills on the part of the worker.

PLACEMENT, TRAINING, AND SUPPORT ISSUES

Job Training Is Based on Data and Relates Directly to Real Work Requirements

Job training must relate directly to real work requirements and be based on data. Job training should focus on critical matches between client skills and job demands, rather than on generic job skills. Because there are important activities involved with jobs that have little or nothing to do with getting the work done, nonwork functions should be included in training as needed. These include general social interactions, workplace routines such as coffee breaks and lunch, and activities away from the workplace. These nonwork functions are often crucial in fostering acceptance and support of the worker with a disability.

Responsible employment specialists collect data on the results of their efforts, whether those efforts involve job development, skills training, or family involvement. It is important for the employment specialist and the client to agree on the goal of an activity and how progress toward, or accomplishment of, that goal can be measured. The measurement of that progress or accomplishment then becomes the data that the client and employment specialist use to evaluate and modify their efforts.

The Amount and Intensity of Support

Depending on the client's need, the employment specialist should vary the amount and intensity of the support provided. People with long-term mental illness vary in the amount and type of support they need to be successful on the job. One person may need a significant amount of job structuring and task analysis, while another may not need any on-site assistance but does require support in problem solving and planning away from the site. A third worker may need moderate amounts of on-site support, but his employer may be willing and able to provide that support. Good support and service is tailor made to consider the employment setting and the need of the client. No matter what the situation is, the support should be nonstigmatizing, reference the natural cues and consequences available on the job, and, when possible, follow the typical training procedures used in a particular workplace.

"John's needing a little extra support today."

The amount and intensity of support vary with individual needs.

Nonprofessionals Are Enlisted to Provide Long-Term Support

Nonprofessionals should be enlisted to provide long-term support when quality standards can be maintained. This standard addresses principles of normalization, as well as recognizing that even long-term paid employment support is not full-time or lifelong. Most workers without disabilities are supported on the job by their families, employers, friends, and co-workers, and there are many workers with disabilities who will testify that this type of support is also available to them as well as preferred by them (Anderson & Andrews, 1990). Nonprofessional support may also allow the employment specialist to stretch what may be scarce service dollars. However, the employment specialist must make certain that the support being provided is actually what is needed for the client and those who have agreed to provide support are willing to continue for as long as it is needed.

In addition, the employment specialist should provide assistance in maintaining the existing friendships and other relationships of the client. This standard reflects the value of natural supports and the importance of employment in terms of the client's life as a whole. People who are moving into employment may need assistance in maintaining personal relationships while spending more of their time and energy at work, or they may need strategies in dealing with their changing role in the family or peer group as they move from "patient" to "client" to "worker." (See Chapter 19 for further discussion of natural supports.)

Job Modification or Reemployment Services Are Available

When it is clear that a worker is becoming dissatisfied with his job, the employment specialist should support him in job modification or reemployment. Reemployment assistance should also be provided to workers who lose or leave their jobs. Many people with long-term mental illness will need to try several different job options before becoming stably employed, a pattern that is not dissimilar to that experienced by workers without disabilities. Therefore, the employment specialist needs to plan for job changes as part of the support program.

Support Is Proactive and Emphasizes Prevention

Support should be proactive, not reactive, and emphasize prevention. The employment specialist must build a system of supports that is not totally dependent on employer panic or on a client's ability to identify a need before an intervention is made. It must be assumed that a client moving into employment will experience difficulties at some point. The employment specialist should offer ongoing support (e.g., individual meetings on- or off-site, telephone contact, group meetings) instead of waiting for a problem to occur.

Support Is Personal and Caring, Not Just Technical

In addition, support must be personal and caring, not just technical. To quote Joe Marrone, "It is difficult for people to provide the level of support people need during a difficult period in their lives (i.e., starting work) when there is no meaningful relationship behind the provision of that support" (1990, p. V-2). It is the relationship established between the employment specialist and the client and often between the employment specialist and the employer that enables the employment specialist to provide effective support. When a client needs support on the job, the reason he calls the local supported agency is not because the agency has an excellent reputation. It is because the client wants to talk to an individual he knows and trusts.

Interagency Cooperation Focuses on Client Needs and Choices

Interagency cooperation must focus on client needs and choices because people with long-term mental illness typically receive services from a variety of agencies, whether it is vocational, residential, mental health, or medical. Cooperative planning, goal setting, and implementation are the keystones of good service. These efforts should focus on client needs and choices in order to circumvent territoriality, power struggles, sabotage, and the like.

CONCLUSION

It is difficult to set up absolute criteria for quality indicators because the bottom line is client control and client choice, but Table 1 reviews 27 quality indicators relating to employment programs. Employment programs should encourage clients to consider many different employment options; allow clients to move in and out of participation in response to personal need; provide access to jobs that match client preference, interests, and skills; and provide or coordinate the training and support needed for client success. Only when every client has these opportunities will employment specialists be providing quality services.

8

THE ROLE OF
STATE VOCATIONAL
REHABILITATION COUNSELORS

The increased inclusion of people with long-term mental illness in vocational programs throughout the United States has forced service providers in vocational rehabilitation (VR) and mental health (MH) systems to coordinate their efforts. Since the 1970s, federal attention to this issue has contributed to the development of formal cooperative agreements between the VR and MH systems in at least 37 states. However, the significant differences between the two systems make it necessary for local practitioners to develop flexible implementation strategies that will be effective for their communities. Although strong links have been forged in some communities, in many others MH and VR counselors view each other with suspicion and frustration (Tashjian et al., 1989).

People with mental illness have been included in vocational rehabilitation since 1954 (Vocational Rehabilitation Act Amendments of 1954, PL 83-565). Although there has been an increase in the number of agencies providing vocational services to people with long-term mental illness, the percentage of successful vocational rehabilitation closures (60 days of employment) has remained stable or declined while the percentage of successful closures for people with disabilities other than mental illness has increased over the same period (Rutman, 1994). Although the percentage of successful closures differs across studies of VR outcomes, people with psychiatric disabilities uniformly have a lower rate than people with other disabilities. Anthony (1994a) reported that after 18 months of VR services only 25% of clients with mental illness had been successfully employed, compared to 50% of those with physical disabilities. An analysis of VR closures between 1984 and 1988 showed that 57% of the clients with mental illness were closed as successfully employed, compared to 76% of clients with hearing impairments and 63% of clients with mental retardation (Rutman, 1994). Marrone (1993) reported in his study that 48% of people with mental illness had successful closures, while 60%–65% of people with other disabilities were successfully closed.

McGurrin (1994) reported figures of 53% for people with mental illness and 61% for people with physical disabilities. Anthony also reported that people with mental illness were just as likely to be found eligible for VR services as people with other disabilities, although they were less likely to exit the system in a permanent job.

Part of the difficulty involved in integrating the two systems is that the VR and MH systems have been developed to meet different needs and goals, and they function in very different ways. VR and MH counselors may share a job title and some of their clients, but they have very different roles in helping people with disabilities gain access to and maintain jobs. Increased understanding of these differences in systems may help identify ways to work with them.

WHY DOES VOCATIONAL REHABILITATION HAVE TO BE INVOLVED AT ALL?

Although in some ways it would be simpler to have the mental health system provide all needed services (including vocational services) to people with mental illness, there are two reasons VR should be involved. First, vocational rehabilitation is a good resource for people with mental illness. In some cases, funding may be available from VR to buy vocational support services (e.g., job coaching) when needed. But even more importantly, most VR counselors offer expertise in job

"Diggs from CIA, Brown from FBI, meet Figwitz from DVR."

Mental health and vocational rehabilitation counselors may view each other with suspicion and frustration.

development, vocational planning, assessment, and job placement that can be very valuable to mental health practitioners and their clients.

Second, people with mental illness should have access to, and responsive assistance from, the same services available to people with other disabilities. People with mental illness make up the largest single client group of those eligible for VR services (Anthony, 1994a; Marrone, 1990).

WHAT DO VOCATIONAL REHABILITATION COUNSELORS REALLY DO?

Vocational rehabilitation counselors have two major roles: they provide services themselves (e.g., vocational counseling, job placement) and they purchase and coordinate other services. Although specialized caseloads are used in a few areas (i.e., most of the counselor's clients have mental illness), most counselors deal with people who have a variety of disabilities. In fact, the typical counselor may have only a few clients with mental illness or other mental disabilities. Therefore, a VR counselor may not have experience in dealing with clients who need intensive and ongoing services, and who may not talk or think very well. In the United States, the average VR counselor has about 100 clients at a time (Tashjian et al., 1989), and about 20% of those served by the VR system have some form of mental illness as a primary disability (Government Accounting Office, 1993).

Although VR counselors have a prescribed structure in which to work, they have a significant amount of latitude within that structure. The steps a client and counselor must go through to reach rehabilitation are fixed and uniform, but the services that are planned for those steps are individually selected by the client and the VR counselor. The counselor then monitors the services as they are provided and adjusts the plan as needed. Figure 1 illustrates the vocational rehabilitation process.

THE VOCATIONAL REHABILITATION PROCESS

Application and Eligibility

The vocational rehabilitation process begins after an individual's application has been received. Eligibility for services is dependent on whether or not an individual applicant has a disability and "requires vocational rehabilitation services to prepare for, enter into, engage in or retain gainful employment" (RehabACTion Advocacy Network, 1992, p. 3). Most people with long-term mental illness meet this criterion if they are receiving mental health services or getting Supplemental Security Income (SSI). Prior to the passage of PL 102-569, the Rehabilitation Act Amendments of 1992, applicants also had to prove that they had employment potential—this was known as the *feasibility test*. Under the 1992 Amendments, individuals are presumed to be capable of employment in integrated settings, regardless of their disability. Therefore, the burden of proof has been removed from the applicant and placed on the agency because VR can only determine noneligibility if they can provide clear evidence that the applicant is not employable. The intensity or cost of services and the support the individual may need to attain employment cannot be used as a reason for VR to deny eligibility. Medical and psychological examinations, or information from recent examinations, may be required (and paid for by VR, if necessary) in order to facilitate the plan develop-

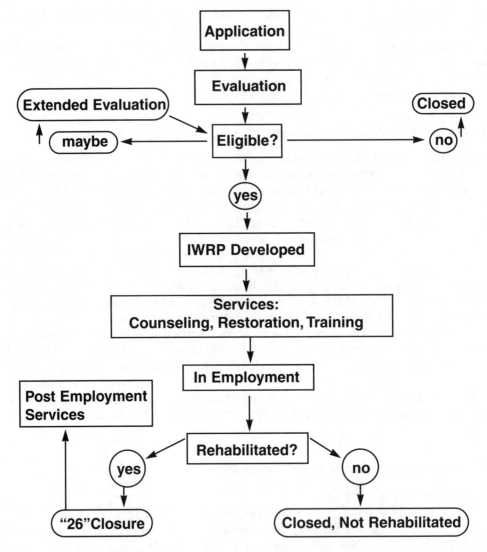

Figure 1.   An overview of the vocational rehabilitation process.

ment. VR is required to determine eligibility within 60 days of application, unless the applicant agrees that an extension is necessary.

Planning and Service Delivery

If the client is found to be eligible, she moves into the planning phase. The planning phase includes the development of an individualized written rehabilitation plan (IWRP) that specifies the vocational goals and services to be provided, an evaluation procedure, and identification of the provider(s) to be involved. According to the Rehabilitation Act Amendments of 1992, the client is a full partner in the planning phase and should work together with the VR counselor to develop the plan. The client should have the right to specify service providers or options in her own plan, and the IWRP should document the client's participation in making choices (West, Kregel, & Revell, 1994). Some VR counselors, especially those who have developed a good working relationship with a vocational service provider (vendor) from whom they purchase services, feel comfortable having the vendor develop the IWRP with the client. Other counselors prefer to maintain control over the process. The rehabilitation plan must lead to employment and should be tailored to meet the needs of the individual by specifying the services to be provided by the VR counselor or purchased from the vendors (e.g., counseling, training, transportation, medical or psychological restoration, education).

Closure

Once a client has maintained employment for at least 60 days her case may be closed as a status 26, which signifies a successful rehabilitation for the VR counselor. Clients closed before reaching 60 days of employment are closed in status 08 or 28 and are not considered to be successfully rehabilitated. Competitive employment, supported or transitional employment, self-employment, homemaking, and sometimes sheltered employment may all be considered successful closures. The number of clients successfully rehabilitated (i.e., closed in status 26) is an important measure of counselor success. Tashjian et al. (1989) reported that 38 states have specific VR counselor performance requirements for the number or percentage of successful case closures to be achieved (e.g., 100 cases opened, 50 plans written, 25 successful closures in status 26 per year).

VR counselors are allocated a limited amount of money to use in serving their clients throughout the year. These funds are usually credited once per year, which can lead to money being scarce toward the end of the 12-month period. Because VR counselors are expected to show successful outcomes in spite of limited financial resources, they must try to meet their clients' needs in the most cost-effective way possible. This pressure occasionally leads to an individual VR counselor being unenthusiastic about working with clients who may need more intensive or expensive services to be successful, although such discrimination is officially not allowed.

Because of limited resources, only 5%–7% of those eligible for VR services actually receive them (Government Accounting Office, 1993). VR is looked at in many areas as a rich source of funds that may be holding out on clients with more severe disabilities. In fact, the VR system is small compared to the mental health system and controls only a fraction of the funding resources. In 1981, the New York State Mental Health Department alone had a budget of $2 billion, while the U.S. VR budget was only $1 billion (Woy & Dellario, 1985). The average amount spent in 1988 to purchase rehabilitative services for each client with mental illness was $1,224 (Government Accounting Office, 1993), which is only a fraction of what it costs to place and support most people needing intensive vocational services. The remaining costs were borne by other public funds (e.g., Medicaid).

Supported Employment

In some states, supported employment services differ slightly from general VR services. Supported employment referrals are sometimes given "interim eligibility" and moved directly into a training status when placed on a job. The VR counselor then has 90 days to complete the background on the application process (e.g., medical exams). This flexibility is an important asset to supported employment programs because the programs are able to receive VR funding for on-the-job training during the first few weeks of employment without waiting for the application to be fully processed. Although this option is legal in all states, not all states choose to use it.

IWRPs written for supported employment clients must include an outline of ongoing support services to be provided after VR funding, an identification of the program that will provide or coordinate the ongoing support services, and the basis for determining that ongoing support services (i.e., funding) are available.

In some areas, a particular VR counselor is designated as a supported employment specialist and handles the majority of the supported employment clients. In others, VR counselors have only a few supported employment clients within their caseload. Although separate supported employment funds exist, the same services (e.g., job coaching) may be purchased with regular VR funds for those clients eligible for supported employment.

SPECIFIC DIFFERENCES BETWEEN
THE VOCATIONAL REHABILITATION AND MENTAL HEALTH SYSTEMS

It is impossible to write a uniform description of the mental health system in the United States because unlike vocational rehabilitation, mental health service systems vary throughout the country. In one state, for example, mental health services are provided by state employees working in mental health clinics but in a neighboring state services are provided by private, nonprofit agencies that contract with county boards who specify what services are needed in that community.

Although there are many basic differences in the way VR and MH services are provided, there are two similarities. First, both systems are pressured to work with reduced levels of funding and with individuals who have the most significant disabilities. In fact, people with less significant disabilities (who might have been served 10 years ago) are being denied services because there is not sufficient funding. The disabilities of the client population are more severe now than they were previously, causing significant consequences in the provision of vocational services. For example, a mental health center with limited funding that is permitted to serve only clients in crisis will probably do very little job placement. Another similarity between systems is the increased emphasis on client choice and empowerment. Both the vocational rehabilitation and mental health systems attempt to actively involve clients in the decision-making processes relating to their own cases, as well as in the management of the agency, development of peer support groups, client advocacy offices, and advisory boards that include clients.

Although the two mentioned similarities are important, the vocational rehabilitation system differs from most mental health systems in several important ways. A brief review of the many different features of the two systems follows. Although most issues are more complex than they appear in this brief review, it is clear that the two systems are quite different in their scope and intention. Table 1 provides a list of the differences.

Goal Oriented versus Process Oriented

The VR system is goal oriented and counselors are expected to get concrete results. However, the MH system has traditionally been process oriented and counselors are judged more by the quality and appropriateness of the treatment provided than by its effect on clients. This is gradually changing with the movement toward "managed care" funding systems that have more emphasis on outcomes.

Table 1. The vocational rehabilitation system versus traditional mental health systems

Vocational rehabilitation	Mental health
Goal oriented	Process oriented
Time limited	Ongoing
Vocational only	Multiple focuses
Many disabilities	Mental illness
Restoration of functioning	Reduce symptoms
Uniform across states	Pluralistic and loosely organized
Federal or state funding	Multiple funding sources
Service brokers	Expert providers
Client driven	Slot driven

Time Limited versus Ongoing

VR services are designed to be time limited, and cases are eventually closed whether or not the client has become employed. MH services are ongoing and may be lifelong if needed by the client.

Vocational versus Multiple Focuses

VR focuses primarily on the vocational issues the client faces (e.g., learning the skills for a job), but MH may deal with all parts of the client's life including medical, vocational, residential, psychological, and recreational aspects.

Many Disabilities versus Mental Illness

VR counselors generally work with people who have many different disabilities. MH counselors usually work with people who have mental illness, although in some states the mental health system also works with people who have developmental disabilities, traumatic brain injuries, or other organic brain dysfunctions.

Restoration of Functioning versus Reduction of Symptoms

The VR process focuses on restoring clients to their highest level of functioning through training and compensatory strategies, while the MH process typically focuses on reducing the symptoms of the illness through treatment. Although many excellent mental health programs do focus on restoring and enhancing functioning levels, this is still an important distinction between the two systems that affects treatment and goal planning. Mental health professionals may say a client is not ready for employment because she is still experiencing symptoms and therefore is not free of disease, whereas the vocational rehabilitation approach would consider what the person is able to do and try to build on that.

Uniformity Across States versus Pluralism and Loose Organization

The VR system is fairly uniform across states and regions and has operating policies set at the federal level; the MH system is primarily state determined, pluralistic, and loosely organized. The VR system in any state typically consists of a state office, regional administrators, and individual counselors who work with clients. The MH system may include public and private hospitals, other institutions, residences, community mental health centers, clinics, and individual practitioners.

Federal or State Funding versus Multiple Funding Sources

By statute, VR agencies receive 78.7% of their funding from federal sources with a 21.3% match from state or other sources. Individual MH agencies arrange their own funding, primarily from state tax funds and public or private insurance reimbursement, but possibly from other sources as well (e.g., VR, SSA, private pay, grants).

Service Brokers versus Expert Providers

Many VR counselors see themselves primarily as brokers who are responsible for arranging a system of needed services. MH counselors see themselves primarily as expert providers who would only rarely purchase services from other providers (Woy & Dellario, 1985).

Client Driven versus Slot Driven

The VR system is client driven (i.e., money is allocated to purchase specific services for a specific client), and the MH system is more slot driven (i.e., money is awarded for providing a given amount of services to any clients who qualify). As the number of mental health managed-care systems increases and moves away from using billable hours to documenting service provisions, this will be even more prevalent.

CONCLUSION

The vocational rehabilitation and mental health systems differ across many important areas and do not automatically coordinate smoothly. However, many individuals with mental illness are eligible for and would benefit from both systems. An understanding of the structure, function, and goals of the systems will enable the employment specialist to better assist people with mental illness in using VR and MH resources to obtain and maintain stable employment.

9

SOCIAL SECURITY ISSUES

In the United States, one of the biggest obstacles an employment specialist must face is encouraging people with long-term mental illness to seek employment even though they have a fear of losing unearned benefits, especially Social Security Disability Insurance (SSDI), Supplemental Security Income (SSI), and associated medical insurance programs. In fact, a 1984 study of factors predicting employment success showed that fear of losing unearned benefits was one of the few things that indicated a higher risk of failure (Anthony, Howell, & Danley, 1984).

The SSI system has undergone extensive modification over the years and has added a realistic incentive to becoming employed by prorating the cash benefits and making it easy to resume benefits if earned income drops. However, the SSDI system remains punitive to people who consistently earn more than $500 per month. Muller (1992) reported that only 3% of all people with disabilities who receive SSDI ever return to work, and Rutman (1994) reported that providers and families were reluctant to encourage people with disabilities to accept employment if it in any way jeopardized their benefits. Rutman also reported that people with disabilities and their families find that work incentives are complex and difficult to understand. Because many people with severe disabilities are likely to have part-time or low-paying jobs, receiving ongoing cash benefits and medical insurance becomes a real factor in deciding whether to seek employment and at what level.

However, there are work incentives available through the Social Security Administration (SSA) to encourage recipients to resume or attempt employment. Employment specialists must understand that the fear of losing unearned benefits is a realistic and important one, and they must be prepared with information on ways to help clients try employment without jeopardizing their benefit status. Anthony (1994a) wrote that in two recent studies of individuals served by a program that provided Social Security advocacy and vocational support, there was no relationship between vocational outcome and benefits received. Anthony hypothesized that through the advocacy services the clients had learned to balance their part-time work and their continued benefits and were no longer fearful of losing their access to benefits.

Service providers are often too conservative about how much a client can do without jeopardizing his benefits. Program directors have been known to say, "None of our clients are *allowed* to work more than 20 hours per week—we don't want to jeopardize their benefits." Although this may work for many of the agency's clients, there may also be clients who could earn substantial wages with support and who might choose to forfeit their beneficiary status in favor of self-support. It is important for the employment specialist to ensure that the client is the one who chooses the road to pursue.

One of the things that makes Social Security work incentives difficult to understand is that the two main programs, SSDI and SSI, have different rules and procedures. Many clients are eligible for both programs and therefore have inter-acting considerations. This chapter briefly outlines the major work incentive programs available under SSI and SSDI and discusses some resources available for more information.

ACRONYMS AND DEFINITIONS

One of the things that makes working with Social Security so confusing are the abbreviations and acronyms that are thrown around with abandon: "After the

"She deserves a raise, but she doesn't need the money—she has Medicaid!"

Providers and families are reluctant to encourage people with disabilities to accept employment if it in any way jeopardizes benefits.

TWP, the EPE begins so you get a check unless you're at SGA." Following is a list of the common terms and abbreviations used.

- *Break-Even Point*—The point, in the SSI program, when the person's gross earnings are high enough that he or she no longer is eligible for a cash benefit.
- *Continuing Disability Review (CDR)*—The review of a person's case to determine whether or not he or she still has a disability. CDRs are done by the state Disabilities Determination Service (DDS).
- *Earned Income*—Income earned by working.
- *Extended Period of Eligibility (EPE)*—The 3-year period after the trial work period (TWP), during which an SSDI recipient receives his or her cash benefit in any month when earned income drops below the substantial gainful activity benchmark (see definition below).
- *Federal Benefit Rate (FBR)*—The base rate for SSI, which is supplied by the U.S. federal government to the states for distribution. Most states supplement the FBR with additional funds.
- *Impairment Related Work Expenses (IRWE)*—Expenses that are paid by the individual, necessary for employment, and disability related (e.g., job coaching).
- *Plans for Achieving Self Support (PASS)*—A program for SSI recipients that allows them to shelter and spend income and/or resources toward a vocational goal, while lessening the effect on their unearned benefits.
- *Social Security Administration (SSA)*—A large federal government agency that administers a number of health and social service programs.
- *Social Security Disability Insurance (SSDI)*—The insurance program that provides benefits when individuals who developed disabilities have paid into the system.
- *Social Security for Disabled Adult Children (SSDAC)*—A form of SSDI benefits paid to a worker's child who has a disability if the worker has paid into the system and has developed a disability, died, or retired. SSDAC is paid only if the child's disability was documented before the age of 22.
- *Substantial Gainful Activity (SGA)*—The benchmark ($500 per month in 1994) that Social Security uses to determine whether a person is employed at a significant level. If a person makes more than $500 per month, he is engaging in SGA and may not be eligible for benefits. SGA is used to determine initial eligibility for both the SSDI and SSI programs and to determine ongoing eligibility for SSDI. In some cases, earnings between $300 and $500 per month *may* also be considered SGA if it appears that the person is capable of working and earning more but is choosing not to or is being paid less than his work is worth in order to limit his earnings.
- *Supplemental Security Income (SSI)*—The welfare program that provides benefits for people with disabilities who have very limited financial resources.
- *Threshold Amount*—In the SSI program, the amount of gross earnings that makes a person no longer eligible for 1619B (Medicaid benefits) alone. Threshold amounts are established on an individual state basis.
- *Title II*—The Social Security Disability Insurance legislation.
- *Title XVI*—The Supplemental Security Income legislation.
- *Trial Work Period (TWP)*—The time period during which a person receiving SSDI first tries to return to work.
- *Unearned Income*—Income from nonwork sources including SSDI, in-kind support (e.g., meals provided without cost, free rent), investments, insurance settlements, veterans benefits, or injured worker payments after the first 6 months.

SSI WORK INCENTIVES

The SSI program is a welfare program designed to provide support for individuals with disabilities who have limited resources and income. In order to be eligible, a person must have less than $500 a month income (SGA) and less than $2,000 in assets at the time of the application. There are some assets (e.g., a car, home, some life insurance policies) that are excluded. Because states often subsidize the FBR, the base amount of SSI a person receives depends on the state or region in which he lives. Marital status and living situation also affect payment amount. In-kind income (e.g., free food, clothing, shelter) and deemed income (i.e., income of a spouse, parent, or immigration sponsor) are also considered when determining the base rate of SSI.

People receiving SSI are also often eligible for Medicaid (e.g., medical coupons), which is the state-administered, federally funded medical insurance program for people with limited resources. It may be necessary to file a separate application for Medicaid. After the onset of the disability there is no waiting period for SSI, so people should be encouraged to apply as early as possible because it is easier to be eligible for SSI before employment. People with substance abuse may have to go into treatment before receiving SSI and must have a representative payee to receive their benefit checks and help manage their income. Table 1 summarizes Social Security work incentives.

Working and SSI

Over the years, various adjustments have been added to the SSI program to make it possible for recipients to earn money and avoid financial penalties for their efforts. In all cases, *amount earned* refers to gross earnings—the figure the Social Security Administration uses to calculate benefit amounts. SSI amounts are prorated according to the following formulas:

1.   The first $65 a person earns does not affect the SSI amount a person receives. If the person has only SSI and earned income, another $20 is excluded, bringing the total exclusions to $85. If the person has unearned income (e.g., SSDI) as well, the $20 is deducted from the unearned income instead.

2.   Earnings (remaining after the exclusions have been deducted) are divided by 2, and the total is deducted from the SSI check. For example, consider a person who was receiving $450 a month from SSI with no unearned income, who then begins to earn $285 a month. The first $85 earned does not affect his benefit. The remainder ($200) is divided by 2, and the result ($100) is subtracted from the SSI check. Therefore, he will continue to receive $350 a month in SSI benefits in addition to his wages of $285, for a total of $635.

$285	Gross earnings
−85	Earned income ($65) and general ($20) exclusions
$200	Earnings after exclusions
÷2	Divide total by 2
$100	Earnings to be subtracted from full SSI amount
$450	Full SSI amount (with no earned income)
−100	Earnings to be subtracted
$350	SSI amount received while working
$285	Gross earnings
+350	Adjusted SSI amount
$635	Total gross income

3. Once the person is earning SGA or more, a CDR will likely be conducted within 12 months to verify that the individual still has a significant disability that is an impediment to working (O'Mara & Pellegrino, 1993a). If after the review it is decided that an individual no longer has a disability that affects his employment, his SSI eligibility will cease. However, if he is determined to still have a disability, he will continue to receive a prorated benefit check and medical benefits up to the break-even point when his income level brings his cash benefit to zero. Using the display above, the break-even point for a base SSI amount of $450 would be $985. This amount is established by excluding the first $85 and then dividing the remaining $900 by 2, and then subtracting this amount from the base SSI amount. The break-even point for each individual depends on the base SSI amount and on whether he has unearned income. Earnings at the break-even point sometimes trigger another CDR, if the last one was done more than 12 months before.

$985	Gross earnings
−85	Earned income ($65) and general ($20) exclusions
$900	Earnings after exclusions
÷2	Divided by 2
$450	Earnings to be subtracted from full SSI amount
$450	Full SSI amount (with no earned income)
−450	Earnings counted against SSI amount
$0	Adjusted SSI amount; Medicaid continues

4. Above the break-even point, the person should continue to receive medical benefits up to the threshold amount. The threshold amount is the level of earnings that has been determined to be sufficient for the person to purchase his own medical insurance. This amount varies across states as a result of differences in the cost of medical services but generally requires earnings of $1,000 per month or more. If an individual has unusually high medical expenses, the individual's threshold may be adjusted, therefore making it possible for him to earn a substantial amount of money and still be eligible for Medicaid. In addition, as long as the person stays below the threshold amount, his enrollment is maintained in SSI (even though he is not getting a check each month), and the person can therefore have his cash benefits reinstated without reapplication if his earnings drop below the break-even point.

There are two requirements that must be met before an individual receives this benefit. One requirement is that the person must not have more than the FBR in unearned income (Koehler & Ellis, 1990). A person earning $1,000 per month, along with $500 a month in unearned income from an insurance settlement, would

Table 1. Social Security work incentives

Program	Supplemental Security Income	Social Security Disability Insurance
Prorated benefit amounts	Yes	No
Trial work period (TWP)	No	Yes
Extended period of eligibility (EPE)	No	Yes
Plans for Achieving Self Support (PASS)	Yes	No
Impairment related work expenses (IRWE)	Yes	Yes
Subsidies	For eligibility only	Yes
Continued eligibility for medical benefits	Yes	Yes

not continue to receive Medicaid coupons even though his earned income was less than the threshold amount. The second requirement for this benefit is that the person must need Medicaid support in order to work. If he uses his Medicaid coupons at least once per year his need requirement will be met, and if he has a year in which no coupons are used Social Security will accept his statement that he plans to use them in the next year as evidence of need. Table 2 addresses the effects of earnings on SSI benefits.

Unearned income (e.g., SSDI) also significantly affects the SSI benefit amount, because the only deduction made on unearned income is the $20 exclusion. For example, if a person was entitled to $450 in SSI benefits and he received $320 a month in SSDI, he would only get a check from SSI for $150 because, after the $20 exclusion, the remaining $300 SSDI amount would be subtracted from his SSI base.

$320	SSDI amount (unearned income)
−20	General income exclusion
$300	SSDI amount after exclusion
$450	Full SSI amount
−300	SSDI amount counted against SSI
$150	Adjusted SSI amount

The $65 earned income exclusion does not apply in this case because there is no earned income, and the SSDI amount is not divided by 2 before subtracting from the full SSI amount.

Programs that Decrease the Amount of Income Considered for SSI

Besides the basic SSI formulae to allow people to improve their financial status by working and receiving benefits, there are two programs used to lower the amount of income considered when determining SGA, break-even, or threshold levels. These two programs, PASS and IRWE, are woefully underused by benefit recipients; in 1993, less than 3% of working SSI recipients were participating in the PASS program, and only 9% of people with psychiatric disabilities were using IRWEs (Social Security Administration, 1993).

Plans for Achieving Self Support   Plans for Achieving Self Support are designed to help SSI recipients eventually become more self-supporting by allowing them to spend money on needed education, training, support, or other resources while maintaining most or all of the SSI cash benefit. For example, a person who is currently working part time as a dishwasher and wants to take community college classes in food service to get a cook's job can write a PASS to cover the cost of tuition, books, fees, and any other education expenses. Another person might use a PASS to pay for the ongoing job coaching services he needs to become more stable in employment.

In order to be eligible for a PASS, a person must meet all SSI requirements (except income and resources) and have earned or unearned income or resources in addition to his SSI check. People can also use a PASS to become eligible for SSI. For

Table 2.   Effect of earnings on SSI benefits

Earnings	Program involved	Benefit(s)
Above threshold	None	None
Between break-even and threshold	1619b	Medicaid only
Between SGA and break-even	1619a	Cash benefit (prorated) and Medicaid
Below SGA	1611	Cash benefit (prorated) and Medicaid

example, Joe may meet the disability requirements but earn $685 a month, and therefore be above SGA and ineligible for SSI. He writes a PASS to buy a car so he can get to and from a better job. He sets aside $250 a month for the PASS, which leaves a gross income of $435. Because this is less than SGA, Joe becomes eligible for a SSI check. After the income exclusion amount of $85 and the divide-by-2 process, his earned income is considered to be $300 a month. After subtracting the $250 that is sheltered in the PASS, the result is what Social Security will consider as income in determining the amount of SSI to be paid.

$685	Gross earnings
−85	Earned income ($65) and general ($20) exclusions
$600	Earnings after exclusions
÷2	Divide total by 2
$300	Countable earnings
−250	PASS amount
$50	Countable earnings after PASS
$450	Full SSI amount (with no other income)
−50	Countable earnings after PASS
$400	Adjusted SSI amount
$685	Gross earnings
+400	Adjusted SSI amount
$1085	Total income
−250	PASS amount
$835	Total usable income

"Congratulations, Mr. Smith!
You've been accepted into our rocket scientist training program."

A PASS is designed to help SSI recipients become self-supporting through education, training, employment support, or other resources.

In Joe's case, staying under SGA more than made up for the extra expense paid on the PASS. Without the PASS Joe had only his $685 in earnings, and with the PASS he has $835 in income plus $250 set aside to meet a vocational goal, plus eligibility for Medicaid.

The same process (using a PASS to make a person eligible for SSI) could have been used if Joe had been receiving SSDI instead of earnings.

$685	SSDI amount (unearned income)
−20	General exclusion
$665	SSDI amount after exclusion
−250	PASS amount
$415	Adjusted SSDI amount
$450	Full SSI amount
−415	SSDI amount counted against SSI
$35	Adjusted SSI amount
$685	SSDI amount
+35	SSI amount
$720	Total income
−250	PASS
$470	Total usable income

The amount of SSI in this example is very small and Joe will end up with $215 less in usable income per month, but he will be setting aside $250 a month for his vocational goal and also will have access to Medicaid benefits because he is now eligible for SSI. These examples illustrate the importance of calculating the financial impact of work incentive programs because of the varying results. People also differ in their willingness to live with less money in order to meet vocational goals. Joe might be so invested in his goal that he is willing to get by with less for a year, while another person might look at the end result and decide not to try the plan.

A PASS can be written to pay for just about any expenses that support a work goal. This could include training, equipment, or supplies to start a business; tuition, books, or supplies for education; job coaching or other supportive services; medication; attendant care or child care; transportation; equipment; tools; uniforms; and special clothing. A PASS is time limited and written for no more than 18 months initially. These plans can be extended for 18 more months and then for a final 12 months if the plan involves education or training. After 48 months, if support is still needed, a new plan would have to be written. Each plan or change in an existing plan must be approved by the Social Security representative responsible for the individual's case.

The work goal for a PASS can include the individual reaching total financial independence, but does not have to. For a supported employment worker, a reasonable goal might be to work more independently or add more hours and tasks to his current job by the end of the plan. A PASS must be individually designed, written, have a feasible goal, show how income and resources will be used to meet the goal, show how money will be set aside (usually in a separate bank account), and approved by a SSA representative. A PASS does not have to be written on a special form and can be written by the person with a disability, a family member, a service coordinator or case manager, a friend, a VR counselor, or anyone else.

If a plan changes or is discontinued before the target date, it is important that the Social Security representative is notified right away. If the person has not saved more than $2,000 through the PASS, the SSA will not try to recover the extra SSI received, but if it is over $2,000 the individual may be denied SSI benefits until he once again meets the resource limitation or sets aside the saved money in a new PASS.

If Social Security does not approve a PASS, the reasons for the decision must be clearly stated to the applicant and the decision can be appealed. If the appeal is not successful, a new plan can be written. An employment support provider must keep in mind that Social Security representatives work with hundreds of beneficiaries each week. Some representatives may process PASS applications very quickly; some may process them very slowly; and others may avoid PASS applications whenever possible. The representatives in local offices may not have experience with the PASS program or be open to learning about it. Each Social Security office should have (or have access to) a work incentive liaison (WIL), whose job it is to understand and implement SSA work incentives. If a support provider has difficulty with his local SSA office regarding a PASS or other work incentives, he might want to call on his WIL for support. If that does not work, a little interagency education might be needed (see Chapter 22).

Impairment Related Work Expense Impairment Related Work Expense is applied to both SSI and SSDI and represents Social Security's acknowledgment that people with disabilities have *special* expenses associated with going to work. These expenses involve adaptive equipment, medication, job coaching, interpreters, mental health counseling, or any other expense that a worker without a disability would not have. Expenses such as tuition, child care, bus passes, or uniforms are not eligible because all workers would be affected to the same degree. However, some items that affect nonwork as well as work time are eligible. For example, the psychotropic medications that a person takes are eligible because they contribute to his employability and also to his stability during nonwork hours. Similarly, a car that is fitted with adaptive equipment so a person can use it to get to work can also be used for nonwork activities and still be considered an IRWE. MacDonald-Wilson (1994) pointed out that charges for individual and group therapy, psychiatric visits, long-distance charges for therapeutic services, residential support services (not room and board), special diets, additional medical insurance, and personal assistance services for psychiatric disability are all acceptable IRWE items for people with mental illness.

Besides relating to the worker's disability, an allowable IRWE expense must be paid for by the worker in the same month the service was provided (a major expense may be prorated over several months), and it must be a reasonable expense given the service or item purchased. An IRWE must be documented with receipts or other records to show that the individual actually paid for the expense.

An IRWE is not time limited, which sometimes makes it the best choice for ongoing expenses such as job coaching or medication. Unlike PASS expenses, which are subtracted *after* the divide-by-2 step, an IRWE is subtracted from earned income *before* the divide-by-2 step. Using Joe as an example, here's how a PASS would compare with an IRWE:

$685	Gross earnings
−85	Earned income ($65) and general ($20) exclusions
$600	Earnings after exclusions
−250	IRWE amount
$350	Adjusted earnings
÷2	Divide total by 2
$175	Countable earnings

$450	Full SSI amount
-175	Countable earnings after IRWE
$275	Adjusted SSI amount

$685	Gross earnings
+275	SSI
$960	Total income
-250	IRWE amount
$710	Usable income using IRWE

With a PASS Joe had $835 in usable income, while with an IRWE he had only $710. Therefore, although a PASS is time limited, it often has the strongest financial benefit in the short run. In addition, a PASS can be written to exclude unearned income (e.g., SSDI) as well as earnings, but IRWEs can exclude only earned income. These examples again point out the importance of the employment specialist knowing how to calculate the impact of various plans and combinations of plans in order to help the worker receive the services he needs and obtain as much money as possible.

SSDI WORK INCENTIVES

SSDI is a program designed to support workers who have paid into the Social Security system and have developed disabilities. Under the Social Security for Disabled Adult Children category, support is also provided for the adult children with disabilities of workers who have paid into the system and have died, retired, or developed disabilities themselves. A requirement is that the adult child was diagnosed with a disability before age 22. There is a required 5-month waiting period to receive SSDI benefits after the onset of the disability, and an additional 2-year waiting period for the Medicare benefits that usually accompany SSDI benefits. People can have many assets and a large savings account and still collect SSDI because SSDI has no resource limitation. They cannot, however, earn very much money and still collect SSDI because the purpose of SSDI is to support workers whose disabilities are too severe for them to continue working.

The SSDI system is less flexible about people returning to work and continuing to collect benefits than the SSI system, where the worker receives gradually decreased SSI payments but still retains eligibility. The most important factor for many people is staying under the $500 SGA level by creatively using work incentive programs such as IRWEs and subsidies to maintain eligibility for SSDI and Medicare.

General Effects of Working on SSDI

The first SSDI work incentive is the trial work period, which allows a person to try working while still receiving benefits. The TWP is the first 9 months in which the person earns at least $200. These 9 months do not have to be consecutive and can add up over 5 years. Therefore, any months in which the person received SSDI *and* earned more than $200 during the last 60 months become part of the trial work period. The SSDI amount is not reduced during the TWP, and any month in which the person earns less than $200 does not count. The TWP is allowed only once for a given determination of disability.

After the individual completes his TWP, a continuing disability review may be conducted, and he enters his extended period of eligibility. The EPE allows the person an extended period to adjust to working without losing his eligibility for benefits. Whether or not the person is earning SGA, the EPE starts at the end of the TWP and continues for 36 consecutive months regardless of employment activity. During the EPE, the person receives full cash benefits for the first 3 months regardless of earned income amounts. After the 3-month period, the person receives full cash benefits in any month in which countable earnings (i.e., after the income exclusions, IRWEs, subsidies) are under SGA. If the earnings are over SGA, the person gets no cash benefit that month. It is all or nothing. It is very important to make sure that earnings are accurately reported to the SSA each month to prevent errors in payments.

After the 36 months, if the person continues to earn under SGA he will continue to receive his SSDI check each month, provided he is not found to have recovered from his disability. However, if he earns over SGA for at least 1 month after the EPE, his cash benefits will stop completely. If he is earning under SGA but Social Security makes a determination that he can perform at the SGA level, he will be paid for the month of determination and two additional months and then all cash benefits will be terminated. In both of these cases, the Medicare benefit will continue for 3 months after the cash benefits end. After that period, Medicare benefits may be purchased by the worker on a sliding-fee scale as long as he is both employed and has a disability. In some states, Medicaid will pay the Medicare premium.

If a person loses his SSDI benefits and subsequently becomes unemployed, he will have to file a new application for benefits. If the new application is approved and he has been off SSDI for less than 5 years and was receiving SSDI due to his own work record (i.e., he is not on SSDAC), the worker will not have to go through a new 24-month waiting period for Medicare.

Programs that Decrease the Amount of Income Considered for SSDI

Impairment Related Work Expense (IRWE) An IRWE can be used to bring countable income down below SGA. For example, Brian, who has used his TWP, begins earning $600 a month and has been receiving an SSDI check of $385 per month. Because his earnings are now over SGA, he no longer gets an SSDI check. But, if Brian uses an IRWE to pay $200 a month for follow-up services, his countable earnings are reduced to $400 a month. By bringing his countable income down, Brian will continue to receive an SSDI check for $385 as well as $600 in earned income. After paying the employment specialist, Brian will have $785 remaining. All IRWEs must be documented and can continue as long as a person is employed.

$600	Gross earnings over SGA without SSDI check
−200	IRWE—the employment specialist
$400	Adjusted gross earnings (under SGA so Brian gets an SSDI check)
$600	Gross earnings
+385	SSDI
−200	IRWE—the employment specialist
$785	Usable income

Subsidies Subsidies are considered to be in effect when the employer is paying the worker more than he is actually earning. The difference between the amount paid and the amount earned is considered a subsidy and is not considered in determining SGA. (Subsidies have no effect on countable income and do not figure in calculating SSI amounts.)

Why would an employer do such a thing? In some cases the employer values attributes about the worker other than his productivity and will pay the worker the going rate or minimum wage even though the worker produces half of what others produce. Or the employer may provide extra time for a break or supervision in response to the worker's disability. If a worker is paid for 4 hours of work per day but gets a half-hour break that no one else in the workplace takes, the pay for that half hour is a subsidy.

Job Coach Subsidy   A job coach subsidy is used when an employer pays the worker more than he is actually earning because the employment specialist is making up the missed production. This type of subsidy is usually short term. For example, during the first 3 months that John is working at Acme Manufacturing he is averaging only 75% productivity, but the employer gets 100% of his work done because the employment specialist is doing the other 25%. Therefore, the employer pays John at 100%, and the 25% of work the employment specialist provided is a subsidy. Supervision provided by the employment specialist can also be considered a subsidy and is calculated by multiplying the number of service hours per month by the worker's hourly wage (MacDonald-Wilson, 1994). Subsidy amounts are deducted from earnings when determining SGA in the same way that IRWEs are.

The employment specialist must be aware that by participating in a subsidy arrangement, the employer and/or the support agency are committed to filing Social Security paperwork testifying that the worker is being paid more than he is actually earning. This may pose a philosophical difficulty for some. It may be necessary to work with the employer in completing the paperwork so that he does not give a glowing account of the worker's performance while the employment specialist is trying to make a subsidy case.

RECEIVING BOTH SSDI AND SSI

A person who is receiving a small SSDI benefit and has limited resources is usually also entitled to some SSI money. SSDI is considered unearned income in calculating SSI, which means that all of it except the $20 general exclusion amount is directly deducted from the base SSI amount. Therefore, a person who gets $270 SSDI but would have been entitled to $450 SSI if he had no unearned income will receive $200 in SSI.

It is important to note that a PASS does not always result in an increase or maintenance of in-pocket income. The employment specialist must learn to accurately calculate the different factors involved in each case in order to help her clients make informed decisions about levels of employment, as well as to effectively advocate with Social Security.

With regard to receiving benefits from both SSDI and SSI, it is important to remember that SSDI and SSI are fairly separate programs as far as Social Security is concerned and will be administered by two separate individuals in the local Social Security office. It is important to make sure that earnings and other changes are reported to *both* representatives. An employment specialist must never assume that they will share information.

SUGGESTED READINGS

Koehler, F., & Ellis, J. (Eds.). (1990). *Project WIN: Work incentives training manual.* Richmond, VA: The Association for Persons in Supported Employment (APSE). One of the best resources for a thorough explanation of benefit programs and especially for doing the calculations involved.

O'Mara, S. (updated by Pellegrino, C.). (April, 1993a). *Understanding and using the PASS work incentive.* Richmond: Employment Support Institute (ESI), Virginia Commonwealth University.

O'Mara, S. (updated by Pellegrino, C.). (April, 1993b). *Understanding Social Security benefits.* Richmond: Employment Support Institute (ESI), Virginia Commonwealth University.

Social Security Administration. (1991). *Working while disabled—A guide to plans for achieving self-support while receiving Supplemental Security Income* (SSA Report No. 05-11017). Washington, DC: Author.

Social Security Administration. (1992). *Red book on work incentives—A summary guide to Social Security and Supplemental Security work incentives for people with disabilities* (SSA Report No. 64-030). Washington, DC: Author.

These manuals provide basic and easy to use information about Social Security programs and include some troubleshooting case studies that are very useful. Both ESI and the Social Security Administration have software that will estimate Social Security check amounts and determine the maximum potential net income using various work incentive programs.

CONCLUSION

Social Security work incentives are difficult to explain and hard to learn. Work incentives try to consider many different individual variables; therefore, for every rule an employment specialist learns, there are invariably exceptions. Another factor is that individual representatives make many of the decisions about eligibility and continuation of benefits and may vary in their expertise. Vocational agencies must make sure that their clients are given the most accurate information possible about how to use the Social Security system to support employment efforts, because the fear of losing benefits is a significant barrier to employment for people with long-term mental illness.

10

RIGHTS OF
WORKERS WITH
DISABILITIES UNDER THE ADA

P L 101-336, the Americans with Disabilities Act (ADA) of 1990, was intended to substantially change and increase the number of opportunities for the inclusion of people with disabilities in the workplace. The law was passed in 1990, and the first employment regulations took effect in July of 1992. Employment specialists who have been working in job placement for some time will recognize many of the "reasonable accommodations" covered by the ADA. Common-sense adjustments that cooperative employers have been making all along include building structure into work schedules, allowing a job coach to provide training on the job, and providing consistent and positive supervision.

BACKGROUND

It is estimated that 42 million people in the United States are covered by the ADA's five titles: Employment (Title I), Public Services (Title II), Public Accommodations (Title III), Telecommunications (Title IV), and Miscellaneous Provisions (Title V). Earlier civil rights legislation said that all individuals must be treated equally regardless of their race, gender, religion, and national origin. The ADA states that people with disabilities must be treated *differently* in order to give them equality. For example, special provisions need to be made to prevent discrimination against people with disabilities when applying for jobs, attending the theater, or riding the bus.

The ADA is not an affirmative action law. It does not require employers to hire a certain number of people with disabilities; it only requires employers to give individuals with disabilities a chance to compete for jobs and to provide reasonable accommodation when needed for them to be successful. Employment provisions of the ADA (Title I) are enforced by the Equal Employment Opportunity Commission (EEOC) and/or by state human rights commissions. Available remedies to proven discrimination include back pay and court orders to stop discrimination.

Private employers with more than 25 employees were required to comply with Title I by July 1992, and those with at least 15 employees by July 1994. Public agencies have been prohibited from discriminating against people with disabilities since PL 93-112, the Rehabilitation Act of 1973, was passed. However, a large percentage of the employers in the United States have fewer than 15 employees and so are exempt from the ADA's mandates. Also, some states already have regulations in place that have stronger requirements than the ADA.

Workers are covered by the ADA if they *have* a disability (defined as a mental or physical impairment that substantially limits one or more major life activities, such as caring for oneself, learning, and working); if they are *thought* to have a disability (i.e., the employer has a perception that the person has a mental illness or has experienced a mental illness in the past, or assumes the person cannot do the job or handle a promotion because of past or current treatment); or if they are *related to* or *associated with* a person with a disability (e.g., the spouse of a person with mental illness). The one exception is that current users of illegal drugs are not covered, although *former* users are.

The Mental Health Law Project (1992) reported that discrimination is prohibited and reasonable accommodation is required in the following areas:

- Application form and process—a person with a disability can take the application home and complete it, or have someone assist her.
- Skill testing—the skills tested must be essential to the job, not general skills.
- The interview—the applicant can bring a support person or can substitute demonstration of skills for a verbal interview.
- Promotion into higher positions—an employer may not deny a job or promotion because he thinks the person will not be able to handle the job.
- Training—workers must be provided slower-paced training or special assistance during training.
- Discharge—performance on nonessential functions of the job cannot be used as a reason for discharge.
- Privacy—employers may not ask about psychiatric treatment.
- Job modification—an employer may not force a person to accept an unwanted job modification.
- Protection from retaliation—an employee has the right to make a claim under the ADA without the employer retaliating against her.

DEFINITIONS OF KEY TERMS

Because the details of interpreting the ADA remain to be negotiated and clarified over time (probably through multiple court cases), the definitions of key terms in the legislation become crucial. Five such terms are discussed here.

Essential Functions

The concept of *essential functions* is at the heart of the ADA's employment provisions. The essential functions of a position are defined as primary job duties that are intrinsic to the position. Other duties are *marginal functions*. An essential function is identified by considering whether others in the same position perform the function and whether removing it would fundamentally change the job. Other considerations include the judgment of supervisors and the work experience of past and present workers. In order to comply with ADA requirements, many employers have rewritten job descriptions to specify clearly the essential functions of each position.

The amount of time needed to perform a task does not necessarily determine whether the task is an essential function because some essential functions may be done during only a small percentage of the workday. For example, a transcontinental jet pilot spends most of her time monitoring the automatic systems of the plane and only a very small percentage taking off and landing, but there is no question that landing the plane is a very essential function of the pilot's job.

The size of the business is also a consideration in identifying essential functions. An office with a large staff may define answering telephones as a marginal function for a file clerk because she does it only when no one else is available, but in a two-person office where there is less flexibility, telephone answering becomes an essential function of the filing job.

Qualified Applicant

A *qualified applicant* is a person who can perform the essential functions of the job, with or without reasonable accommodation. Therefore, a person who can per-

"You said 'Trust me! They're accessible!'"

Employment specialists should recognize the "reasonable accommodations" covered by the ADA.

form the essential functions of a job cannot be screened out because she is unable to perform the tasks that are considered marginal functions. For example, a person who does not drive can still be a qualified applicant for a dishwashing job in a restaurant where the past dishwashers occasionally drove to the store if the cook ran out of supplies.

A person who can perform the essential functions only if reasonable accommodations are made also must be considered a qualified applicant and cannot be screened out on the basis of needing accommodations. However, a person who does *not* have the requisite skills, experience, education, and other job-related requirements would not be considered a qualified applicant, even if she has a disability.

Reasonable Accommodation

Accommodations are changes in procedure or process, equipment, and work space that act to compensate for the disability experienced by the worker. The person with a disability may request reasonable accommodations (i.e., those that do not impose "undue hardship") and the employer is required to meet her request. Accommodations vary according to the needs of the individual worker and the work situation. These accommodations include modifications to improve physical accessibility, specialized equipment, assistance with the essential functions of the job (e.g., a reader, a job coach), or the transfer to a vacant position if a disability occurs after employment and the person is no longer able to do her former job. Transferring essential functions to other workers is not considered a reasonable accommodation, although transferring marginal functions would be. The request for accommodation must come from the employee or applicant, because the employer is not responsible for providing accommodations if he is unaware of the need for accommodations.

Undue Hardship

The concept of *undue hardship*, an action requiring significant difficulty and expense, will develop over time as it is negotiated based on different court cases because it is a likely defense employers will use against charges of failure to provide reasonable accommodations. The financial and other resources of the employer are considered in deciding whether a requested accommodation would cause undue hardship. When appropriate, the resources of the parent company would also be considered. For example, purchasing an additional computer for an accountant with mental illness to use at home might be an undue hardship. However, if the office is part of a national chain that employs 1,000 accountants, the cost of the accommodation would no longer impose an undue hardship. If finances are the stumbling block, the company must consider other ways to pay for the accommodation. For example, if vocational rehabilitation agrees to fund a special work station, the company must allow the accommodation in the workplace. If allowing the previously mentioned accountant to work at home meant that the secretary had to routinely leave her work to deliver needed documents or that the person's clients routinely had to be seen by other staff because she was not available in the office, allowing the accountant to work at home could be considered an undue hardship because it disrupts others in the workplace. The presence of a job coach could also be considered unduly disrupting in some workplaces, and therefore could be denied.

Direct Threat

An applicant who is considered to be a *direct threat* to the health or safety of herself or others can be screened out of a particular job. This reason not to hire a person with a disability can be used only if verified by a professional on a case-by-case basis. Evidence of a moderate threat is not enough because the decision must rely on objective, factual evidence not subjective perceptions, irrational fears, patronizing attitudes, or stereotypes. Fears about the risk to the worker in the employment environment (e.g., the stress of a particular workplace would cause a relapse) may not be used to exclude the person unless there is a strong past history supporting such fears.

IMPLICATIONS FOR WORKERS WITH LONG-TERM MENTAL ILLNESS

Applying and Interviewing

Employers are prohibited from asking applicants if they have a disability, if they have ever been hospitalized, or if they have ever received treatment. They must describe the job duties and performance standards (i.e., essential functions) of the position and ask if the applicant can perform them. They may also ask for evidence that the applicant can perform the essential functions, such as references or information about related work experience. For example, the interviewer can not legally ask "Wouldn't your illness make it difficult for you to handle working with customers?", but questions like "Do you have experience working with customers?" or "What do you think you would do if an angry customer came up to your register and started yelling?" are legal and fair. Medical examinations cannot be required until after a conditional offer of employment has been extended and must then be required of *all* applicants, not just those with disabilities.

Workers do not have to disclose their illness (or past illness) during the application phase in order to be covered by the ADA later. People who have long-term disabilities or who develop disabilities after employment may ask for accommodations at any time during employment. However, if the employer does not know about an existing condition, he is not obliged to make accommodations, which brings up important questions about disclosing information about the worker's illness and subsequent disability. Some people have no hesitation about sharing this sort of information and may need coaching on the appropriate times and places to talk about it. Others may prefer to disclose as little and to as few people in the workplace as possible, while others may not want *anyone* in the workplace to know. Each of these may be the right decision for a given individual in a given situation; there are no hard and fast rules. The employment specialist must talk through the situation with the worker ahead of time so she can be assisted in making decisions about what to disclose, when, and to whom.

Once on the job, the employer may share confidential information with a supervisor, manager, and first-aid and safety personnel if those individuals need the information in order to provide accommodations. However, he may not tell people who do not have a specific need to know.

Typical Accommodations

The accommodations that are generally needed by people with mental illness tend to be less obvious than the accessible sidewalks and bathrooms needed by people with physical disabilities. Mancuso (1990) commented that most accommodations for people with mental illness are inexpensive or free, but require sustained changes over time.

The particular accommodations needed by a worker vary according to the type of functional limitations experienced and the needs of the workplace. Mancuso (1992) and Parrish (1992) reviewed common accommodations for workers with mental illness and suggested that changes in the following areas are most common.

The supervisory process The supervisory process could involve assigning the worker to a different supervisor, training the supervisors to provide clear feedback to the workers, scheduling daily planning sessions, using a particular supervisory style, or establishing written agreements for supervisory issues.

Provision of human assistance Assistance to workers by allowing job coaching, designating a co-worker for peer support, or pairing workers with mentors.

Flexibility in work scheduling Flexibility in work schedules could include allowing time off for medical or mental health appointments, paid or unpaid hospital leave, changing shifts, job sharing, keeping a job open when the worker is unable to attend work, reassigning the worker to another position, or allowing a self-paced work load.

Physical arrangement of the workplace Physical arrangements could include providing a closed shielded work space to avoid distractions or removing objects that cause undue anxiety.

Restructuring job duties Restructuring job duties by changing task procedures, building structure and routine into the job, or having requests or assignments made in writing.

Adjustments in workplace policies Adjusting policies to permit personal telephone calls for support, working at home, or using sick leave for emotional illness.

"Jones, Line 2, it's your psychiatrist.
Hey, he sounds like my psychiatrist!"

Being open about a disability enables others at the workplace to provide support and accommodation.

Akabas (1994) discussed examples of reasonable accommodations that have been made for people with mental illness. One example involved a person working the night shift who was able to switch to a more desirable day position for medical reasons (documented by a psychiatrist). In another situation, an easily distracted person was moved to a more secluded worksite where she was less distracted. A third situation involved a teacher who was having difficulty managing her classroom and was assigned a mentor to show her coping skills. In each of these examples, if the reasonable accommodations had not been made, the worker might have been fired for documented nonperformance.

Many employers are concerned about the cost or difficulty of providing accommodations. However, according to Douglas (1994), the average financial cost of accommodations provided to workers with mental illness was less than $100. Employers cannot use financial cost as an excuse to deny accommodation if another source (e.g., vocational rehabilitation, self-pay) of funding is available.

Fabian, Waterworth, and Ripke (1993) identified 231 job modifications (a mean of 5.1 per job) in a study of 30 individuals with mental illness placed in 47 jobs. The most common job modification was providing orientation and training to supervisors (38.1%), followed by modifying the work environment to provide on-site support (16.4%), and modifying time schedules (15.6%). Other categories included modifying work rules or procedures (10%), performance expectations (7%), job tasks (5%), and modifying workplace social norms (6%), as well as orienting co-workers (3%) (in some cases more than one type of accommodation was provided). They also reported that there was a link between the higher number of job accommodations and longer time on the job. The authors commented that the lack of information about reasonable accommodations for people with mental illness is a barrier because support personnel are not informed about the range of accommodations that might be requested.

Enforcement

Employers are prohibited from firing or punishing individuals who use the ADA or who assist others in doing so. A person is advised to first try to work things out informally with the employer, but if this is not successful the person must file a complaint with the EEOC within 180 days of the alleged violation. The worker may also file a complaint with the state equal rights enforcement agency or with both the state and federal agencies. Rayton (1993) reported that in the first year, more than 11,500 Title I complaints were filed with the EEOC, and 9.8% of those complaining had a mental illness. The most common charge was wrongful discharge, followed by refusal to make accommodations and refusal to hire.

CONCLUSION

Although the ADA is an important tool for increasing awareness and supporting the right of people with disabilities to compete in the workplace, there continues to be a need for skill development and long-term support. To empower rather than stigmatize workers with mental illness, Parrish (1992) emphasized recognizing the individual's strengths and contributions to the employer instead of focusing on the limitations of disability. Ideally, the worker, employer, and employment specialist should work together to determine adjustments needed to accommodate the worker with a disability, and the individual should be involved in making all the decisions concerning her position.

It is important to balance the need for disclosure of a disability or needed accommodations with the individual's right to confidentiality and nonstigmatizing support. For example, a worker might have difficulty balancing a particular work schedule with her medical treatment, but be reluctant to ask for a change in schedule because she has not told her employer that she has a disability and prefers not to. Therefore, to avoid disclosing information about her illness, the worker is denying herself access to accommodations that might make her job easier. This is a decision that each individual client will have to make for herself, possibly with support and assistance from the employment specialist.

The impact that the ADA has on the employment of people with disabilities will not be known for years. In 1994, 2 years after the employment provisions took effect, two thirds of all adults with severe disabilities in the United States were still unemployed, and 85% of the discrimination claims filed under the ADA in the first 2 years were brought by people who were already employed (Kaufman-Rosen & Springen, 1994). It is possible that employers who have always been flexible and accommodating will continue to be so because it is good for their business, while employers who have never been interested in integrating people with disabilities into their work forces will continue to be resistant. However, the ADA has brought the issue of workplace accommodation and accessibility into the public eye and given service providers a perfect opportunity to increase education efforts on the value of workers with disabilities.

Additional information on the Americans with Disabilities Act can be found at state VR agencies, the Job Accommodation Network (JAN) (1-800-526-7234), Independent Living Centers, city and state Offices for Individuals with Disabilities, and the Equal Employment Opportunity Commission (1-800-USA-EEOC).

III

THE JOBS
AND THE CLIENTS

11

CLIENT SCREENING AND ASSESSMENT

Screening and assessing clients in supported employment is a controversial issue. People who believe in consumer empowerment and inclusion insist that the only legitimate reason for assessment is to identify training and support needs. They also believe that every client is entitled to community-based employment regardless of his limitations or functioning level. "Is it reasonable to make decisions about people's lives based upon how they compare with normative data or with our preconceived notions and perceptions? Is it reasonable to deny individuals with disabilities opportunities for regular lives and regular jobs based on our own limitations as trainers and facilitators?" (Garner, 1989b, p. 4). However, people who believe in traditional vocational evaluation see a valid role for assessment when deciding which clients a specific program should accept and to which jobs clients should have access to. Botterbusch (1989) wrote,

> If one accepts that no evaluation is necessary prior to placement, then placement simply means putting a person on a job and then seeing if he/she learns the required tasks and related social skills. This is obviously wasteful of resources, inhumane to the worker, and unfair to the employer. (p. 31)

Many supported employment providers have difficulty with traditional assessment because the typical aptitude tests, work samples, and behavior checklists generally predict only the difficulties that individuals with severe disabilities will experience in community employment. Traditional vocational evaluation attempts to determine whether a person is qualified for the "average" job, while supported employment assumes that all worksites are unique, and a careful job match or use of compensatory strategies can reduce the impact of many disability-related limitations (Menchetti & Udvari-Solner, 1990). Powell et al. (1991) stated that assessment tools are often inappropriately used to make predictions about future employment potential, rather than to determine whether functional limitations make an individual eligible for services. Therefore, the controversy about assessment partly involves the way that assessment information is used—specifically, whether the information gathered during assessment is used to screen an individual or if it is used to identify remedial activities or compensatory strategies.

Another concern about assessment involves the realism of the measures used and the settings where the assessment is done. Because people with disabilities have been excluded in the past by standard assessment measures that may or may not have had any relationship to a person's ability to do a particular job, supported employment advocates recommend a *functional assessment* approach. Functional assessment is done in as realistic a setting as possible, considers only issues that are relevant to a specific job or job type, and focuses on ways that the worker's disability affects his vocational performance and need for support.

WHY ASSESSMENT?

With all the concern about the use and validity of assessment, what value does it have for clients and vocational service providers? The assessment process provides information that is crucial for the clients and employment specialists to make good decisions during the rehabilitation process. These decisions include whether an individual should try work, whether a given agency can provide the kinds of opportunities and services needed, what the individual's long-term vocational goals are, what kind of work an individual should try, and what kinds of support will be helpful to the individual. Client assessment should be an ongoing process that uses all the information available to make decisions, rather than a one-shot, formal testing and evaluation regimen.

For example, if an employment specialist is helping a client decide if he should move from a work crew to an individual transitional employment position, she must start with good information about the parameters and demands of the job (see Chapter 14). The client-related information the employment specialist uses to assist and advise the client will come from many different assessment sources including written referral information, reports from the client's crew supervisor, the client's long-term vocational goals, the client's expressed opinions about the two jobs, and the employment specialist's observations of the client's behavior and knowledge about his situation. Some of these sources will be somewhat formal and directly address vocational skills and weaknesses, while others will be more subjective (e.g., the "gut feeling" factor). The client's experience as he moves into his new job also becomes part of the record and is considered in subsequent decision making.

BASIC ASSESSMENT GUIDELINES

There are certain basic guidelines that increase the probability of making the assessment process both humane and useful. This is especially true when analogue tests or situations are used to simulate work or nonwork activities (e.g., paper-and-pencil tests, psychological evaluations, simulated work samples). Although all assessment procedures should be justifiable in terms of the information they yield, assessments that are not done in the targeted work environment (e.g., analogue tests or situations) and relate only in a general way to employability must be evaluated carefully to ensure that the information they provide is worth the time and trouble.

The Assessment Process Should Involve and Empower the Client and His Family and Friends

The assessment process should involve the client and relate to his personal goals and objectives and to the requirements of a specific job, not to a generic list of skills. The process itself should empower the client and his family and friends by assessing and reinforcing competencies that the client already possesses, as well as identifying limitations. To a person who has never been successfully employed and has little confidence in his capabilities, learning through assessment that he actually has valuable skills (even if they only involve getting to work on time every day) can boost his confidence.

Performance in One Setting May Not Accurately Predict Performance in Another Setting

Ideally, assessment should be done in the real work setting or at least in a very similar setting because performance in one setting may not accurately predict performance in another setting. Although this guideline is true for everyone in employment, it is especially important for people whose disabilities prevent them from easily generalizing behavior across settings. Another reason it is risky to predict success in a given job based on vocational assessments done in other settings

"Where's the new guy?"

Working successfully in a job involves much more than just doing the tasks needed.

is that working in a job involves much more than just performing the necessary tasks. For example, a standard aptitude test may determine that an individual would do well as a welder. However, even though the test may determine that he can perform the welding involved in a given job, if he cannot deal with the social climate on that particular job or he has difficulty communicating with the boss, he is not going to do well in that job in spite of his welding skills.

Supported Employment Involves Providing Any Needed Skills Training After Placement

Because clients in supported employment are provided any needed training after placement, it is not necessary for individuals to know everything to be eligible for employment. The job-readiness model used in the past caused the exclusion of many individuals who would have done well in a supported job, but were screened out because they lacked some of the skills needed for employment.

A Reasonable Balance Must Be Maintained Between Assessment and Placement

There needs to be a balance among assessing the worker's skills, finding him employment, providing training, and providing support. One common complaint about vocational services in the past was that participants were repeatedly assessed but left with no job or training after the assessment. Work samples and job trials may provide valuable information, but they can also be time consuming to develop, set up, train, and supervise. They can take as much time as a paid job and not yield any more information.

ASSESSMENT PRIOR TO RECEIVING SERVICES

Employment programs often require that people with disabilities are assessed before being accepted as clients because the programs believe their resources are finite and limited. The staff of an agency may believe that they lack the knowledge or skills needed to serve some clients or that they have a limited funding base that requires them to try to select clients who have the greatest chance of success (or, conversely, those who have the most severe disabilities). They may believe that their access to jobs in the community is limited, which encourages them to be selective about who is given access to those jobs. These limitations may really exist or they may reflect inaccurate assumptions, but they affect the way services are provided and who has access to them. Most programs therefore do have some eligibility requirements that must be met before a client can have access to vocational services. The collection and review of this information can also help identify the possible first steps and support needs of the individual (e.g., whether the person will start in a volunteer job, a work crew, or an individual placement). Screening criteria often used by vocational programs include residential stability, awareness of the illness and its effects, freedom from substance abuse for a specified amount of time, and the motivation to work, which is often proven by participation in daily structured activities. There are two major concerns involved in setting up eligibility requirements.

The first concern is that diagnosis, symptomatology, and tests of intelligence, aptitude, and personality do not predict employment success for people with long-term mental illness (Anthony, 1994a). The most powerful indicator of vocational success for a person with mental illness is his employment history. Work adjustment skills and social skills are also related to vocational success (Anthony,

1994a). However, these indicators may all be improved by training and support, and therefore are questionable as screening tools. As a result, there is no quick and easy test that can predict whether a given individual has the potential for being successfully employed if needed supports are provided.

Second, setting up criteria for receiving services implies three obligations: to make sure the criteria have a valid relationship to the activities and services provided, to express the criteria in measurable and objective terms, and to make sure that potential clients have a way to meet those criteria. For example, if a program specifies that a potential client must have a stable residential situation before being eligible for vocational services, then three tests must be applied.

1. Is a stable living situation necessary for someone to be employed?
2. How is a stable living situation defined?
3. Does the client have access to the services he needs to establish a stable living situation?

If potential clients are required to demonstrate motivation by participating in daily structured activities, does the program provide a range of appropriate and interesting activities from which clients can choose? If a client's only choice is to stuff envelopes in a work activity center or sit around watching TV and smoking cigarettes in a day activity program, his refusal to participate might indicate a *high* motivation for desirable work. In fact, a study showed that when people with schizophrenia had the opportunity to work for pay, their participation and functional behavior levels were far better than when their only option was unpaid activities (Bell et al., 1993). It is important to remember that the issues often used as screening criteria may be only reflections of the client's current environment or lack of support, not indicators of potential success. Screening considerations should function as indicators of the service and support needed rather than as barriers to eventual participation.

ASSESSMENT TOPICS

There are three types of information gathered in any vocational assessment process. The first type of information includes the preferences of the individual. Does he want to work? Why? In what kind of job is he interested? The second type of information includes the skills, abilities, and limitations the client brings to the employment process. Does he know enough about working to make good decisions about the kinds of jobs to pursue? What social, vocational, or academic skills does he have? Does he have behavior patterns or communication styles that may interfere with his success on some jobs? The third type of information includes the support(s) the person needs or is likely to need, and the support(s) to which he currently has access. What are the most effective approaches to working with this person? What kind of off-site support does he need? What kind of a work environment might be most successful?

The individual characteristics of the potential worker to some degree frame the assessment issues. A person with good job skills and a prior history of employment may need information about the limitations caused by the illness and the possible compensatory strategies. However, a person with severe disabilities who has a very limited employment history may need help in identifying any strengths or abilities that might be assets in employment.

Preference Issues

Interest and Motivation   A client's interest in, or motivation to, work is a very common criterion used for eligibility; it is also one of the most questionable. Motivation is directly related to the choices people think they have and to the success people believe they will have in those choices. Many people who have long-term mental illness have never been successful in a job or in any vocational activity. A person who does not think he has any chance of being successfully employed will not be very motivated to seek employment. Many clients need encouragement, gentle pushing, and the chance to gain access to successively more challenging employment activities. Employment programs should be very cautious about using motivation as a screening criterion.

For some people the question of whether to work, or whether to work for money, is a legitimate one that has little to do with motivation. For example, a person who is very interested in employment might be worse off financially if he takes a job that pays more than a token amount, and a person who is 57 and had worked for 30 years before becoming ill may decide that early retirement sounds just fine. Ideally, the employment specialist should help the client choose whether to seek employment based on solid information and legitimate choices, not the client's fear of failure or limited skills.

Vocational Preferences and Interests   It is essential for the employment specialist to understand the client's vocational preferences and interests. What kind of a job does this person want? Days or nights, full- or part-time, inside or outside, blue collar or professional? Does this person have a work history? Does he have enough information and experience in working to set reasonable vocational goals? How much support will he need to accomplish this? This initial assessment might also include helping people decide the best level of employment activity for them, as long as there are multiple choices available. Some clients may want to go right into an individual independent placement, while others prefer (or need) on-the-job support, group employment, career development, job exploration, supported education, or transitional employment.

Type of Vocational Support Preferred   It is also important for the employment specialist to understand the kind of vocational support preferred by the client. Is the client comfortable with the idea of on-site support? Is he comfortable with skills training, or would he prefer to try a job within his current level of skills so he can gain access to the job more independently? Does he prefer ongoing support provided by the supervisor? Or would he rather receive support from a peer group?

Skills, Abilities, and Limitations

The employment specialist must understand the client's skills, abilities, and limitations in order to provide appropriate support. The following are some specific areas that may be important:

Adaptive skills: Competence in adaptive skills or having access to the support systems needed to maintain acceptable levels of grooming and living skills, are often used as a prerequisite for services or as a factor in matching workers to jobs because different work environments require different levels of grooming.

Basic vocational skills: Can the client work independently? Can he concentrate and remain on task? Solve problems? Ignore distractions? Take initiative? Follow directions? Accept feedback? Tolerate frustration?

Behavioral appropriateness and stability: Does the client verbalize or act out troublesome behaviors such as destructiveness, suicidal gestures, withdrawal, and inappropriate sexual behaviors? Does he demonstrate socially inappropriate behavior or have bizarre appearance habits? If so, can he control them with intermittent support?

Academic and other specific vocational skills: What specific skills can the client draw on from previous employment or education?

Work-related skills: Apart from the specific task demands of a job, does the client have the related skills needed to succeed? This includes such areas as attendance and time management, appearance and grooming, dependability, cooperation with others, and managing leisure time.

Social skills: Does the client have social skills that will support his integration and acceptance on the job? Can he initiate conversations, understand jokes, respond to requests, and eat in public without offending tablemates?

Physical limitations: Are there strength, endurance, or dexterity issues that need to be considered in job development and matching?

Support Needed and Available

Information about the following issues will help determine the type(s) of support needed, and potential resources for that support:

Stability in symptoms and medications: This does not mean absence of symptoms but rather that the level of symptoms is stable and that the client is managing his medication consistently (or has the support he needs to have his medication managed).

Residential stability: A client's residential stability is an important factor for employment. People who are moving into a new apartment every month or living with various friends may not be able to attend work consistently.

Past or present substance abuse: Past or present substance abuse may affect a client's choices. Many programs and VR agencies will not accept individuals who are active users. Some programs require current participation in treatment, while others require specified periods of sobriety.

Available support: What kinds of formal and informal support does the client have available? Is he involved with other agencies? Does he have family support? Community support? Church support? Peer group support? What supports are currently active, and which are potential?

Employment resources: Are there potential employers in the family, among friends, or in the client's neighborhood? Does the person have a job to which to return?

Effective approaches to working with the individual: How does the client learn? What kind of a relationship would he prefer to have with the employment specialist? What kinds of reinforcement does he prefer?

Illness awareness and management: Does the client acknowledge his illness? Does he recognize symptoms? Is he consistent with his medication, counseling, or other treatment components? Does he know what his signs of decompensation are? If he is taking medication, does he know what side effects to look for?

Characteristics of supportive work environments: What kind of a work environment would best support the client? How much supervision will he need?

What accommodations is he likely to need in the workplace? What kind of a social environment seems best?

ASSESSMENT METHODS

The best way to predict whether a person will be successful in a job is to have him take the job, provide support, and see how well he does. However, this is an expensive assessment approach, one that puts both the client and employer at risk of experiencing what may be a very unsuccessful situation. Therefore, employment specialists generally use other assessment methods, less accurate but also less costly, to gather information needed to make vocational decisions.

Some of these methods are *analogue approaches* that put the individual into situations that are comparable to the job situation and then consider his performance. Others are *ecological* or *functional approaches* that examine the individual's behavior in a real work situation or something very similar. Besides working directly with a client in assessment activities, the employment specialist may be able to help the client gain access to other assessment resources within the community. For example, interest and aptitude testing, neuropsychological evaluations, or testing of physical limitations may be available through vocational rehabilitation, a community college, the local YMCA, or other community resources.

PROFILE: JESSICA

Jessica had just been referred to David, an employment specialist working at a community vocational program. Jessica's case manager explained to David that he and Jessica had both decided that it was a good time to look into returning to work and he wanted Jessica to begin with some assessment activities. Jessica had completed the referral form, and in it had described herself as unsure about her vocational goals.

David and Jessica met and developed an assessment plan that included the following:

- Conversations between Jessica and David to review her past work history, vocational skills, and job preferences. Some of these discussions would include other people (e.g., Jessica's parents or her case manager) and others would be just between the two of them
- Telephone calls from David (with Jessica present) to her previous employer to clarify her job duties and employment strengths
- Job exploration activities, including visits to employers and library research into different vocational areas to increase Jessica's knowledge about employment and enable her and David to test her skills at completing projects independently
- A referral to vocational rehabilitation

Although David had access to a lot of information in Jessica's file, most of it was developed during day treatment and was questionable for employment use. Before he met with Jessica, David asked the case manager if there were any personal safety or therapeutic issues he definitely needed to know. Because the answer was no, David decided not to read Jessica's file until after he had met with her a few times and become acquainted with her in an employment counseling environment. This gave David a chance to form his own opinions about Jessica before exposing himself to a lot of other input.

Analogue Assessment Approaches

Talking with the Client   Talking with the client can help increase his investment in the employment process and provide firsthand information about his communication skills, appearance, work skills, and interests. This approach is not as effective if the client has limited communication skills or if his self-report is purposely or inadvertently inaccurate.

Talking with Family Members or Friends   Talking with the client's family and friends can provide another viewpoint on strengths and limitations and also help them get invested in the employment process while assessing their potential support and level of understanding. However, it is important to remember that family members and friends are usually not objective reporters and may have a vested interest either in getting the individual accepted for services or in proving that his disability is too severe for him to work.

Talking with Other Service Providers   Talking with other service providers may yield more objective information about the client, but it is important for the employment specialist to remember that even other professionals may have hidden agendas. A mental health counselor who does not understand supported employment or who does not value employment as therapeutic may paint a very bleak picture of the client's capabilities. It is also important to remember that the person's behavior in one setting (e.g., counseling sessions, day treatment) may have no relationship to his behavior in an employment situation.

Reading Reports on Current or Previous Employment or Nonwork Activities   Information about current or previous employment, whether paid, sheltered, or volunteer, may provide useful information about the client's work and social skills. Reports on participation in nonwork activities are sometimes substituted. As in other situations, it is important to remember that behavior may not generalize across settings, and the demands in one activity may be very different from those involved in another. For example, a person may be very comfortable and productive in a clubhouse program, where demands are variable, but still have difficulty in a competitive job where the work must be done. In addition, the person writing the report may have openly or inadvertently reflected her own biases about the client along with information about the client's performance.

Reading Reports on Previous Educational Activity and Accomplishments   Reports on a client's educational activity and accomplishments can yield valuable assessment information, providing the reports are fairly recent. However, there often is a substantial gap between the time a person with long-term mental illness leaves school and the time he returns to employment, and therefore school records may be quite dated and of limited use.

Medical and/or Psychological Evaluations   Medical and psychological evaluations vary in their usefulness depending on when they are done, whether the evaluator is familiar with employment demands, and whether the evaluation addresses the functional effects of any medical or psychological issues. The employment specialist can often improve the usefulness of these standard evaluations by giving the evaluator specific functional questions to answer about the individual, and then giving her feedback as to what parts of the evaluation were useful and why.

   Standardized Aptitude and Interest Tests   Standardized aptitude and interest tests are among the most suspect of the measures used to assess people with long-term mental illness. Most of these tests have respectably high reliabilities but low predictive validity and have not been validated for people with severe disabilities (Menchetti & Rusch, 1988). Some clients, especially those with higher levels of intellectual functioning, may profit by using some of the traditional interest inventories to spark discussions about desirable vocational areas and goals. Table 1 compares the analogue assessment and ecological and functional approaches.

Ecological and Functional Methods

   Guided Visits with Employers   Guided visits with employers are very useful for clients who have a limited exposure to employment and may not be able to identify appropriate and interesting vocational goals. The process of visiting different employment settings, usually in the company of the employment specialist, can be a useful way to identify interests and preferences.

   Observation   Observation of client performance on a job or in a setting that is as job-like as possible will provide information about a client's general work skills, the best approaches to working with him, and the type of environment he prefers. Observation may take place in the context of a work sample, transitional employment, sheltered employment, work activity, or volunteer work. It is helpful for the employment specialist to spread the observation across several different jobs or settings in order to increase the information about vocational preferences, characteristics of supportive work environments, and skills exhibited in response to different demands. It is also helpful for the observation period to be long enough to gauge changes in performance over a period of time and under different circumstances. However, the desirability of multiple settings and extended time periods must be balanced with the client's right to gain access to paid employment in a timely manner.

   Work Samples   It may be possible to set up work samples that correspond with the tasks involved in the job away from the job, as a screening or training approach. A person who was considering a data-entry job might want to try entering similar data on the mental health center's computer after determining from the employer what the data look like.

   Community-Based Assessment (Paid or Unpaid)   It may be possible to negotiate a community-based assessment (trial work period) with an employer so that the client can try a job for a specified period of time in order to assess how his current level of performance relates to the job requirements. This is an excellent way to assist people to try various work environments and skills without making long-

Table 1.   Assessment approaches

Analogue approaches	Ecological and functional approaches
Talking with the client	Guided visits with employers
Talking with family members or friends	Observation of client performance in employment or other settings
Talking with other service providers	
Reading reports on current or previous employment or nonvocational activities	Work samples
	Community-based assessment (paid or unpaid)
Reading reports on educational activity and accomplishments	
Medical and/or psychological evaluations	
Standardized aptitude and interest tests	

term commitments. This type of community-based assessment can help the client gain experience, gather information about preferences and skills, explore interactions between himself and the work environment, test support systems and identify support needs, explore learning styles, and explore career possibilities. Dineen, Ford, and Oswald (1994) suggested that community-based assessments are a poor choice when there are no permanent community jobs to move into, the worker has a recent history of dangerous behavior, the worker needs the support of an employment specialist and none is available, the worker does not understand the difference between temporary and permanent, the assessment plan is not designed to look for answers to specific questions, or the community rehabilitation program (CRP) is unwilling to follow the U.S. Department of Labor guidelines described below.

Issues of pay and insurance coverage in community-based assessments can be resolved in several ways.

1.   The person can work as a volunteer in an organization (e.g., a hospital) that is nonprofit and has an existing volunteer program that also includes people without disabilities. In this situation, the worker is not paid and is covered by the organization's volunteer program liability insurance.
2.   The person can be hired by the employer on a temporary basis and paid like any other worker. The employer's liability insurance covers the worker.
3.   The person can be paid by the community rehabilitation program on an hourly basis. Because the worker is an employee of the community rehabilitation program, he is covered by the CRP's insurance while working.

"Today, the arboretum...tomorrow, corporate law!"

Community-based assessments are an excellent way to assist people to try work environments and requirements without making long-term commitments.

4.   In 1993, the U.S. Department of Labor Employment Standards Administration released the following guidelines under which a worker with disabilities may participate in unpaid community-based assessment with for-profit employers. The guidelines specify several criteria for this type of assessment, including:

   • Participants must have disabilities and need intensive support.
   • Participation must be under the general supervision of rehabilitation organization personnel.
   • Assessment activities are specified in the individualized written rehabilitation plan (IWRP) developed with a VR counselor or CRP employment specialist.
   • The activities of the worker do not result in an immediate advantage to the business (i.e., there is no displacement of paid employees), and the person's work efforts are made to satisfy the IWRP and not the labor needs of the business.
   • The number of unpaid assessment hours may not exceed 215 *per job*.

Liability insurance coverage is an important issue in unpaid assessments because the worker is not paid by the employer and is therefore not covered by the employer's liability insurance. Community rehabilitation programs can purchase fairly inexpensive insurance to cover workers who participate in unpaid assessments and are strongly encouraged to do so.

Although there are potentially many advantages to helping people gain access to unpaid assessment experiences in the community, it is important to remember that the guidelines mentioned are in place to protect workers from being exploited by working for nothing. Once the assessment questions have been answered, the worker should be moved into a permanent, paid job.

JESSICA, PART 2

Jessica's assessment activities showed that she was a person who wanted to work because she needed money and saw working as a "normal" thing to do. She was not enthusiastic about returning to work as a cashier (the job she had held before becoming ill), but did not have many other vocational skills. After visiting several community employers, Jessica chose to do a volunteer temporary placement at the local library. The assessment questions to be addressed during this placement included the level of job structure Jessica needed, her computer skills, her ability to handle customer questions, and the level of support her parents were willing to provide on an ongoing basis. Things went well at the library, but Jessica decided she would rather have a job that did not involve as much customer contact. She was very interested in a position as a parts clerk at a large auto repair shop where she could use her computer skills for locating parts, do the inventory, and have little contact with customers. However, Jessica was unsure about whether she could do the job. David arranged to get a copy of the software used to track parts so Jessica could experiment with it at his office. Reassured, she accepted the position.

ASSESSMENT FORMS AND FORMATS

It is not easy to come up with an assessment form that summarizes all the possible information needed to make a good decision about vocational activity. A good assessment form addresses the important questions, uses clearly stated criteria, and specifies who is doing the assessment (so that possible biases may be taken into account). It is important to remember that the form is not the same as the assessment, but rather it is used to summarize information taken from assessment sources (e.g., observation, interviews, community-based assessments). Figures 1 and 2 are suggested forms for summarizing assessments of background, referral, general training, and support issues. For further structured assessment forms refer to Mcloughlin, Garner, and Callahan (1987); Moon, Goodall, Barcus, and Brooke (1986); and Powell et al. (1991).

CONCLUSION

Assessment activities can make an important contribution to the quality of the employment services provided by an agency. They can serve to educate the client and his family about employment options and begin to develop a good relationship between the client and the employment specialist, as well as identifying client's skills, interests, and support needs.

REFERRAL AND BACKGROUND INFORMATION

This form is intended to be used to help answer questions about whether you would benefit from the services we might provide and about support you might need. The information should be updated as each new vocational decision point is reached.

Name: _____   Date: _____

Date of birth: _____ Sex: _____   Social Security number: _____

Address: _____   Telephone: _____

_____   Marital status: _____

What is your living situation (with whom, how long, type of setting)?

What are your transportation options for getting to work?

What is your current income source?

What is your current occupation or activity?

What is your vocational goal?

How much education have you had? Are you interested in getting more education?

What jobs have you had in the past? Why did you leave?

Are you currently involved in any treatment programs? What are they?

_____

(continued)

Figure 1.   Referral and background information on potential workers with disabilities. This form should be completed by the client, with or without assistance.

Figure 1. *(continued)*

When was your first hospitalization? Have you been in the hospital during the last 2 years?

Are you currently taking any medication? If yes, what are the effects and side effects of the medication?

How do you know when your illness is becoming worse? What do you usually do about it?

Have you ever been treated for substance abuse? Do you use alcohol or other drugs currently?

How is your physical health? Do you have any medical problems that would prevent you from doing any job? If yes, what are they?

Why are you interested in employment at this point?

What strengths do you think you would bring to a job?

What things do you think you might have trouble with on a job?

Do you have friends or family members who might provide support for you when you start working? Who are they?

Are there other people who might give us more information about you? Who are they?

SUMMARY OF GENERAL TRAINING AND SUPPORT ISSUES

This form is designed to be used to help answer questions about the general training and support an individual with long-term mental illness might need prior to or while moving into employment. Some of these questions are:

"What kinds of issues might profitably be addressed in preemployment training?"
"What kinds of nonvocational skills and supports might be enhanced before employment?"
"What strengths does this person bring to possible employment?"
"What training and support needs will have to be addressed in the job-matching and placement process?"

The information used to complete the form might thus be collected or updated before referral for vocational services, before preemployment activities, as a person moves from preemployment into employment, or any time a new vocational decision point is reached.

Client's name: _____ Date: _____
Rater (name and role): _____
Setting(s) in which these issues were assessed: _____
_____

From the types of resources used for assessment below, check all that apply:
_____ Direct input from the client
_____ Direct knowledge of/experience with client
_____ Input from significant others
_____ Input from other professionals
_____ Other (specify): _____

SECTION I: VOCATIONAL GOALS AND RESOURCES

1. Rate the individual's clarity of vocational goals. Please circle the answer that best applies.
    a. Person has not worked and is not familiar with different jobs.
    b. Person has limited work experience and is not familiar with different jobs.
    c. Person has worked in several jobs and has no preference.
    d. Person has worked in several jobs and has definite preference, or definitely wants to return to previous type of employment.

2. Vocational preferences and interests: What type of a job does the person want? Why? What factors seem to be the most important to him or her? Be as specific and complete as possible.

3. Are there potential employers in the family, among friends, or in the person's neighborhood? Can any of these yield business or employer contacts for job development leads?

_____
(continued)

Figure 2.   This form is designed to be used to help answer questions about the general training and support an individual with long-term mental illness might need prior to or during his transition into employment. The information used to complete this form should be updated before referral for vocational services, before preemployment activities, during the transition from preemployment to employment, or at any time a new vocational decision is reached.

Figure 2. *(continued)*

4. Rate the individual's self-confidence. Please circle the answer that best applies.
   a. Shows a firm belief in his or her own abilities; tries to solve problems alone
   b. Has moments of doubt, but is usually confident
   c. Has moments of doubt that undermine his or her belief in abilities
   d. Frequently doubts abilities; depends on others for assistance

5. What strengths does the person have to draw on in employment?

SECTION II: WORK-RELATED SKILLS

Please circle the answer that best applies.

1. Misses 1 day per month or less	yes / with support / no
2. Starts work on time	yes / with support / no
3. Is appropriately groomed and dressed for work	yes / with support / no
4. Assists fellow workers on joint projects	yes / when asked / no
5. Manages adaptive skills (e.g., eating, sleeping, health issues)	yes / with support / no
6. Manages leisure time effectively	yes / with support / no
7. Manages basic living skills (e.g., shopping, money management) effectively	yes / with support / no
8. Has physical strength and endurance that is:	high / average / low

Comments:

SECTION III: SOCIAL SKILLS

Please circle the answer that best applies.

1. Initiates social interactions	yes / with support / no
2. Responds to social interactions	yes / with support / no
3. Seeks the company of others	yes / with support / no
4. Understands others/grasps receptive language	yes / with support / no
5. Is understood by others/grasps expressive language	yes / with support / no
6. Selects appropriate conversation topics	yes / with support / no

7. Socially inappropriate behavior and/or bizarre appearance
   a. Are present and not controlled (specify)
   b. Are occasionally present and are controlled with support
   c. Have been present and are currently controlled
   d. Are not an issue for this individual

Comments:

SECTION IV: BASIC VOCATIONAL SKILLS

Please circle the answer that best applies.

1. Independent work	high / medium / low
2. Ability to focus attention on task	high / medium / low
3. Problem-solving skills	high / medium / low

(continued)

Figure 2.   *(continued)*

4.	Ability to work despite distractions	high / medium / low
5.	Flexibility/acceptance of change	high / medium / low
6.	Neatness and accuracy of work	high / medium / low
7.	Initiative	high / medium / low
8.	Ability to follow verbal directions	high / medium / low
9.	Ability to follow written directions	high / medium / low
10.	Appropriate acceptance of feedback	high / medium / low
11.	Frustration tolerance	high / medium / low
12.	Independent task sequencing	high / medium / low
13.	Ability to tolerate interruptions	high / medium / low
14.	Usual work rate	high / medium / low

Comments:

SECTION V: ACADEMIC SKILLS

Please circle the answer that best applies.

1. Reading ability   none / simple / fluent
2. Writing ability   none / simple / fluent
3. Mathematical skills   none / counts / add or subtract / complex

Comments:

SECTION VI: SPECIFIC VOCATIONAL SKILLS

Describe any particular vocational skills gained from previous jobs or other experiences or education.

SECTION VII: TROUBLESOME BEHAVIOR

Does the person have any troublesome behavior, including destructiveness, suicidal gestures, anger and assault, extreme withdrawal, or inappropriate sexuality? Please circle the answer that best applies.

1. Regularly verbalizes and acts out in one or more ways
2. Often verbalizes and/or acts out in one or more ways
3. Occasionally verbalizes and/or acts out in one or more ways
4. Infrequently verbalizes in one or more ways; does not act out
5. Neither verbalizes nor acts out

Specify problem areas (if applicable):

Specify approaches that have been useful in helping the client control troublesome behavior (if applicable):

(continued)

Figure 2.   *(continued)*

SECTION VIII: ILLNESS AWARENESS AND MANAGEMENT
Please circle the answer that best applies.

1. Does the client acknowledge his or her illness?   yes / sometimes / no
2. Does he or she recognize symptoms?   yes / with support / no
3. Can he or she control symptoms?   yes / with support / no
4. Does he or she take prescribed medications consistently?   yes / with support / no / NA
5. Does he or she know individual signs of decompensation?   yes / with support / no
6. If taking medications, is he or she aware of possible side effects? yes / with support / no / NA
7. Does he or she attend other treatment activities consistently?   yes / with support / no / NA

Comments:

SECTION IX: AVAILABLE SUPPORT
To what formal supports (e.g., medical, psychological, recreational) does this person have access?

To what informal supports (e.g., family, friends, neighbors, church members) does this person have access?

Rate the individual's ability to gain access to these supports.
1. Does not have or is not aware of possible supports
2. Is aware of supports, but does not use them
3. Is aware of supports, but uses them only in crisis situations
4. Is aware and uses supports to meet basic needs

SECTION X: CHARACTERISTICS OF SUPPORTIVE WORK ENVIRONMENTS
What kinds of conditions or supports will enable this person to work? How much supervision will be needed? What kind of social environment will work best? What kinds of accommodations or compensatory strategies are likely to be needed? Are there any environmental conditions that should be avoided?

(continued)

Figure 2.   *(continued)*

SECTION XI: EFFECTIVE APPROACHES TO WORKING WITH THE PERSON

How can this person be best supported as he or she moves into employment? What type of communication works best? What kind of relationship does he or she prefer to have with the employment specialist? What kinds of things are reinforcing? Are there any approaches that should be avoided? Be as specific and complete as possible.

12

CAREER DEVELOPMENT,
TEACHING JOB-SEEKING SKILLS, AND JOB CLUBS

Career development, teaching job-seeking skills, and participating in job clubs are activities that share an important characteristic: They are all ways that clients are helped to participate in the choose phase of employment.

CAREER DEVELOPMENT

Rationale for Career Development Activities

Assistance with career development is a service that is not usually provided by supported employment programs. Instead, programs have generally just developed entry-level jobs and then made those jobs available to any participant who might be interested and have the skills required. However, as supported employment has continued to develop as a rehabilitation approach, career development has gained recognition as a vital component of employment services.

Career development is particularly important for people with long-term mental illness. Mental illness often strikes during late adolescence or early adulthood, a period when people typically explore career options and identify personal vocational preferences. It is during this period that most people are finishing high school, perhaps going on to college or technical school, getting their first jobs, trying different career areas, and making long-term career plans. People with mental illness may have spent this period moving in and out of the hospital, or at best living in the community and trying to manage the symptoms, limitations, and the stigma of their illness. Even people who had made career plans or had established a career before becoming ill may need to explore other vocational options because of the long-term effects of the illness. For example, a woman who had been a high school teacher and tennis coach before becoming ill might be interested in returning to work but is unable to handle the time and stress involved in her former job. Career development activities allow individuals to consider their current skills, interests, and abilities in considering alternative career paths.

Bingham (1988) wrote that most people with mental illness have not progressed beyond the exploration stage of career development. This stage involves developing an orientation to work, understanding the meaning of work, trying out work roles, developing occupational preferences, and setting vocational goals. Anthony and Blanch (1987) agreed that many clients with long-term mental illness were unsophisticated with regard to career development and suggested that poor job retention occurs partly because clients are employed in jobs that they did not choose. Anthony et al. (1984) suggested that people with mental illness can develop new interests and values when new knowledge and experiences are provided through the rehabilitation process. They also identified the kinds of career development skills that people with long-term mental illness typically lack; these include the following:

- Identifying interests and abilities
- Identifying occupations that relate to interests or abilities
- Evaluating occupational alternatives based on personal values
- Listing more than one work alternative
- Developing a career plan
- Identifying symptoms that hinder career plans

Career Development Approaches

When considering possible career development approaches, the employment specialist must remember that offering a range of activities does not guarantee that good vocational decisions will be made. People with mental illness often need

"But, this is a career!"

Career development is a service not usually provided by supported employment programs.

encouragement to try out different options and support to sort out the experiences in order to make decisions. The particular activities provided to a client depend on her level of skills and disability and her knowledge about employment.

One approach to career development involves activities that take place within the agency (i.e., a mental health agency or community rehabilitation program). These activities include reading about occupations, discussing and clarifying past experiences and present preferences, collecting information from family members and friends, and sometimes taking and interpreting standard vocational interest or aptitude tests. The employment specialist may also be able to help some clients clarify their employment goals by analyzing different aspects of jobs. For example, a client who wants to work in a dental office may be assisted to identify exactly what it is about that particular job that is appealing to her. Is it the public contact? The prestige? The working hours? The feeling of safety because she would be working with medical personnel? The uniforms? The fact that her father is a dentist and she is familiar with that environment? The soothing music generally played in dental offices? By analyzing the appealing aspects of a desired job, an employment specialist may be able to identify other jobs that share those characteristics and should also be considered.

A second approach to career development involves moving into the community to collect information about different jobs. This may include researching different jobs in the library, talking with people who do a particular job (i.e., informational interviews), or observing people doing the job (i.e., job shadowing).

A third approach to career development involves an activity that is very time consuming, but it provides useful information in making long-range plans. This approach involves having the client try targeted jobs with the goal of analyzing her experiences and using the information to make subsequent decisions. This may take the form of transitional employment or short-term job trials (paid or unpaid), volunteer positions, and sheltered or semi-sheltered work (e.g., clubhouses, rehabilitation facilities). This approach allows clients to experience jobs that are quite different from the ones they had originally targeted in order broaden their experience with employment before making long-range plans. Agencies that support clients in volunteer positions or unpaid trial work periods must follow the U.S. Department of Labor Employment Standards Administration guidelines to avoid risking exploitation on the client's part and possible financial consequences (e.g., payment of back wages, fines) for the employer (see Chapter 11).

A fourth approach to career development involves helping the client use the information and experiences she has collected to make good decisions about her vocational goals and plans. Many clients do not have good decision-making and analysis skills and cannot easily learn these skills merely from observing others who are involved in the same process. Direct instruction in decision-making skills may need to be provided.

A fifth approach to career development involves drawing on the experience and expertise of peers for support and information. Support groups that involve other clients who are also in the career development process, as well as clients who have moved into employment, are often able to provide valuable encouragement and realistic feedback to new participants. This may be done one-to-one or in the form of job clubs, employment dinners, and other similar methods.

The activities involved in the career development process lead to the identification of differences in work tasks and characteristics and the expression of per-

sonal preferences reflected through the individual's interests, values, and apti-
tudes. The employment specialist and client then may use this information for the
job development and the job-seeking process. Career development and planning
should not take place only before a person gets her first job, but should continue (as
needed) as she moves through multiple employment experiences toward stable
employment and the fulfillment of long-term goals.

TEACHING JOB-SEEKING SKILLS

Rationale for Teaching Job-Seeking Skills

Employment specialists often spend years developing the skills and contacts needed to provide job development for their clients. Therefore, it may seem strange to
try to teach clients the skills to find their own jobs. In some cases the client may
prefer to find her own job development so that the employer remains unaware of
the client's disability. In other cases the employment specialist may not have the
contacts or expertise needed to provide access to advanced job opportunities in professional or technical fields.

   People who have a limited level of functioning and are seeking entry-level jobs
may still benefit from learning job-seeking skills and participating in finding their
own jobs. People who actively participate in a job search generally feel greater own-
ership of a job and may have a stronger commitment to success (Anthony & Blanch,

"You said you wanted to fly!"

Trying targeted jobs is a type of career development activity an employment specialist can offer to his clients.

1987). Learning the skills needed to find a job and achieving at least some success in the process may build a client's confidence. Another reason for teaching these skills is that as agencies try to serve large caseloads with limited staff, having the clients involved in the job-seeking process helps stretch the limited resources available.

However, not all clients are able to or have an interest in learning job-seeking skills and taking part in job development. Some clients will need to have all or most job-seeking activities done on their behalf by the employment specialist. The employment specialist and the individual client should jointly decide what roles they will play in the job development process.

Many clients will need to learn specific job-seeking skills before they are able to effectively participate in job identification and development. The medical treatment and counseling used to control the symptoms of mental illness will not necessarily result in improved skills in contacting employers and writing résumés. Actually, most people in general lack good job-seeking skills; this is a characteristic that is not limited to people with disabilities.

Job-seeking skills are best taught through direct instruction because many people with mental illness do not easily learn by observing and therefore will not benefit much from seeing others in society identify and find jobs. A combination of direct instruction, practice, feedback, and reinforcement is the most efficient way to help clients develop the skills needed to participate in the job-seeking process.

Approaches to Teaching Job-Seeking Skills

Job-seeking skills may be taught in one-to-one sessions, with the employment specialist providing individualized tutoring and instruction. However, job-seeking skills are often taught in group settings in order to take advantage of peer experience and support and to use the employment specialist's time more efficiently. These groups generally meet at least once a week and are usually facilitated by an employment specialist or other vocational service provider. The areas usually involved in job-seeking skills classes or groups include the following:

1. Communication skills (listening, assertiveness, nonverbal behavior, self-disclosure, providing and accepting feedback)
2. Vocational awareness (assessing past training, experience, and employment; local hiring practices and market trends)
3. Job-finding skills (finding job leads, arranging interviews, interview skills, applications, résumés, cover letters)
4. Appropriate behavior (grooming and hygiene, accepting feedback, conversation topics)

These skills are taught through a combination of written materials, prompts, modeling, role playing (with or without videotape), instruction and feedback, enhanced cues (e.g., a list of interview information on a 3" × 5" card), and reinforcement for effort and improvement. The purpose of these classes is to improve and reinforce the organization and communication skills needed to find a job through active instruction and participation. These classes vary in length and intensity depending on the program.

Some programs combine ongoing skill instruction and review with peer support and problem solving, as in a weekly support group meeting. Others take a more structured approach (based on the job club model) and provide more intensive skill instruction over a briefer period of time (e.g., 3 hours per day for a week).

JOB CLUBS

Rationale for the Job Club Approach

Job clubs were developed by Nathan Azrin in the 1970s as a way to apply behavioral principles to vocational counseling (Azrin & Besalel, 1980). The job club approach combines direct instruction and practice in various job-seeking skills with support and reinforcement from the counselor and other club members, in an environment where a full-time job search is expected. The job club approach has been proven successful in many experimental studies with various types of clients, including people with long-term mental illness (Azrin & Phillips, 1979; Eisenberg & Cole, 1986; Jacobs, Kardashian, Kreinbring, Ponder, & Simpson, 1984; Rutman, 1994). McGurrin (1994) reported that job clubs have been impressive in terms of the length of time needed to find employment, starting salaries, the low cost to the social service agency, and the success rate of 65%–85% of the participants with mental illness finding employment.

It is important to understand that many job clubs sponsored by agencies are actually loosely structured support groups for clients seeking or maintaining jobs. Although these groups are often useful, they are quite different from the formal job clubs developed by Azrin (see Chapter 21).

Job Club Procedures

Azrin and Besalel (1980) wrote that the goal of job clubs is "to obtain a job of the highest feasible quality within the shortest feasible time period for all participating job seekers" (p. 1). They described the job club method as a structured collection of procedures that many counselors have used to help people find jobs, but only in a casual way (e.g., résumé writing, practice interviews). The job club approach is differentiated from other approaches by a standardized, consistent, intensive use of every prescribed procedure with all clients. The job club counselor should follow certain specific approaches in working with the clients. These include taking a positive approach and attitude with clients, primarily spending time identifying and reinforcing what the clients are doing correctly, and using the positive social influences of the group to encourage and reinforce effort and achievement.

The *brief talk* and *automatic rotation* rules are two job club procedures. The brief talk rule recommends that the counselor explains new procedures only briefly to the clients before moving into role playing and other types of practice. This ensures that the clients actively participate. The automatic rotation rule recommends that the counselor interacts with each client in the group for a set amount of time by approaching each in turn regardless of what she is doing. This ensures frequent personal interaction between the counselor and the clients and prevents one person from monopolizing the attention of the counselor or group. The job club approach is a very directive approach to counseling because it uses a set of specific activities and skills. The counselor is not viewed as a discussion leader but as a knowledgeable source of encouragement and feedback.

During the first week of participation in a job club clients are provided with training and practice in such skills as identifying possible employers, writing résumés, interviewing, asking friends and associates for job leads, and contacting possible employers. After the first week, the focus is on continuing to identify leads and set up interviews. Clients track their own efforts and progress with the help and reinforcement of the counselor.

Bond and Boyer's (1988) review of vocational programs for people with long-term mental illness reported that several studies showed that Azrin-model job clubs have been successful in helping people with mental illness, especially those with less severe disabilities. People with problems such as substance abuse, depressions, and anxiety disorders were more successful in finding jobs than those people with schizophrenia and bipolar disorders (Bond & Boyer, 1988). Eisenberg and Cole (1986) reported on a modified job club for people with long-term mental illness that met for 2 hours daily for 5 months. The first hour each day was spent developing personal and vocational goals and learning social, verbal, behavior, and writing skills. The second hour was spent reviewing job leads and making telephone contacts. In an average of 24 days, 61% of the participants found employment after participating in an average of three interviews.

Jacobs et al. (1984) also used a modified job club approach to help individuals with their transitions out of a mental hospital. The job club components they adopted involved the use of an environment that contained the supplies and professional support needed to look for a job, peer reinforcement systems, the breakdown of the tasks involved in finding a job, and a full-time commitment to job seeking. To better accommodate the needs of their particular client group, the authors also provided remedial training in job-seeking skills, daily goal-setting sessions with each participant, problem-solving (i.e., counseling) sessions relating to the job search, a close liaison with mental health treatment personnel, monetary reinforcers for attendance, assistance with daily living skills, and a weekly support group after employment. In this self-selected client group, 76% of the participants were successful in finding jobs.

The job club approach is a proven method to help people with or without disabilities become employed. Some people with long-term mental illness may need more structure and support than is typically provided in job clubs, and many will be unable to maintain employment without ongoing support. However, many of the guidelines and techniques developed by Azrin are directly applicable and may greatly profit those served by employment specialists.

CONCLUSION

Career development, job-seeking skills, and job clubs are all important topics for the employment specialist to discuss with his clients. The choose phase is essential for people with long-term mental illness because it allows the clients to explore their career opportunities and preferences, learn how to look for jobs on their own, and provide support for each other in the process.

13

JOB DEVELOPMENT

Job development is perhaps the one task performed by employment specialists that arouses the strongest emotions: They either love it or hate it. Many social services workers feel uncomfortable with the responsibility for developing jobs (Burnham-Thornton & Graham, 1988). Job development involves going out into the community to sell the program and the program participants, and it takes a different set of skills from those needed to work with people with disabilities. The world of business may seem like foreign territory to someone who has spent her career as a social services provider. However, as employment specialists become familiar with the personnel needs of businesses in their area and begin to have successful placements they develop confidence in their skills, the abilities of their clients, and the contribution that workers with disabilities make to the work force. Job development then becomes an opportunity to provide excellent service both to the client and to the employer. This chapter discusses the basic principles of job development and addresses some issues that relate uniquely to people with mental illness. DiLeo and Langton (1993); Fabian, Luecking, and Tilson (1994); Mcloughlin, Garner, and Callahan (1987); and Shafer, Parent, and Everson (1988) are all excellent resources for more thorough information about job development procedures.

PURPOSE OF JOB DEVELOPMENT

The primary reason for job development is to convince employers to hire people with disabilities. Therefore, the majority of job development activities involve educating employers about the value of including workers with disabilities in their work force and presenting clients' specific abilities in the best possible light. Job development contacts also provide important information about the employer including whether her particular business has job opportunities that would be valuable to clients who might work there. At the same time that the employment specialist is trying to get the employer to consider hiring a client, she and the client are considering whether this employer's job offers what the client wants or needs.

161

AGENCY MISSION DEFINITION

It is crucial for all agency staff to understand and accept the goals and values that are the basis for the services provided. For example, a mental health agency may have the executive director visiting the local Kiwanis Club luncheon one month to ask for donations on behalf of "the poor people with disabilities" served by the agency. The following month the employment specialist is there describing the clients as able workers and contributing society members who are striving to fill a valued role in the community. The next month the job developer from the same mental health agency is there telling the business people about the wonderful employment services she can offer, guaranteeing that no job is too menial or low paying for her dedicated, eager workers. What is the true picture? How is the community supposed to view the agency's services or the clients it serves? Is the agency marketing the services it provides, or is it marketing the clients it represents? Does the agency have minimum standards for the jobs that are developed? A unified understanding of the agency's mission and how employment fits into that mission will help agency staff work effectively with the clients and the community.

GET TO KNOW THE COMMUNITY AND VICE VERSA

The next step in job development involves getting to know the local business community and helping them get to know the agency and the clients it serves. One way to accomplish this is through networking with local business and service

"I don't have a business card...but we're
in the phone book under mental illness and suicide prevention."

Employment programs must think about the way in which they are viewed by the community.

groups, including business and professional organizations (e.g., the chamber of commerce) and community service organizations. Joining these groups gives the employment specialist a chance to make personal contacts with potential employers, educate others in the community about workers with mental illness, and to learn about the world of business. Specific information about the local labor picture can also be obtained from the U.S. Department of Labor, the state employment service, the private industry council (PIC), and the state's department of vocational rehabilitation (which may have its own job development program set up). The local United Way organization often has detailed information about the business community including the size of businesses and the names of the people in charge of the businesses. Networking with the business people on the boards of directors at local service programs can often open doors to other contacts. Businesses that supply goods or services (e.g., heating oil, travel arrangements, janitorial supplies, equipment repair) to the community rehabilitation program are also good sources for job leads or referrals. Presentations to non–business-related groups (e.g., church groups) may provide exposure and education to a wider audience, which over time may lead to possible referrals.

When contacting potential employers, an employment specialist must remember that she and her agency have valuable skills and services to offer. DiLeo and Langton (1993) suggested that employers are interested in being able to gain access to the following employment resources:

1. Information about the employment provisions included in the ADA
2. Job analyses
3. Successful employer practices in hiring workers with disabilities
4. Job accommodation strategies
5. Training for co-workers and managers in supporting and interacting with employees with disabilities

Offering one or more of these services is an excellent way for an employment specialist to develop a relationship with an employer.

The needs of the clients being served will determine which employers should be targeted for contact. Mcloughlin, Garner, and Callahan (1987) suggested that a structured process for prioritizing employers will clarify direction and increase effectiveness. They suggested that the employment specialist should start with personal referrals when targeting potential employers, then move to those employers who seem to match targeted clients, then to those thought of as most likely to hire individuals with disabilities, then to those employers with the most transportation options, and finally to those whose businesses are located near other placement sites for efficient follow-up. It is important for the employment specialist not to neglect already existing connections the client may have with potential employers (e.g., personal contacts, friends, family) because this is how most people in the United States find their jobs.

No matter which issues the employment specialist uses to prioritize contacts, it is important to have a system to keep track of job development activity. A tracking system ensures that prospects are neither ignored nor contacted multiple times by different people.

Although some communities have thousands of possible employers, others may have only a few. The employment specialist must remember that all she has to do is find one job at a time. Job development does not require an ability in sales;

it requires someone who believes in the quality of what she has to offer and is willing to keep at it until she is successful.

APPROACHING EMPLOYERS

Meet in Person

The most effective approach to job development is to arrange a face-to-face meeting with the individual who actually has the authority to make hiring decisions. This may or may not be someone in the personnel department. It often works best if the employment specialist makes the initial contact with the manager or owner of the business to show her how hiring workers with disabilities would be to her advantage. Ideally, this initial meeting will result in a referral to the personnel department with a positive recommendation.

Some programs arrange face-to-face meetings over the telephone, while others send an introductory letter before calling for an appointment. No matter what method the employment specialist uses to make the initial contact, it is important for her to remember that when calling employers she is not asking for favors, but rather offering something that could potentially be very valuable to their businesses. It is generally best for the employment specialist to give only a limited amount of information on the telephone, and save lengthy descriptions for the meeting.

"How fortunate, Mr. Perkins, I've been
wanting to tell you about our employment program."

The most effective approach for the employment specialist is to discuss the clients and the agency with a potential employer in a face-to-face meeting.

Gather Information

Before the employment specialist meets with an employer she should gather information about the business so she can make her presentation relevant to the needs of that particular company. It is important to find out the nature of the business, the jobs the company offers, the key personnel, the employment picture in the community, and how the company is affected by the economy.

Clarify the Goal

Before meeting with an employer, the employment specialist should be clear about what she hopes the result of the meeting will be. The goal of the initial contact is to get an appointment within a certain period of time. The goal of the first appointment may be to give the employer information about the clients and services and leave with a second meeting set up to tour the business, observe a specific job, bring someone in for an interview, or meet with another person at the business.

The Initial Meeting: Screen the Employer and Potential Jobs

Initial meetings should involve a two-way exchange of information. At the same time that the employment specialist is presenting information about the program and the clients, she should begin the process of collecting information about the employer and the jobs potentially available at that business. Guidelines for the initial meeting are listed in Table 1.

Initial meetings also should be brief. During these meetings many agencies use printed and/or photographic materials to hand out during the presentation or to leave behind after the meeting. These may include business cards, letters of introduction, brochures, fact sheets, or portfolios of photographs of clients in work settings. All the materials should present an image of the agency that is consistent with the mission and goals of the agency.

Job development materials should be developed specifically for each different purpose, rather than trying to meet multiple needs with a single product (Mcloughlin et al., 1987). For example, a brochure used with potential employers should probably look very different from that used with potential clients.

Perhaps the biggest job development mistake made at this point is to get too eager and accept any job offer, and in doing so get clients involved in jobs that are not appropriate or desirable for them. An employer may be very friendly and open to the idea of hiring a worker with a mental illness, but unless she can offer a quality job that matches the needs and interests of a particular client, the employment specialist will not be able to do business with her at that time.

Table 1. Guidelines for the initial meeting

Be prepared, organized, and professional.
Dress as expected by the company.
Do homework on the company beforehand.
Be consistent in presenting the agency's mission and values.
Be enthusiastic and confident.
Have props ready.
Do not use rehabilitation jargon; learn business language.
Expect and prepare for objections.
Do not be shy about asking for referrals.
Be clear about the goal of the contact: a follow-up meeting, a tour, or an interview.

Arrange a Mock Interview

One effective approach to dealing with an employer who is hesitant to consider hiring a worker with a disability is to ask the employer if she would be willing to donate 15 minutes of her time to do a mock interview with one of the clients. There is no obligation to hire the individual, and the employment specialist is only asking for a chance for the client to practice being interviewed by a real employer. Most employers will agree to this as long as it can be done at a convenient time. After meeting one or two of the clients the employment specialist is trying to place, employers may feel more comfortable about the possibility of hiring a worker with a disability. At the very least, the client gets a practice interview out of it. Asking to bring a potential worker or workers in for a guided tour is another variation on this approach that provides clients with exposure to possible jobs as well as building contact between the employer and individuals who have disabilities.

TALKING TO EMPLOYERS

Because mental illness is often an invisible and poorly understood disease, employment specialists who are doing job development may be challenged by the stigma and fears employers may have about people with mental illness. Fear and stigma can be reduced when employers are educated by reading written materials, contacting other employers who have hired in the past, or getting to know clients personally. The services promised by the job developer (e.g., training on the job, long-term support) can also reduce concerns about hiring people with disabilities and the stereotypes perceived by people because of the media. Kirsner, Baron, and

"He wants a job so badly, he'll do anything"

Probably the biggest job development mistake the employment specialist can make is to get too eager to accept any job offer.

Donegan (1994) reported on a study of 120 employers who had hired workers with mental illness through supported or transitional employment programs. They found that the promise of support from the employment agency (e.g., assistance with training, on-the-job support, troubleshooting) was the primary reason employers made the decision to hire a person with mental illness. Other factors that encourage employers to hire a person with a disability include a sense of altruism, prior personal or family experience with mental illness, and endorsements from other employers (Rutman, 1994).

Marrone (1990) suggested the following guidelines for talking to employers about psychiatric disabilities.

Stress the Positive Aspects of the Client's Functioning

The employment specialist should emphasize the client's skills and strengths, not his disability. The important question is whether the person can do the job at this point in time, not what difficulties he may have faced in the past. Armed with information about the business and the potential worker, the employment specialist can point out ways in which both the employer's and the worker's needs can be met.

Do Not Volunteer Negative Information

Although the employment specialist should be honest when answering direct questions relating to job duties, she should not volunteer negative information about the client's past or present functioning.

Avoid Using Medical Terms

The employment specialist should avoid using medical terms. Labels like "schizophrenic" or "manic-depressive" are not relevant to the employer's hiring decisions and may cause the employer to make inaccurate assumptions about the applicant's potential as a worker. It is more useful to give information about the functional effects of the disability and supports or accommodations that may be required.

Mention the Disability in Relation to a Significant Life Event

If possible, the employment specialist should mention the client's illness in relation to a significant life event such as the loss of a family member, getting through the teenage years, or a divorce. This frames the illness in a context to which everyone can relate. For example, the employment specialist might say, "He went through some tough times emotionally after his divorce and was unable to work for a while."

Explain the Chronic Nature of Mental Illness

It may be useful to explain the chronic nature of mental illness through comparisons with physical illnesses such as diabetes because both illnesses are invisible, require consistent medication, and may have vocational implications. Comparisons help the employers understand the role mental illness might play in employment by relating it to more familiar medical issues.

Use Business Language

Use business language when talking to employers (i.e "job," not "placement" or "worksite"). It is a good idea for the employment specialist to role play her presentation with a few employers who can be counted on to give good feedback (e.g., members of the board or business advisory council).

Keep the Emphasis on Work Skills

Whenever possible, the employment specialist should keep the emphasis on work skills, not on psychiatric problems. Specific questions can often be redirected once the specific concern is clarified. For example, if the employer asks, "Will this person flip out on the job?" the employment specialist can respond, "Are you concerned that he will make co-workers uncomfortable?" and then provide specific reasons why the worker can do the job: "He just finished a 3-month volunteer job and got along great with the other workers."

Do Not Divulge Confidential Information

The employment specialist must remember that it is important not to divulge information about the client that is confidential, especially information that is not directly related to performance of the job. Employers are usually curious about people with disabilities especially if they have not had much contact with them. Questions about the person's residence, their past history, and their illness are natural and may be difficult to sidestep in the context of a friendly and positive discussion. It may be possible to suggest that the employer save those questions for her interview with the client and then redirect the conversation to the skills the client can bring to the job. However, it is not always easy to be honest about the client's limitations or need for special support without disclosing confidential information about his disability. It can be very useful for both the client and the employment specialist to practice fielding questions that might be asked by employers in order to reach an agreement about how to talk about the client's individual situation and to get comfortable with the answers. Employment specialists must always remember that they need specific permission from the client to share any information with an employer. It is also important to remember that employers covered by the ADA (i.e., all employers with 15 or more employees) can ask only about a person's ability to perform a job, not whether he has a disability (see Chapter 10).

Listen to the Employer

An employer who believes that the employment specialist is attentive and responsive to her concerns, spoken or unspoken, will be much more receptive to what the employment specialist has to say.

Be Persistent

Any good salesperson knows that it takes multiple contacts to close a deal that is advantageous to both parties. Cook, Razzano, Straiton, and Ross (1994) reported that the percentage of employers who hired a worker with a disability increased in direct relationship to the number of times the employer remembered being contacted by the placement agency. Developing employer relationships by investing time and energy does pay off in terms of job opportunities. Another study found that job developers invested 76 telephone calls, 11 mailings, and four face-to-face meetings for *each* successful placement (Cook, Solomon, Jonikas, & Frazier, 1990).

De-emphasize Special Financial Incentives

Some employers may be interested in financial incentives such as special wage structures, on-the-job training reimbursement, or the Targeted Jobs Tax Credit. It is better to emphasize the skills and positive attributes that the clients have to offer an employer than it is to focus on the fact that the employer can hire them for less money than they would pay another worker. Emphasizing the financial benefit leaves the worker vulnerable when the period of reimbursement is over and the employer is expected to cover the full cost of employment. If financial incentive programs are available and the employer expresses an interest, the employment specialist must be prepared with specific information, but she should not use these incentives as a major marketing strategy.

WHO IS RESPONSIBLE FOR JOB DEVELOPMENT?

The question of who should be responsible for marketing and job development has implications for program design and staff skill development.

Clients

When possible, clients should be involved in the job development process at the level at which they are comfortable. Not only does client involvement bring additional resources to job development, it may encourage investment in the job once the placement is made. Some clients may do all job development on their own, while others may not want to get involved until the interview phase. Clients who are interested in participating may need training and support in the most successful methods and techniques (see Chapter 12). DiLeo and Langton (1993) suggested that clients might participate in their job search by listing the people in their social network, calling prospective employers, getting references from prior employers, writing or copying their résumés, touring workplaces, or writing or dictating letters to employers.

Employment Specialists

Employment specialists are often the most appropriate and successful job developers (Fadely, 1987). Although it may be difficult for the employment specialist to incorporate job development activities into her other responsibilities, the employment specialist offers a single contact person for the employer, which in turn contributes to good communication and continuity. In addition, employment specialists who provide job development for their own clients are more accurate when screening jobs and representing the clients' capabilities. An employment specialist who is going to be responsible for training and supporting a worker in a given job is generally more careful about what jobs are accepted and more accurate in representing the program's services to the potential employer. She may also be able to advocate more effectively because she knows more about the clients she represents.

When the employment specialist is responsible for developing jobs for her clients she has more investment in the placements, which may encourage her to provide better services as the placement is made.

Specialized Job Developers

Specialized job developers are often used by larger agencies to make all initial and developmental contacts with potential employers. This approach provides a solution when large caseloads make it difficult for the employment specialists to contact employers or to maintain continuity in those contacts. Having a specialized job developer also improves the coordination of job development efforts across the agency because the same person would generally contact all possible employers. However, it can be challenging to make sure that job development and client service staff work together and see themselves as having identical goals and objectives, although their tasks may differ. The point at which a job possibility is passed on to the next staff person is a common time for arrangements to fall apart, and care must be taken to structure and emphasize complete and open communication.

SHOULD JOB DEVELOPMENT BE GENERIC OR CLIENT SPECIFIC?

The question of whether to focus on generic or client-specific job development is an important one in planning job development. Generic job development focuses on developing jobs for a pool of people with long-term mental illness. Ideally this approach generates many job possibilities, which are then matched against the pool of possible workers to see whether any would fit the position and are interested. The larger the client pool and the greater the number of job offers, the higher the likelihood of a good job match. The advantage of this approach is that it allows the employment specialist to develop relationships with many potential employers without worrying whether an appropriate client is available at the time. The disadvantage is that when the job opening is compared to the pool of potential workers, the workers with the fewest skills or the most severe disabilities are less attractive than those who are more skilled or have less severe disabilities. Therefore, the same individuals tend to be passed over every time a job is filled and eventually sink to the "bottom of the pool."

Client-specific job development has the advantage of allowing the employment specialist to strongly consider an individual client's interests, skills, and preferences when deciding which jobs and employers to pursue. This model is often an employment specialist's only choice when the client needs a very particular work environment (e.g., strongly prefers only a very specific job, needs to have a job created for him due to his limitations). The disadvantage is that it can be very time consuming and therefore quite costly. It usually is less efficient to approach an employer who has been targeted for only one individual than it is to approach an employer who might be appropriate for several clients.

Some programs try to work around this issue by doing client-specific job development but consider other clients for any job possibilities that are not appropriate for the targeted client. Other programs do general job development but try to prioritize their clients with the most severe disabilities first for each job opening even if it means modifying the job to fit the client.

No matter what route is chosen, the issue of making sure that jobs are developed for *all* clients is an important one that should not be left to chance.

CONCLUSION

Job development is a crucial part of the employment services needed by people with mental illness. Well-done job development can serve to educate the community and reduce the stigma associated with mental illness as well as to identify specific job opportunities. The job development process also sets the stage for the important steps that follow: job analysis, job modification, and job–client matching.

Effective job developers remember that they have valuable services to offer employers, including access to excellent, prescreened employees and their own expertise. Their enthusiasm and commitment to the value of the people with disabilities are the most important job development tools.

14

CHOOSING AND BUILDING THE RIGHT JOB

Once career goals have been identified and possible jobs have been developed, the employment process continues with activities to select or build the best possible job opportunity for a client. These activities are actually a continuation of the job development process, in which employers and job positions are initially evaluated.

THE IMPORTANCE OF JOB ANALYSIS, MODIFICATION, AND MATCHING

Not every person with long-term mental illness will need an employment specialist to screen, select, or modify potential jobs, but many people do need assistance in this area because their illness has left them with significant residual intellectual impairments or because their vocational knowledge and experience are limited. The amount of assistance needed by an individual client depends on her level of functioning, her experience with employment, her interest in managing or completing the process on her own, and the level of other nonwork issues with which she is dealing. Although some clients may be searching for professional-level positions, most will start employment in entry-level jobs for the same reasons that many people without disabilities do; they are easy to get into, routine, and generally do not call for a lot of decision making or complex tasks. An additional advantage is that entry-level jobs can often be modified or restructured in order to meet the needs of the individual worker.

Job analysis, modification, and matching are activities that overlap and often happen at the same time. The information gained in the job analysis is used to match workers with jobs and to determine possible job modifications. Similarly, the needs of a particular worker who is considering a job are used to determine what the job modifications should be. Also, the possibility of modifications or restructuring may determine which workers are able to do the job. Job analysis, modification, and matching are among the most important skills an employment specialist can have because the key to success in job placement is the close match between the employee and the job requirements (Akabas, 1994).

Job Analysis

A written job analysis is a necessity when the employment specialist will be providing intensive on-the-job training and support. It can also be used to support job matching and modification efforts. After the client takes the job, the completed job analysis becomes the basis of the training plan, provides a benchmark for measuring worker progress, and is the basis for an agreement with the employer regarding the job.

Job Modification or Creation

When job analysis begins, an employer may have no positions that meet all the needs of any potential employees. Fortunately, it is often possible for an employment specialist to work with an employer to identify tasks and create a specific, modified position within the business. This job modification or creation approach is usually unfamiliar to employers, who may automatically assume that none of the jobs in their business can be performed by a worker with a disability. The employment specialist may be able to specify tasks currently done by other employees that could be combined into a job that would be appropriate for the supported employee. In other cases the employment specialist may be able to modify an existing job by negotiating for the removal of particular tasks (perhaps in exchange for other tasks) that would make the job a better match for a given client.

Job Matching

Assuming that the situation is one in which the employment specialist is actively involved in helping the client select a job, the job-matching process is a crucial one. The two main considerations in this process are whether 1) the worker can meet the demands of the employer; and 2) whether the employer can provide the necessary wages, supports, and other benefits to meet the individual needs of the employee and his chosen lifestyle (Garner, 1989a).

Job matching is a business and a rehabilitation decision. If it is done properly, it increases the likelihood of client success and builds self-esteem by minimizing problems, capitalizing on skills, and finding a work environment in which the person can be successful. However, if job matching is done poorly, it can not only jeopardize client progress but also ruin a hard-earned relationship with employers in the community.

EFFECTIVE APPROACHES TO JOB ANALYSIS, MATCHING, AND MODIFICATION

Job Analysis: Collecting Information About Existing Jobs and Tasks

Job analysis and assessment take place at four levels. At level 1, general information is collected about the employer and the business. The question asked at this level is "Would this employer potentially be good for any of the agency's clients?" Level 2, often called job analysis, involves gathering information about the jobs available at the business by looking at descriptions and schedules of tasks. The question asked at this level is "What jobs does the employer have to offer at this point?" Level 3 involves the general procedures used to do each task, and Level 4 is a more detailed analysis of procedures for a given task, known as task analysis. Levels 3 and 4 answer the questions "How are tasks done?" and "Are there better ways to do them?"

Information collected at these levels is used to make decisions about screening an employer, creating or modifying jobs, job matching, training approaches, and evaluating worker performance. Table 1 shows the relationship among the four levels of assessment, the decisions made, and the methods for collecting information at each level.

The employment specialist may not need to assess each potential job at all four levels. For example, if the employer is one with whom the agency has worked in the past, starting with the first level might be redundant. If the job being considered appears to be well within the capability of the target client and the employment specialist will not be providing on-the-job training, levels 3 and 4 would not be necessary. Job assessment should take place at the level(s) that is pertinent to each individual situation.

The process of collecting information about jobs and employers begins in the job development phase. As the job developer collects information about a business, he is also analyzing the company to determine if any of his clients would want to work there (level 1). This involves questions about the company's attitude toward their employees (i.e., are they disposable or valued?), the safety of the workplace, the social climate, and the probable longevity of the business. For example, an employment specialist once looked at a possible job in a fish-packing plant where all of the workers were recent immigrants. The only people who spoke English on the job were the managers, and they had little contact with the production staff. Although some of the clients (all English speakers) might have been interested in the job, the social isolation they would have experienced would have made it difficult to maintain employment. In another situation, the employment specialist was looking at potential positions at a restaurant during the job development phase and discovered that the restaurant manager changed every few months, making it an unstable work environment. Figure 1 is a form for assessing general employer information.

One study reported that workers with mental illness were more likely to remain employed when employment situations included 1) an opportunity to learn on the job, 2) the freedom to organize work, 3) clear supervision, 4) a trusting social climate, and 5) tasks that required a working relationship with co-workers (Floyd, 1982). Although each worker will have different needs, these characteristics may be general areas to consider when the employment specialist and the client are making the initial screening decision. Akabas (1994) suggested that there is little documented research regarding job characteristics that contribute to employment

Table 1. Job assessment levels, decisions, and methods

	Level 1	Level 2	Level 3	Level 4
Assessment	General employer information	Job analysis	Job procedure	Task analysis, more detailed descriptions
Purpose of decisions	Initial screening	Job identification, modification, matching, training, and evaluation	Modification, matching, training, and evaluation	Modification, matching, training, and evaluation
Method of assessment	Discussion, observation, and job description	Discussion, observation, job description, and working the job	Discussion, observation, job description, and working the job	Discussion, observation, job description, and working the job

JOB ASSESSMENT: LEVEL 1
GENERAL EMPLOYER INFORMATION

This form is intended to summarize the information needed to initially screen an employer and decide whether the site would be appropriate for any potential workers. The information required can be collected through interviews with the employer and employees, observation of the workplace, and/or any written job descriptions that might be available.

Date: _____

Business name and address: _____

_____

Contact person: _____

Telephone: _____

Job development lead from whom? _____

What are the transportation options?

What type of business is it?

What are typical job titles? Possible job titles?

What is the number of employees?

What is the annual rate of turnover? What were the reasons for the turnover(s)?

What are the typical hours, shifts, and pay rate?

What benefits are available?

Are there overtime requirements? Are the employees members of a union?

_____

(continued)

Figure 1. Level 1. General employer information needed to do initial employer screening. The information required can be collected through interviews with the employer and employees, observation of the workplace, and review of any written descriptions that might be available.

Figure 1. *(continued)*

What are the education requirements?

Are there any tests, licenses, or certifications required?

Does the employer have experience with workers who have disabilities?

Is there openness to job restructuring?

Is the employer interested in Targeted Jobs Tax Credit (TJTC)? On-the-Job Training (OJT) funds?

What are the application procedures? Who is involved in the hiring decisions?

What is the typical new employee training?

Are there opportunities for advancement?

Are there employee social groups and nonwork activities?

What is the physical appearance of business?

What are the environmental conditions?

(continued)

Figure 1.   *(continued)*

What is the general atmosphere?

What are some valued employee characteristics?

What are the absolute don'ts for employees (e.g., pet peeves, reasons for termination)?

Person conducting analysis: _____

Based on (specify who was interviewed and/or observed to collect this information): _____

_____

outcomes for people with psychiatric disabilities. She also suggested that workplaces that pay attention to the needs of employees, provide opportunity for growth and development, respect and celebrate diversity, and encourage teamwork and participation are good places for all workers, including people with mental illness.

Once the business has passed this initial screening and an interest or at least a willingness to consider employing a worker with disabilities has been indicated, the employment specialist begins the job identification and analysis process (i.e., level 2). The employment specialist often begins level 2 with a tour of the business operations and then moves on to activities such as observing the existing positions and tasks performed by current workers, having discussions with employees and supervisors, and reviewing the existing written job descriptions. Level 2 analyses might be done on several possible jobs with a given employer. Table 2 summarizes the guidelines for successful observations and discussions.

As the employment specialist develops and refines the job analysis, he should have the employer regularly review it and approve it when it is complete. If an

Table 2.   Guidelines for job observations and discussions

Get permission from the supervisor(s).

Introduce yourself to the workers and explain why you are there.

Treat the current employee as the expert and phrase questions accordingly.

Avoid discussing grievances, conflicts, or salaries; accept worker statements at face value.

Ask open-ended questions.

Pay attention to social climate and culture as well as to the job tasks.

Wear the same type of clothes worn by other workers, and follow workplace rules regarding breaks, smoking, and so forth.

Take careful notes.

Verify job data and technical terms with the supervisor.

Remember a position may be created that would work for someone.

employer continues to add or change tasks in a client's job, it may be difficult to finalize the job analysis. Although some adjustments in a job are normal and can benefit the worker, continued changes after the second week on the job may be a sign that the job is not stable and the employment specialist will have a difficult time fading from the jobsite. Therefore, it is important for the employment specialist to include the employer in the creation and approval of the job analysis from the beginning, and throughout the job analysis process.

Some programs find it useful to use structured forms to analyze and collect information about possible jobs, employers, and tasks. Figures 2 and 3 are examples of formats for collecting this information (see Chapter 11). Most programs eventually adapt existing forms to meet the needs and preferred styles of their staff members. The issues typically assessed at the job analysis level include the tasks involved, the level of supervision, the dexterity and strength required, independence, variability in schedule, academic skills, social skills, potential natural supports, openness to unusual behavior, and working conditions.

If the employment specialist will be providing on-the-job training, it is often useful for him to do the job for a period of time in order to collect information about procedures and task analysis (levels 3 and 4) before beginning to teach the job to the client. Although this approach (working the job) is not appropriate for situations in which the client prefers not to disclose her disability or for jobs that require sophisticated skills or knowledge, it can provide benefits in unskilled or

"Quick, hand me the wrench!"

Workplaces that encourage teamwork and participation are good for all workers.

JOB ASSESSMENT: LEVEL 2
SPECIFIC JOB ASSESSMENT

This form is intended to facilitate the assessment of specific job opportunities with a given employer. The information needed to complete the form might be collected through a combination of discussion, observation, written job descriptions, or working the job.

Job title: _____ Date: _____

Business name: _____

Hours, shifts, and wages: _____

Special clothes, equipment, and other necessities: _____

Opportunities for advancement: _____

Rater: _____

Type of resources used for assessment:

    Discussion with supervisor or manager (specify):

    Observation of workers (specify):

    Written job description:

Briefly list major tasks, including time done, setting, and tools/equipment used:

Task	Time done	Setting	Tools/equipment

(continued)

Figure 2.   Level 2. This form is intended to facilitate the assessment of specific job opportunities a given employer has to offer. The information required for this form may be collected through a combination of discussion, observation, written job descriptions, or working the job.

Figure 2.   *(continued)*

SECTION II: WORK-RELATED SKILLS

Rate the following issues as they relate to this job by circling the answer that best applies:

1. Attendance (person misses 1 day
   per month or less)   not important/important/crucial
2. Punctuality (person starts work
   on time)   not important/important/crucial
3. Appearance   not important/neat and clean/special requirements
4. Cooperation with others (assists
   fellow workers, answers questions,
   works on joint projects)   not important/important/crucial
5. Physical strength and endurance
   (specify in Comments section)   not important/important/crucial
6. Dexterity   not important/important/crucial
7. Other physical demands
   (reaching, lifting, etc.; specify in
   Comments section)   not important/important/crucial
8. Orienting   small area/one room/several rooms/building/grounds

Comments:

SECTION III: SOCIAL SKILLS

1. Receptive language (understands others)   not important/important/crucial
2. Expressive language (is understood by others) not important/important/crucial
3. Interactions with customers   not important/important/crucial
4. Interactions with supervisor   not important/important/crucial
5. Interactions with co-workers   not important/important/crucial
6. Socially inappropriate behavior and/or bizarre
   appearance   acceptable/somewhat ok/not ok at all

Comments:

SECTION IV: NEED FOR BASIC VOCATIONAL SKILLS

1. Working independently   low/medium/high
2. Ability to focus on task   low/medium/high
3. Problem-solving skills   low/medium/high
4. Ability to work in spite of distractions low/medium/high
5. Flexibility/acceptance of change   low/medium/high
6. Neatness and accuracy of work   low/medium/high
7. Initiating work   low/medium/high
8. Following verbal directions   low/medium/high
9. Following written directions   low/medium/high
10. Independent task sequencing   low/medium/high
11. Tolerating interruptions   low/medium/high
12. Fast work rate   low/medium/high
13. Adjustment to work rate changes   low/medium/high

Comments:

(continued)

Figure 2.   *(continued)*

SECTION V: NEED FOR ACADEMIC SKILLS

1.	Reading ability	none/simple/fluent
2.	Writing ability	none/simple/fluent
3.	Mathematical ability	none/count/add and subtract/complex
4.	Time telling	none/to the hour/to the minute/to the second
5.	Money management	none/simple/complex
6.	Computer skills	none/simple/fluent

Comments:

SECTION VI: SPECIFIC VOCATIONAL SKILLS

Describe any specific vocational skills needed to do this job.

SECTION VII: CHARACTERISTICS OF WORK ENVIRONMENT

Are there any potentially dangerous components? If yes, what are they?

What level of supervision would be provided?

Is there integration with co-workers?

Does it appear that there will be cooperation and support from the supervisor?

Does it appear that there will be cooperation and support from co-workers?

How is the atmosphere (relaxed, tense, etc.) in the workplace?

How is the work environment (noisy, cold, dark, etc.)?

JOB ASSESSMENT: LEVEL 3
JOB TASK PROCEDURES

Job title: _____ Date: _____

Business name: _____

Special terms or equipment used: _____

Describe how each task is done, including the time performed, where performed, and with whom (if applicable), how quickly, where supplies are kept, applicable criteria, and so forth. Descriptions should be done at a level of detail that would allow another person to either teach the task or determine whether the worker is doing it correctly.

Task: _____ Time(s) done: _____

Task: _____ Time(s) done: _____

Task: _____ Time(s) done: _____

Task: _____ Time(s) done: _____

Task: _____ Time(s) done: _____

Task: _____ Time(s) done: _____

Task: _____ Time(s) done: _____

Task: _____ Time(s) done: _____

Figure 3.   Level 3. Information on the job task procedures.

semiskilled placements where the employment specialist will be providing on-the-job training. Working the job provides an opportunity for the employment specialist to clarify and refine the job analysis and to structure and modify the tasks involved. At this stage, the employment specialist can identify natural cues and consequences as well as possible teaching approaches. The employment specialist also gains credibility with the employer and co-workers as he shares their daily work load.

There are situations in which it may be helpful to have two employment specialists involved in the job analysis for half a day or a day so that one can learn or perform the job while the other records the procedures and routines. Some programs with specialized job developers continue to have the job developer involved in the job analysis activities, alone or alongside the employment specialist; others turn over the whole job analysis responsibility to the employment specialist.

In some situations, it may be useful to complete a detailed task analysis on certain duties in addition to the job analysis. A detailed task analysis may be useful in situations where the potential employee has severe limitations that might affect her ability to do the task, the task is more complicated than it looks, it is unclear what the best approach to doing a task is, or the task requires specialized skills or abilities. Some people believe that task analysis is an esoteric tool that is only useful when teaching people with limited intellectual functioning, and therefore is not needed in supporting individuals with long-term mental illness. However, anyone who has ever followed a recipe or used the assembly directions to put together a bicycle (two task analysis variations) can attest that task analysis is a useful tool in many learning situations. Barcus, Brooke, Inge, Moon, and Goodall (1987) have written an excellent resource for learning about task analysis.

Job Matching: Client Needs and Job Requirements

Good job matching involves collecting extensive information about client(s) and job(s) and then helping the client(s) use that information to make decisions about the jobs. There are few decisions that have such a major potential impact on the employment specialist or on the client because deciding to support a client in a given job may mean committing time for months. Although everyone may be potentially capable of being employed, not everyone can succeed in every job. Job-matching decisions are often too quickly done in proportion to the amount of work that will result for both the client and the employment specialist.

Every employment specialist will become involved in a job-matching process at some point in his career. Even programs that try to develop only specific jobs in response to a client's goals and preferences will at times end up with job possibilities that are available to other clients, because the target client was not interested or because the employer had more than one job possibility available. Also, many clients have learned to depend on professional opinions to make decisions about their own lives and will work hard to get the employment specialist to provide advice about a particular job opportunity. Therefore, employment specialists have an impact on the job-matching and selection process even if they try their best to have the client make her own decision.

There are three common pitfalls in the job-matching process. The first involves a lack of information about the vocational demands of the job, the social climate in the workplace, or the client's capabilities. An employment specialist can avoid this by doing careful job analyses, spending time in the potential workplace, or possibly arranging a trial work period before either the employer or the worker makes a permanent decision.

The second pitfall occurs when service providers become overanxious to make a placement because the employment specialist has been idle or the client has been waiting a long time for a job opportunity. In these situations, there may be a tendency to place people in jobs that are not quite right for them instead of holding out for the right opportunity. Experienced employment specialists learn (often by an awkward experience) that job matches that look great at the beginning may not turn out well and job matches that look marginal from the start are rarely successful. The time spent training and supporting clients in marginal job matches would be better spent continuing to identify and develop a job that better meets the client's needs.

The third pitfall involves ignoring client input about the type of job that interests her. This is a difficult area because many clients do not know what kind of job they want or they have unrealistic employment expectations. The employment specialist therefore must strike a balance between supporting the client's preferences and helping her become educated in her employment expectations.

Beyond client and job assessment, a third category of information sometimes contributes to job-matching decisions. Many programs have too few job opportunities or, more commonly, not enough staff time to keep every potential worker employed. Therefore, as a job opportunity arises and there is more than one worker who could potentially do the job, a decision must be made as to which client has priority and should be offered the job first. This can be a difficult decision and is best handled by setting program policy ahead of time. Some of the factors used to do this prioritization include financial need, previous placements, length of time unemployed, level of disability, and probability of success. For example, a filing job is developed at a local insurance company and three skilled clients are interested. However, there is only one position available. If the program has no policy on job matching, the opening will probably be offered to the person who is best known to the employment specialist or to the person with the best social skills. In order to balance these factors, agencies may choose to develop policies stating that each job opening is first offered to the person who has been waiting the longest, the person who needs the money the most, or the person who has the most severe disability and is therefore least likely to have another opportunity in the near future.

It may be useful to have more than one staff person involved in job matching, especially if the person who developed the job is involved. An employment specialist who has invested a lot of time in developing and analyzing a job and who has developed a relationship with the employer and co-workers may have a difficult time making an objective decision about whether the job is a good match for any client. This can lead to making a poor job match just because the employment specialist does not want to waste the time and energy already invested in the employer.

There are times when the employer will want to participate in job matching by interviewing a candidate or candidates and making a hiring decision. This may or may not be to the client's advantage. Many clients who are perfectly capable of doing a given job are not impressive in an interview situation and unless the job requires communication skills, the interview may not give the employer a good sample of relevant work skills. Clients who will be participating in interviews

often benefit from specific training in interviewing skills such as attire and grooming, social greetings, providing information, résumé development, and answering
common questions. Some programs use videotaping and role playing to help
clients practice for interviews. It may be useful for the employment specialist to
take an active role during the interview, especially if the client has limited communication skills or if the employer seems uncomfortable with the situation. The
ADA requires reasonable accommodation (if needed) in the application process. A
reasonable accommodation could include having the interview at another location, having the employment specialist accompany the applicant, or using a work
sample rather than a formal interview.

Issues that are generally considered in matching jobs and workers include the
following:

- Would this be a good job for anyone (i.e., considering staff turnover, transporta-
  tion, wages and hours, safety, opportunities for integration, social support, con-
  sistency of supervision, job duties, stability of company)?
- Which workers are interested in such a position?
- Which workers have transportation?
- Which workers have the job skills needed or could develop them (i.e., vocational
  and social)?
- Is there family and/or mental health support for this placement (if applicable)?
- Which workers have the highest priority?

When matching jobs and workers, the employment specialist must remember
that many people with disabilities have had limited work experience and may not
look like good candidates for any job. Clients who are repeatedly passed over for job
opportunities need specific job development and modification to build a job that
matches their skills and limitations. It is important to balance the need of the program to be successful with the need of a worker with fewer skills to have a chance
at employment.

A good program will acknowledge that giving good service to workers with
significant disabilities means that some job matches will be risky and that not all
placements will be successful. The employment specialist must realize that if all
his placements are successful, he is probably being too conservative about with
whom he chooses to work and the kinds of jobs he helps people get into. Supported
employment services are intended for people with severe barriers to employment;
thus, providing good service involves taking calculated risks.

Job Structuring and Restructuring

Employment specialists often spend a good deal of their time building structure
into jobs where none existed before. The job analysis and task analysis processes
represent examples of added structure. Having adequate structure on the job
makes it far easier to track and assess progress and to analyze the reasons for problems on the job when they arise in the future.

In some cases the needed changes go beyond simply adding structure and
begin to involve more significant changes to the existing job. Businesses often have
enough flexibility to change tasks if the request is presented diplomatically and
with consideration for the effect on the business and on co-workers. This is almost
always true for the entry-level service jobs commonly done by workers with disabilities because the jobs tend to turn over so often, they end up being rather loose-

ly defined. However, job restructuring also often works for jobs that require more skilled workers. There are very few skilled workplaces (and supported employment programs are no exception) that have not informally adapted jobs to meet the individual needs and preferences of the staff who work there.

It is sometimes best for the employment specialist to wait until the new worker is in place before asking for significant changes in the job. If the employment specialist walks in on the first day and starts talking about all the things the worker cannot or will not do, the employer is not going to be impressed or cooperative. After the worker has had a chance to demonstrate her competence and strength and has established relationships with others on the job, her perceived value as an employee may balance her need for changes in the job.

The following are examples of common types of structuring and modification.

Establishing Time Criteria for Task Completion   Where the existing job description may not specify how long it should take a janitor to clean a bathroom, the employment specialist may want to develop a standard to use as a comparison when assessing job performance.

Establishing Consistent Routines   Some workers may perform better, at least in the beginning, if they have a consistent work routine to follow each day. If this type of consistency is not already a feature of the job, the employment specialist may be able to work with the employer to develop it.

Establishing Checkpoint Times Throughout the Day   Many workers with mental illness have a difficult time pacing their work in order to complete all assigned tasks. Frequent checkpoint times (i.e., telephone calls returned by 11:00 A.M.) may assist the worker in consistently meeting the needs of the workplace.

Establishing Consistent Procedures for Each Task   Establishing consistent procedures for each task makes it easier to provide consistent teaching and ensures that the employer's expectations are met. A written record of consistent procedures also can assist in making a transition from one employment specialist to another or from the old supervisor to a new one, especially if the procedure preferred by the worker (or the employer) differs from that generally used and would not be easily understood.

Changing the Routine   In some cases, it may work better for the client to adjust her task schedule by doing tasks at different times of day or in a different order. For example, a worker who is more alert during the morning hours might profit by changing a schedule that has her most demanding task occurring at 2 P.M. In other cases, it may help to do a task more than once a day in order to make the task easier (e.g., emptying heavy garbage cans).

Using Jigs or Other Aids   The employment specialist may decide to use jigs (i.e., devices to help hold a tool or the material being worked on) or other aids to help the client. Although more commonly thought to pertain to workers with physical disabilities, jigs and other aids can also assist workers with psychiatric disabilities to work around limitations (e.g., distractibility, poor decision making, hand tremors caused by medication side effects).

Changing Tasks   It may be advantageous for the employment specialist to negotiate for the removal of certain tasks from the job description, perhaps in exchange for other tasks. For example, a worker was fearful of using a narrow stairway that led to some infrequently used (once per day) files. The employment specialist was able to exchange that 30 minutes of filing for a brochure preparation task that was being done by another employee.

Using Written Agreements with Employers

Some programs have found it useful to use written agreements with employers to whom they are providing on-the-job training and follow-up services. Although not legally binding contracts, written agreements can be useful to clarify responsibilities and employment arrangements and perhaps guard against unreasonable expansions or additions to a worker's responsibilities. Therefore, the agreement functions as a communication tool and as a protection for the supported employee by making clear the conditions under which the client is accepting employment. However, unless the written agreements are carefully developed, they may sound like they have legal implications that might make employers nervous about working with the agency and/or a worker with disabilities.

Written employer agreements typically include job duties, work hours, wages and benefits, arrangements for performance evaluations, arrangements for supervision and for interacting with the employment specialist, possible changes in status and what they depend on (e.g., moving from part- to full-time), and the responsibilities of the employment specialist, including tentative timelines.

Written agreements are an important way to clarify and communicate employment expectations for all those involved in the employment process. An employment specialist who chooses to use agreements must write them in simple, everyday language and must not try to make them sound like legal contracts. Also, the employment specialist should not assume that the employer will actually *read*

"I thought you said you provided training!"

Written agreements are an important way to clarify and communicate employment expectations.

the agreement; he must try to spend some time reviewing it with her. Figure 4 is an example of a written employer agreement.

CONCLUSION

Job analysis, job modification, and client–job matching are important tools for the employment specialist. Carefully done, they make it possible to help people achieve their employment goals, whether by adding structure and routine to make a job fit a person who has difficulty with variability or by identifying a skilled and challenging position for someone who would become bored in a more routine job.

EXAMPLE EMPLOYER AGREEMENT

Employer:	Greenwood Bakery
Contact:	John Employer
Address:	7220 Greenwood Avenue
	Seattle, Washington
Telephone:	783–0000
Employee:	Joanne Employee
Address and telephone:	
Employment specialist:	Gary Coach
Telephone:	543–0000
Effective Date:	February 14, 1995

This agreement outlines the duties and responsibilities of both the Greenwood Bakery (the employer) and Support, Inc. (the agency) in relation to the employment of Joanne Employee in the position of janitor. It outlines basic information relating to Joanne's employment and is meant to help Joanne be successful at the Greenwood Bakery. Updates and changes to the agreement will occur as necessary, and may be initiated by any involved parties.

I. JOB INFORMATION

Duties: The attached job analysis describes the tasks to be done by Joanne and was approved by John Employer on February 10, 1995. Tasks include washing dishes and cleaning various pieces of equipment including the refrigerator, walls, drawers, shelves, proof boxes, mixers, floors, bathrooms, fryers, and so forth.

Work hours: 11 A.M.–4 P.M. Tuesday through Saturday, with one paid 15-minute break.

Wages and benefits: Joanne will begin work at a wage of $6 per hour, with raises occurring according to the Greenwood Bakery personnel policies (generally 50 cents after 6 months and review every 6 months thereafter).

Benefits include 1 day of paid sick leave per month, 1 week paid vacation after 1 year, and worker's compensation. Health benefits are available on an employee-pay basis after 6 months. Joanne may also take up to 3 additional unpaid weeks of sick leave per year if needed (as arranged through discussion with John).

Joanne receives 50% off on any bakery items purchased.

(continued)

Figure 4. An example of an employer agreement that is completed after the client gets a job.

Figure 4.   *(continued)*

II. TENTATIVE TIMELINES

Week 1: Gary will accompany Joanne to the job each day and will stay throughout the shift. John will provide Joanne with the typical training given to new employees, while Gary will provide any additional training and support necessary. Although Gary will be available at all times, John will be responsible for supervising Joanne.

Week 2: Depending on Joanne's performance, Gary will be on site 3–4 hours of Joanne's shift each day.

Week 3: Gary, Joanne, and John will have a meeting to reassess job duties and make any needed changes. Depending on these changes and on Joanne's performance, Gary will reduce his time on site to probably 2–3 hours daily.

Weeks 4–6: The fading process will continue with Gary eventually coming in once a day, then every other day, and then once per week.

III. PERFORMANCE EVALUATION

Gary and John will share responsibility for evaluating Joanne's performance during the training period. Because the Greenwood Bakery does not typically use written performance evaluations, the format developed by Support, Inc., will be used to identify Joanne's strengths as well as ongoing areas for training and improvement. This will be done after the second, fourth, and sixth week and then less often in the follow-up phase.

In addition, Gary will be responsible for collecting training data that support Joanne's task acquisition and document her improvement.

Joanne is interested in adding baking tasks to her job. This will be discussed once she is able to complete her initial tasks to John's standards within the time allotted.

IV. FOLLOW-UP SUPPORT AND TRAINING

Support, Inc., will assist Joanne and the Greenwood Bakery in maintaining this job and in expanding Joanne's role and responsibilities. This assistance could include retraining, job restructuring, advocacy, communicating with others involved, consulting with Joanne's supervisor and co-workers, or any other support that might be useful. If Joanne needs to call in sick, the bakery will cover her work just as they would with any other employee.

IV
ON THE JOB

15

INITIAL ACTIVITIES

As the new employee prepares for and starts his new job, there are several areas that need attention. Some workers may be able to handle all of these areas gracefully and independently, while others will need the employment specialist, the case manager, or family members to assist with many or most of them.

This chapter reviews some of the early details involved in starting a job. Subsequent chapters describe the teaching approaches, behavior management, natural supports and integration, and fading activities that represent the bulk of the employment specialist's involvement in job placement.

BEFORE THE FIRST DAY

Communication with Others on the Support Team

Before employment begins, the worker and/or the employment specialist needs to inform significant others about the upcoming change in his status. Significant others may include the VR counselor, the mental health counselor and/or caseworker, the medical specialist, the current supervisor (if involved in a transitional employment or other agency-sponsored vocational activity), the Social Security representative, the residential provider, family members, or anyone else who has been or will be providing support for the individual.

Transportation

The employment specialist may need to help make arrangements for transportation to and from the job. This may include identifying walking routes, developing car pool resources, getting a private automobile tuned and ready to drive, identifying and practicing bus routes, or having the employment specialist transport the worker himself. No matter what the arrangements are, they should be in place (or at least in development) before the first day on the job.

Rescheduling Appointments or Other Activities

When a person agrees to work at a job for a certain number of hours or days, he may need to reschedule appointments (e.g., with mental health counselors, medical personnel) around his work schedule. There may also be other activities the worker has planned that will need to be shifted to other times or days including routine activities such as grocery shopping, laundry, or cleaning the house. The employment specialist may also need to provide assistance in rethinking how the worker will continue to have access to clubhouse activities or other supportive and social events.

Double-Checking Medication Levels

This may also be a good time for the worker to schedule a medication check and discuss the possibility of temporarily increasing medication levels during the first few weeks of work if an increase in symptoms is anticipated or noticed. This is a decision that must be made on an individual basis, because increased medication levels may also increase drowsiness, restlessness, or other impediments to good job performance.

Clothes, Equipment, and Food

The worker may need assistance in obtaining special clothing or equipment required for the job. This may include business attire or specialized uniforms, or groceries to pack a lunch or cash to buy one.

"This job has everything...except convenient transportation."

Some workers may need assistance in gaining access to or arranging transportation.

Prework Routines

Some workers may not be prepared for the routine of getting ready for work (i.e., showering, fixing and eating a meal, packing a lunch, etc.) and may need assistance in planning their time. An organized approach may help reduce the stress that is inherent in moving into employment. If time allows, some individuals might profit from going through the routine of getting ready for work a day or two before they actually start the job.

Employment Paperwork

In some cases it may be possible or even required to complete employment paperwork (e.g., application forms, tax forms) before the first day of work. Some employers also require a preemployment physical examination before starting work.

Planning for Stressful Periods or Decompensation

For many workers it will be helpful to discuss a plan for dealing with periods of stress or exacerbation of symptoms. Advance discussion about such issues as the support resources available to the worker (e.g., mental health, peer support, family, employment specialist, other friends) and positive approaches to dealing with stress (e.g., exercise, journals, positive self-talk, relaxation) may reassure the new worker that although periods of stress are to be expected, they may not mean the end of the job. Some workers and employment specialists negotiate possible extended leave as a condition of employment, while others decide to be less explicit with the employer about the possibility of decompensation.

Thinking About Disclosure

Most co-workers are curious about a worker with disabilities joining their crew, especially if an employment specialist comes to the job with the new worker. They will have questions and concerns about the type of disability and how that disability will have an impact on the worker's performance. It is a good idea for the employment specialist to discuss these interests and concerns with the new worker so that he is prepared for the questions that may be asked and has a chance to decide what information he would like to share and what information he would prefer not to share. The way in which disclosure is handled should also be discussed. Some clients prefer to answer all the co-workers' questions themselves, while others may prefer that the employment specialist sit down with the co-workers before the first day (without the worker being present) and answer all their questions so that the worker does not have to deal with the questions himself.

Visiting the Jobsite

It may be helpful for the employment specialist and the worker to make one or more visits to the job before the first day of work. This gives the new worker a chance to get acquainted with the environment, identify key areas in the workplace, practice transportation arrangements, and possibly meet some co-workers before he begins.

THE FIRST DAY

Transportation Assistance

Some workers may need assistance in gaining access to or arranging transportation after the plan has been determined. This may mean driving them to work, riding the bus with them, or making sure the car pool picks them up.

Orientation to the Jobsite

Orientation to the jobsite is an important first-day activity if the worker has not been there before. Learning the location of primary work areas, locker space, bathrooms, break and lunch rooms, and time clocks helps a worker feel comfortable on the job. These introductions should be done by the employer or a co-worker depending on what is typical for the job. The employment specialist should remember that the first few days of a new job are likely to be stressful even for workers without disabilities and even simple information about work routines may need to be repeated before it is fully understood.

Introductions to Co-workers

Meeting co-workers is another important first-day activity. As with the orientation, these introductions should be made by other employees or the employer rather than the employment specialist. New workers may need to be reminded that it is normal (not pathological) to have difficulty remembering the names of several new people when first introduced.

New Employee Training

The employer should provide the worker with the usual training and orientation typically given to new employees, even if it will be grossly inadequate for the purpose of teaching him the job. The employment specialist's role during this training is to provide quiet support as needed, while noting any areas that may require further instruction. It may also be helpful for the employment specialist to reassure the worker that she *will* review and support any areas that are not mastered after the initial training period.

Additional Training and Support

As the worker moves through his first day on the job, the employment specialist begins to augment any training provided by the employer with any individualized instruction and support needed by the worker. This may mean teaching and reteaching tasks (see Chapter 16), assisting the worker to manage his behavior, reinforcing learning and correct performance, doing some of the tasks to reduce the pressure, and/or helping the worker to interact with co-workers. At the same time, the employment specialist models natural interactions with the worker in order to educate and reassure the supervisor and co-workers who may be concerned about sharing their workplace with a co-worker who has a mental illness. The employment specialist may also work directly with the supervisor and co-workers to help them develop an effective style of interacting with the worker and to identify potential natural support resources.

Mcloughlin et al. (1987) suggested that the employment specialist should explain that the reason she is needed on the job is that the worker has been unemployed and needs extra training to be able to perform his job like everyone else. They also pointed out that the employment specialist's attitude and professionalism influence how others perceive the worker.

THE FIRST WEEK

Employment support activities during the first week on the job vary according to the worker's capabilities, the other support available, and the needs of the workplace. The employment specialist's role is to do whatever is necessary to help the worker succeed on the job without doing so much that the client, co-workers, and employer become dependent or fail to invest in the placement themselves.

Unfortunately, this may leave an inexperienced employment specialist with a lot of questions. How much time should she spend on the job with the client? How does she know when to teach, when to help, and when to stand back? Should she be an anonymous presence spending as little time as possible in the workplace or should she try to build relationships with people at the job in case her client needs support down the road? There are no easy answers to these questions. This is where the employment specialist's good judgment and experience (i.e., common sense) allow her to assess the situation and make decisions that provide the needed support without being unnecessarily intrusive. There are three things that might make the employment specialist's efforts more successful.

Plan Ahead

The employment specialist can plan ahead by thinking through all the areas that need to be addressed before and during the first week, and trying to anticipate anything that might go wrong.

Be Aware of Behavior

The employment specialist must be aware of the fact that her behavior in the workplace, whether she is providing training or on-site support, is a powerful influ-

"Hi, I'm Lenny's job coach."

The employment specialist should try to blend in with the culture of the workplace.

ence. The employment specialist should blend in with the culture of the work-place (e.g., dress, schedules, other expectations), while at the same time projecting a professional and supportive image that shows confidence in the client's abilities and in the employer's good judgment in choosing to hire him.

Prepare for Stress

Experienced employment specialists realize that the first week of a placement can be stressful for them as well as for the new workers. Staying in touch with fellow employment specialists, getting some exercise and plenty of rest, and taking an occasional break will make it possible for the employment specialist to continue to provide good service to clients and employers alike. Above all, staying focused on the values that underlie the employment specialist's efforts—values that support the right of people with disabilities to live and work in their communities—will help to make those inevitable stressful days go more smoothly.

CONCLUSION

Regardless of the type of job or the client's abilities and limitations, there are certain activities that need to take place as a job begins. The employment specialist's involvement in these activities may range from total responsibility to minimal oversight, but careful attention to details, such as transportation arrangements or plans for decompensation, may make the difference between eventual success and failure.

16

LEARNING THE JOB

lthough many people with mental illness are able to learn job tasks through the training and instruction typically provided to new employees, others will need specific instruction over a longer period of time. Studies have repeatedly shown that an active approach to teaching and reinforcing appropriate behaviors helps clients learn much more effectively than environmental or milieu therapy (Anthony, 1982; Marshall, 1989; Mueser & Liberman, 1988). It is not enough just to help people gain access to new environments; employment specialists also need to actively help people learn the vocational, social, and other skills needed to be successful in those environments. The most successful approach to teaching job skills combines knowledge developed in two disciplines: adult learning and behavior modification.

THE BEHAVIORAL APPROACH

Characteristics of the Behavioral Approach

A behavioral approach requires a belief that behavior is learned and therefore can be unlearned, and that this past learning, rather than character flaws or personality attributes, determines how a person acts. This approach involves an understanding that behavior has a purpose (or did have one in the past) and that even injurious behaviors may serve definite and complex social functions. Intervention procedures that are intended to help people change their behavior must take the purpose of the behavior into account and develop appropriate behaviors to replace inappropriate ones. For example, June works in a grocery store and irritates her co-workers by repeatedly telling them the details of her illness and treatment. This behavior clearly gets the co-workers to pay attention to her, even though the attention may seem negative. Helping June change her behavior requires not only getting her to stop talking about the inappropriate topics, but also helping her learn and practice more positive ways to get attention. (Recognizing that a behavior is serving a legitimate purpose does not mean that the behavior must be allowed to continue in its present form.)

In the above example, June's unwanted conversation served the important purpose of getting co-workers to pay attention to her. It also put her job in jeopardy and needed to be replaced by more acceptable behavior.

In considering the purpose and function of behavior, employment specialists should keep in mind that the behavior of people with mental illness may be in response to stimuli that are not apparent to others; that is, what looks like illogical behavior may make perfect sense to a person with a severe disability whose ability to interpret and sort through external events is seriously impaired.

Behavior is a response to specific cues (obvious or not), is maintained by reinforcement, and can be increased, decreased, or eliminated through interactions between an individual and her environment, specifically by the use of contingent reinforcement.

The behavioral approach depends on the observation and measurement of skills through the collection and summarization of data, which are used to measure progress, provide evaluative information to the worker and employer, and monitor the effectiveness of the training. Training must be individualized and should take into account the unique past history of the learner and the characteristics of the environment.

Using a Behavioral Approach to Teach in the Community

There are several factors to consider and guidelines to use when developing teaching programs for use in community-based jobs. The employment specialist's role is at times a very public one. How an employment specialist performs in his job reflects on his clients and may have an impact on their acceptance by those who share the workplace, as well as on the perceived employability of people with disabilities in general.

There Should Be a Limited Amount of Control Community-based jobs generally feature a good deal of variability and a limited amount of control over the environment. There may also be pressure to complete the job and to be aware of all the significant factors in what may be an unfamiliar, constantly changing environment. At the same time, the employment specialist is responsible for helping the worker develop needed skills and behaviors.

Procedures Must Be Unobtrusive The teaching procedures used must be unobtrusive and as normal as possible given the needs of the individual worker and the work situation in order to facilitate both integration and maintenance of performance after the employment specialist has faded from the job.

Programs Must Be as Simple as Possible Programs cannot be complex or difficult to implement and maintain, especially if they involve others in the work environment and need to continue after the employment specialist has faded from the jobsite.

Changes Must Occur Relatively Quickly In community-based jobs, a worker's behavior or performance generally must change at a higher rate than would be necessary in a rehabilitation setting. Rapid improvement builds worker confidence and employer investment and reassures those involved that eventual success is likely.

Support May Be Limited The employment specialist may have limits imposed on the support he may provide because of client preference, caseload demands, or funding arrangements.

Change Is to Be Expected In the real world, workplaces are not static. In fact, the supervisor, co-workers, tasks, and production demands are highly likely to change over time. Employment specialists should help clients learn positive approaches to dealing with the changes that will eventually occur in the work environment.

The Best Approach May Be Changing the Environment, Not the Worker   The goal of every placement is a comfortable fit between the worker and the job. The best approach for doing this is to help the worker improve her job performance, which has the added benefit of leaving the worker with stronger, transferable skills. However, sometimes the most effective and reasonable thing to do is to modify the job or the work environment to accomplish the same goal. For example, in a situation in which a person is distracted while working at a desk close to a main hallway where many co-workers come and go, enhanced cues, practice sessions, and feedback might be used to help the worker become better at working in spite of distractions. A more direct approach might be to help the person negotiate with the employer for a more secluded work space.

TEACHING ADULTS AS ADULTS

Several issues differentiate the ways in which children and adults learn. Employment specialists who are aware of adult learning principles can use them to develop more effective approaches when teaching their adult clients with disabilities. This is especially important information to use when supporting individuals with long-term mental illness whose intellectual functioning may be at or above average levels.

Motivation

One of the biggest differences in the ways adults and children learn is that children usually enjoy learning for learning's sake, while adults learn because they see it as a means to a desired end (Zemke & Zemke, 1988). Therefore, the rationale for learning a skill is an important issue when working with adults and should be clearly explained and understood. Adults are often motivated to learn new skills as a coping mechanism for changes in their lives and may have difficulty learning things that are not clearly needed at the present time.

Another reason adults may be motivated to learn new skills is to increase self-esteem. For example, a person invests hours in relearning to drive a car (a skill she had before her illness) and is proud that in one way she has lessened the gap between herself and her former peers. Another person works hard to finish her college degree and gains confidence from her successful efforts as well as from the recognition she gets.

The point at which an adult becomes aware that she needs to learn something to accomplish a personal goal (or avoid punishment) is the point at which she will be the most motivated to learn a particular skill. This is what is known as a *teachable moment* (Zemke & Zemke, 1988). Table 1 lists some ways to use adult learning principles to increase motivation.

Table 1.   Motivation

Relate needed skills to changes in environment.
Explain the rationale for learning new skills.
Relate new skills to self-esteem and personal goals.
Pick teachable moments.

Learning on the Job

Another important difference in the way children and adults learn is that children are generally comfortable in the "learner" role and are not as self-conscious about making errors in the learning process. However, adults see themselves as having a lot to lose in the learning process. Adults fear they will lose face, status, and credibility if they admit that they do not know something or make mistakes. Therefore, learning situations must be set up in ways that provide error-free learning, while respecting the adult's equal status with the teacher. This is no less true for adults with disabilities than for anyone else.

Effective adult teaching draws on the fact that adults bring experience and knowledge to the learning situation. Adults like to actively participate in the learning process, and they generally learn better through discussion and rehearsal than through lecture and demonstration. They like to be involved in selecting the things to be learned rather than having the selection made for them.

In general, adults learn more slowly than children, partially because adults try to make fewer mistakes in the learning process. Children tend to try all sorts of responses to see what might work, while adults tend to wait until they think they know the right answer. However, slower learners tend to retain their new knowledge better than those who seem to learn quickly. Therefore the person who approaches learning cautiously and progresses slowly may be more consistent in the long run.

It is important that the expectations of the teacher (e.g., the employment specialist) and the learner (e.g., the client) agree on what will be taught, how it will be

"Well, Ed...this just could be your teachable moment!"

Adults learn best when there is a clear link to achieving a personal goal or avoiding negative outcomes.

taught, and why it is important to be taught. Adults are reluctant to spend time learning things they do not see as useful or things that have been selected by someone else. Table 2 illustrates adult learning issues on the job.

Teaching Designs

The issues listed above have implications for the ways in which instructional approaches are designed. Although each individual will have unique learning styles and needs, the following guidelines will generally increase the effectiveness of teaching designs.

Relate New Knowledge to Things Already Learned   The speed of learning can be increased by relating new concepts or information to things the learner already knows. This approach also shows respect for the skills and experiences the adult learner brings to the teaching situation and implies that the employment specialist will need to spend time getting to know the worker in order to understand previous skills and experiences the worker can use as frames of reference for new information.

Conflicting Knowledge Is Integrated Slowly   Knowledge that conflicts with things already learned is absorbed slowly over time. For example, a new method for doing a very familiar task will likely be integrated slowly over time, or a person who has always thought of herself as a poor worker will need a great deal of time and many successful experiences to change her self-image.

"I knew that!"

Adults fear they will lose face if they admit that they do not know something or if they make a mistake.

Table 2.   Learning on the job

Adults believe they have a lot to lose when learning new skills.
The expectations of the teacher and the learner need to match.
The learner's experience and knowledge should be utilized.
Adults tend to learn slowly but make fewer mistakes.
Active participation should be built into the learning process.

Stick with a Single Focus and Emphasize Applications   The most effective approach is to teach one task, skill, or concept at a time and keep it as simple as possible, while using examples, practice, and direct skill building rather than emphasizing theory. As stated previously, adults learn best when it is clear how the new knowledge is needed and will be applied.

Minimize Risk Taking   Situations that allow the worker to learn without making many errors or taking many risks will generally be more positive and comfortable for her. Minimizing the risk of making errors can be accomplished by teaching tasks in small steps while providing positive correction and reinforcement. This is one principle of adult learning that may be even more salient for learners with long-term mental illness because as a group they tend to have low self-esteem, little self-confidence, and a history of failure (Jansen, 1988).

Self-Managed Learning Is Preferred   To the degree possible, the worker should control the learning process by deciding what skills to learn and identifying how she would like to be taught. Ideally, the learner selects the preferred teaching process, pace, and content and the employment specialist serves as a resource.

Vary or Combine Instructional Approaches and Media   Every person has a preferred learning style, which may involve written information, verbal instructions, modeling, rehearsal, or some combination of the above. Using a variety or combination of instructional styles may make it more likely that the preferred style will be included, and will therefore help workers learn in spite of internal or external distractions. However, some individuals with mental illness (particularly schizophrenia) may have difficulty processing input in more than one modality at a time and may do best with one stimulus at a time (e.g., giving verbal instructions without eye contact or gestural prompts). Table 3 summarizes elements of effective teaching design.

ISSUES THAT IMPEDE LEARNING

Above and beyond the principles of behavior change and adult learning, there are specific workplace issues that impede the teaching and learning processes. These may be issues relating to the worker's mental illness or issues relating to the employer and the workplace. Some of the most common are described below along with suggested compensatory strategies.

Table 3.   Teaching designs

Relate new knowledge to skills already learned.
Integrate conflicting knowledge slowly.
Maintain a single focus and emphasize applications.
Minimize risk taking.
Provide opportunities for self-managed learning.
Vary or combine instructional approaches.

Mental Illness Issues

Although each person manifests mental illness differently and experiences any of a variety of social and cognitive problems, some issues are fairly common. Associative intrusions (e.g., hallucinations, delusions, illogical thinking) may be a barrier to learning because they interfere with logical thought process. Distractibility makes instruction less efficient. The learner may become overloaded when faced with information that is complex or varied or may have a difficult time learning because of the stress involved with functioning in a new work environment. An inability to interpret social interactions correctly may interfere with accurately understanding communicated information, and a lack of ability to generate alternative approaches to situations may lead to frustration or poor decision making (Mueser & Liberman, 1988).

Table 4 outlines some of the more common ways that mental illness manifests itself in regard to learning and suggests compensatory strategies for dealing with them.

Employer Issues

In some situations, it is the employer's actions or procedures that may interfere with the learning process. One common situation is that the lines of communication and decision making are not clear. For example, the plant manager may have given instructions to the worker on Monday that were changed by the shift manager on Tuesday, and on Wednesday the plant manager wants to know why his instructions were not followed. The best solution to this problem is for the worker

In some situations it may be the employer's actions or procedures that interfere with the learning process.

Table 4.   Mental illness issues that impede learning

Issue	Description	Compensatory strategy
Associative intrusion	Hallucinations, delusions, or illogical thinking interfere with processing new information or communication; sometimes these are vocalized.	Present information in small units. Monitor thought processes with frequent questions; have the worker think aloud. Use thought-stopping or other intrusive stimuli to break into perseveration. Use praise or mild censure contingent on responses.
Distractibility	Decreased ability to filter and process important information from the environment and ignore unimportant events.	Keep tasks and steps brief and focused. Use frequent prompts. Redesign work area to limit distractions and clutter. Post simple graphic charts. Use visual as well as verbal instructions.
Overloading	Information is too complex or too varied to be assimilated at the speed at which it is being presented.	Use task analyses to break down tasks. Reduce novelty through repetition of tasks and steps. Present information in multiple formats, or, alternatively, limit the number of formats used.
Stress reaction	Heightened reactions to the normal stresses of learning a job can increase symptoms and interfere with comprehension.	Pace training individually, keeping performance demands low and feedback positive. Plan a positive way to deal with anxiety. Allow for escape or time out from training when needed.
Misinterpreting social interactions	Confusion and distraction caused by trying to interpret social interactions interferes with comprehension of information communicated verbally.	Monitor thought processes by having the worker think aloud. Use written instructions as cues. Have worker record concerns in a journal to be shared later. Role play and rehearse social interactions.
Lack of ability to generate alternate approaches	Confused thought processes or limited work experience make it difficult to create or choose among approaches to problem situations.	Cooperatively develop alternate approaches. Develop decision-making rules. Develop and identify on-the-job resources for problem solving.

and the employment specialist to sit down with all the managers involved and develop a joint agreement describing lines of communication and decision making.

In another common situation, the employer changes the expectations for the job after the training has begun. For example, after originally agreeing that the worker may take a month to learn the job (with the employment specialist's help), after 3 days the employer then says that the worker must be independent by the next week. In other situations, the employer may continually change the agreed-upon job description by adding tasks or failing to supply promised safety equipment.

One way to try to safeguard against these changes is to start the job with a written employer agreement (see Chapter 14). If changes are later requested by the employer, there is written documentation of the original arrangements. If the employer refuses to acknowledge or comply with the original agreement, the worker and the employment specialist can together decide whether to continue with the job placement or to seek other employment.

TEACHING JOB SKILLS AND JOB-RELATED SKILLS

Building a Model

The first step in teaching a job is to have a clear understanding of the desired outcome. It is necessary to know the characteristics of the perfect worker in a given job before deciding how best to help a client move in that direction.

This process begins by completing a job analysis to determine the vocational and social requirements of the job. Job analysis generally involves observing co-workers, identifying and recording tasks, reviewing written job descriptions, possibly working the job to test the analysis, and reviewing the job analysis with the supervisor or employer (see Chapter 14). While the employment specialist completes the job analysis, he should also note and record any formal or informal non-work expectations that are held for employees. What is talked about at lunch? Do employees take turns bringing donuts for the morning coffee break? What kind of behavior is valued in the workplace?

Combining the job analysis and the social expectations produces the model of the characteristics, skills, and behavior of an ideal worker for the workplace. Comparing this ideal expectation to the client's actual skills and behaviors yields information about what needs to be built into the environment or into the worker's repertoire to help her succeed in employment.

Once the employment specialist understands the model and has identified areas of remediation and support, he will then provide intervention, direction, and assistance in three ways:

- Adding structure
- Providing and/or strengthening cues
- Providing and/or strengthening reinforcement

Adding Structure

The first type of assistance is adding structure to the job because many people with long-term mental illness have difficulty being flexible and dealing with variety. Adding structure is a process that starts with the initial job development and analysis when the employment specialist tries to identify and encourage consistency in schedules and demands. The outcome of this process is the job analysis or task list, which can be used by the worker and/or the employment specialist. It can be a written list that names the tasks to be done and the times to do them, or a checklist that the worker can use to track her task completion. The level of specificity and complexity depends on the needs of the worker and the characteristics of the job.

Task Analyses If the worker is having difficulty mastering tasks using job analysis-level training, task analyses are usually written and used to teach the tasks step by step. Task analyses list the sequential steps involved in each task and provide detailed information about how each step is done. They are usually developed or at least adapted to meet the specific needs of the individual worker. The need to use a task analysis does not necessarily imply intellectual limitations. They are very useful in situations in which a task must be done a certain way, the task is very complicated, or the worker is very unfamiliar with the task. A recipe is an example of a task analysis that is commonly used.

   Forward and Backward Chaining   Another way to add structure is forward and backward chaining. This refers to teaching a task one step at a time, adding more steps as initial steps are mastered. In forward chaining, the worker is taught the first step of the task and the employment specialist completes the subsequent steps. Once the first step is mastered, the worker moves on to the second step and the employment specialist takes over with the third step. Gradually the worker takes over completion of the whole task. Forward chaining has the advantage that the worker learns the steps in their natural sequence, while being able to focus on learning one step at a time.

   In backward chaining, the employment specialist completes all the steps of a task except the last. The worker then does the last step, completes the task, and has the satisfaction of task completion. Once the last step is mastered, the worker begins on the next-to-last step, and so forth. An advantage of backward chaining is that the worker has the satisfaction of completing the task successfully; backward chaining is especially useful when the initial steps are more complicated or demanding than the following ones.

   Shaping   Another approach to adding structure to a job is shaping or *successive approximation*. Rather than expecting the worker to meet the ultimate criterion for a task immediately, the employment specialist helps her set intermediate goals that can be reached more quickly, gradually shaping the worker's performance more closely to the criterion. For example, a worker who is learning to package custom eyeglasses for mailing may be working toward an ultimate goal of 15 pairs per hour but may start with a goal of 8 pairs per hour (with the employment specialist making up the rest of the production). This goal is raised gradually until the worker meets the production criterion.

   Preinstruction and Rehearsal   Preinstruction and rehearsal can add structure by helping the worker learn needed skills before they are required on the job. This may involve role playing, practicing tasks, or discussing situations that might arise and identifying good and bad ways of dealing with them.

   The employment specialist will often need to prioritize issues that need to be addressed when helping the worker set training goals. These issues may include learning the procedures for certain tasks, meeting production standards, coordinating nonwork issues in order to get to work on time every day, and learning to interact comfortably with co-workers. The priorities for each worker will be determined by her individual needs and the needs of the workplace.

Providing and/or Strengthening Cues

Much of what is considered training or instruction involves providing cues for behavior or strengthening cues that already exist in the workplace. Cues are signals that tell people what to do, when to do it, how to do it, and with whom. Common workplace cues include appointment books, the clock on a desk or wrist, the items in a "to do" box, the movement of colleagues as they head toward the lunchroom for a staff meeting, and the boss peeking in the door and asking, "How close are you to getting your monthly reports done?"

Prompting Prompts are cues provided by the employment specialist to get the worker to initiate, finish, or self-correct a task. Prompts can be provided in several ways and vary in their level of obtrusiveness. Although the needs of the individual worker and workplace must determine the types of prompts used, many employment specialists advocate a *least-prompts* procedure to anticipate and avoid errors (Barcus et al., 1987). This procedure guides the worker through the performance of job tasks, interrupting her before errors are made so that she avoids making mistakes and learns to complete the job correctly from the beginning. Least-prompting begins with a natural cue, perhaps the completion of the previous task. The employment specialist waits for self-initiation of the next task and provides reinforcement if the worker does it correctly. If the worker does not initiate the task or does it incorrectly, the employment specialist provides a verbal prompt, once again providing reinforcement if the worker begins the correct task. If the verbal prompt is not sufficient, gestures or modeling of the next step is provided, moving on to physical prompts if necessary. Each subsequent prompt should be provided as soon as the employment specialist realizes the worker is not making the correct choice, instead of waiting until an error has been made.

Verbal prompts are typically used in most workplaces. They can be either direct (e.g., "Try lifting the handle a little higher"; "I wonder if it would work better to finish the telephone messages before starting today's entries"), or indirect (e.g., "What do you need to do now?"). The employment specialist must be careful not to make assumptions about the worker's ability to understand verbal prompts. Because some people with long-term mental illness may have difficulty understanding verbal instructions or prompts, it may be helpful to combine them with

"Great, I get the cartooning job coach!"

The types of prompts used should be determined by the needs of the worker and the workplace.

gestural or written prompts or to have the worker repeat or demonstrate the instruction before assuming comprehension.

Verbal prompts used later in training may involve referencing natural cues in the environment rather than specifying the correct action. A prompt to go to lunch becomes "What time is it?" rather than "It's time to go to lunch." Shorter prompts are usually more effective.

Gestures   Head nods, hand signals, and facial expressions are all gestures that provide information nonverbally and can be useful with workers who have difficulty processing verbal information or who work in noisy environments. Gestures may involve simulating the desired action, pointing at the next step, or just making a questioning movement, such as raising the eyebrows. Gestures may be easier to fade than verbal prompts.

Modeling and Demonstration   Through modeling and demonstrating, the employment specialist completes the task and points out natural cues as the employment specialist works. This technique is often used to train new workers without disabilities (and therefore is fairly unobtrusive) and provides information in a second medium (nonverbal) that may strongly complement verbal instruction.

Physical Prompts   Physical prompting can involve manipulating fingers, placing the employment specialist's hand over the worker's as she goes through a task, touching the worker's hand or elbow to move her to the next action, or nudging the worker toward the next step. These types of prompts should only be used when other types of prompts have been ineffective or when physical prompts are commonly used with others in the workplace. The employment specialist must make sure he does not block the worker's view of the task while he is assisting her.

Although any type of prompts may be either reinforcing or punishing to a given individual, physical prompts tend to be particularly positive or negative. For example, the employment specialist must be aware that some people may be very uncomfortable with being touched and therefore are unable to learn from the prompt, while others may find the employment specialist's proximity comforting and may have difficulty working independently after becoming used to the employment specialist's presence.

Augmenting Cues   Augmenting cues that are already found in the workplace is a very effective teaching technique. This might involve moving a clock so that it can be seen by the worker, developing a written checklist of tasks that can be used to check progress during the day, adding labels to switches so it is easy to tell if they are on or off, or color coding a filing system. Often the augmentation can be done in such a way that it is either unobtrusive to other workers or helpful to everyone in the workplace.

Providing an Example   Providing a concrete example of the correct process or the finished product can help a worker learn task procedures or quality standards. A poster depicting a correctly folded and inserted brochure, a correctly assembled camp stove, or a grant proposal that had been successfully submitted all can serve as examples to use to guide the worker's efforts.

Verbal Rehearsal   A powerful yet subtle way to cue task performance is through verbal rehearsal. It can range from having the worker repeat an instruction (e.g., "I need to sweep the kitchen floor") to having her answer an open-ended question (e.g., "What do you need to do next?"). By having the worker verbally rehearse the next step, a link can be made between the natural cues and the proper task sequence.

Providing and/or Strengthening Reinforcement

The fourth step in teaching jobs involves making sure that the worker gets consistent feedback and reinforcement for her efforts. This completes the learning cycle and is crucial to task acquisition and maintenance.

Role Playing and Practice Sessions   Role playing and practice sessions provide a forum for providing feedback away from the work setting. They give the worker an opportunity to identify and try approaches and responses that might be effective on the job without interfering with completing the job. Many workers find it better to develop alternate approaches to situations in a supportive environment away from the pressures of the job. These approaches can then be called on, perhaps with cuing assistance, when needed.

Reinforcers   The major tool in the employment specialist's bag is reinforcement. Everyone responds to reinforcers in a variety of everyday situations. Reinforcers that get people through their workday include the knowledge that they are getting paid (i.e., a token reinforcer), the social interactions with their colleagues, clients, and others (i.e., social reinforcers), and the feeling of accomplishment that they have done a task well (i.e., internal reinforcers). As people with mental illness move into employment situations, they may require time and support in order to identify and acknowledge the reinforcers available in the work environment. In some cases, the work environment currently set up may not deliver reinforcers on a consistent basis. The employment specialist's job becomes that of helping redesign the workplace to make reinforcement available and/or helping the worker recognize reinforcement when it is offered.

PROFILE: TERRY

Terry has taken a job in a dental office. Her tasks involve sterilizing the dental tools, preparing the packs of tools for the dentist's use, and making telephone calls to remind patients of their appointments. Some of the reinforcers generally available in this work environment include praise and compliments from the dentist and other staff, crossing off the name of each patient called, completing each pack of tools and moving it to the cupboard, finishing the tool work and seeing the area cleaned, going to lunch and having breaks, participating in social chitchat with the staff, listening to the music piped in for the patients, and getting a paycheck every 2 weeks. Some of these reinforcers were easy for Terry to appreciate, particularly the paycheck and lunch breaks. However, she had difficulty with the praise at first because she did not take it at face value. When the dentist would tell Terry she was doing a good job, Terry's response was something like, "He's just saying that because he feels sorry for me. He'll probably fire me as soon as I make a mistake." By gently challenging this interpretation and repeatedly pointing out other staff members' responses to praise, the employment specialist was able to help Terry gain confidence in the sincerity of the dentist's praise. However, there was one reinforcer Terry never did learn to value: the dental office music. After hearing the orchestral version of one particular song too many times, Terry asked for and received permission to wear headphones at work.

The most effective reinforcers for employment specialists to manipulate are those that are least obtrusive to the routines of the workplace, that occur naturally in the work environment, and that are valued by others in the workplace because they are the most likely to be available on a continuing basis. Typical kinds of reinforcers found in workplaces include social praise or compliments, physical contact (e.g., handshakes, high fives, pats), smiles, having access to valued activities, bonuses, raises, promotions, and the removal of less desirable parts of the job.

Reinforcers can be idiosyncratic and must be individualized. Employment specialists and employers must realize that what is reinforcing to one person may be punishing to another. In all cases, the effect is more important than the intent. For example, a worker who may be pleased with a private word of praise might be embarrassed when praised in front of her co-workers. The timing of reinforcement also affects its power. In order to be most effective, reinforcement should be clearly linked with the desirable behavior and should occur soon after the target behavior. Reinforcing a new behavior every time it occurs will build the behavior quickly. Fading reinforcement to an unpredictable and intermittent schedule will be most effective for maintenance.

Correction   Correction provides feedback on errors that are being or are about to be made by the worker. Generally, the best approach to correction is to first interrupt the worker gently as soon as it is clear that she is making an error. The employment specialist should then provide the kind of cues or assistance that will most likely help the worker to complete the step correctly, and then back up a step and allow the worker to repeat the step correctly (with appropriate assistance).

When using correction procedures, it is important to maintain a positive attitude so that corrections do not become punishing. Conversely, the correction procedure may itself be reinforcing, which causes some workers to err on purpose in order to be corrected. The ideal correcting procedure should be experienced by the worker as neutral—neither reinforcing nor punishing.

It is usually best to use the least amount of instructional power that will accomplish the step. This includes such things as the following:

- Beginning with the most natural assistance and increasing only as necessary
- Modifying the procedures selected according to environmental conditions
- Using physical assists only when necessary and fading them as soon as possible
- Trying to follow the company's existing procedures for communicating information and training as much as possible (Mcloughlin et al., 1987)

TEACHING DIFFICULT STEPS

An employment specialist may need a more structured approach when teaching tasks or steps that the worker is having difficulty learning. In general, such techniques as practicing the step repeatedly (i.e., massed trials), providing specific and concrete cues, developing specific decision rules, providing structured aids, and using verbal rehearsal are effective in learning difficult steps. Table 5 summarizes some effective approaches to teaching difficult steps.

MEASURING PROGRESS

There is probably no topic that makes inexperienced employment specialists cringe faster than data collection, unless it is job development. People who are not accustomed to using behavioral technology when helping their clients learn gener-

Table 5.   Teaching difficult steps

Issue	Teaching strategy
Discriminations between minimal differences (e.g., weeds versus flowers, filing by dates)	Providing multiple practice trials Presenting examples in easy-to-difficult sequences Making the relevant dimension easier to judge (enhanced cues)
Discriminations along a continuous dimension (e.g., hot and cold, clean and dirty)	Starting with extreme examples to learn relevant dimensions and then using positive and negative examples that get closer to the boundary Trying to establish a measurable criterion (e.g., using a thermometer)
Simultaneous discriminations across more than one dimension (e.g., files that are dated after 1988 and are from Alaska addresses)	Performing discriminations sequentially (e.g., separating Alaska files, then placing in order by date) Repeating practice trials, varying the irrelevant dimensions of the examples so the worker learns to focus only on the relevant factor(s)
Nonvisual discrimination (e.g., filling a mower with gas)	Modifying the task design (e.g., sensor on gas pump automatically shuts off when tank is full, gas is first measured into a visible container, then added to mower) Identifying and attending to cues that correlate with relevant outcome (e.g., number of turns with screwdriver relating to tightness of screw)
Simultaneous manipulations (both hands)	Teaching one hand at a time before combining them Modifying the task design

ally are afraid that data collection will be inconvenient, unwieldy, too structured, and more trouble than it is worth. However, collecting the right kind of data enables the employment specialist to recognize and plot progress (or lack of it), to make objective decisions, to evaluate and adjust training methods, to reinforce himself as well as the worker, and to demonstrate progress to the employer and funding agencies. Data collection also facilitates communication and information sharing, and focuses the employment specialist's attention on prioritized training objectives. Table 6 outlines five different rules for data collection.

Data usually describe the worker's behavior (e.g., units completed during a shift) or the employment specialist's behavior (e.g., number and type of prompts). They may be collected throughout the workday, throughout a task, or during probes made at specific times. Data can be used to measure the time it takes to complete a task, the amount of time that goes by without the occurrence of a problem behavior, the volume of work completed, the number of social interactions initiated, or any key issues for the client in the work environment. The simplest form of data collection that still provides the necessary information is generally the best.

Table 6.   Data collection rules

Know the purpose of the data to be collected.

Collect data at levels appropriate to the purpose.

Collect data in units that are adequate.

Establish and maintain formats and procedures for analyzing data.

Make decisions based on data trends.

At the beginning of training it is often difficult, if not impossible, to collect data for every step. Instead, it often works well to identify trends and potential problem areas over the first few days. As the worker learns more of the job, the employment specialist will be able to make better decisions about areas in which a worker needs additional training and data that should be collected. Many programs use some variation of the Virginia Commonwealth University system, which records a symbol representing either independent performance of a step or verbal, modeling, or physical prompts (Barcus et al., 1987).

Summarizing data reduces the probe-to-probe and day-to-day variability of worker performance, illustrates the degree and direction of behavioral trends, allows comparison with past performance, and provides a permanent record of worker progress and a standardized system for communicating that information. This can be done by graphing (i.e., days of the week on the horizontal axis, prompt or behavioral information on the vertical axis), charting a bar graph, entering weekly averages in a table, or any other way that makes the data useful for making training decisions.

If the data do not seem to accurately reflect the worker's progress, possibly the wrong data are being collected. It is also possible that the employment specialist may be ignoring facts about the worker's performance that are inconsistent with the employment specialist's own assumptions. For example, the employment specialist wants to believe the worker is improving although the data show no change, so he assumes the data are wrong rather than challenging his own reading of the situation. If data are not giving the employment specialist useful information, it may be helpful to monitor a different variable, use smaller time intervals, weigh the tasks differently, or adjust the criteria to reflect the reality of the workplace. If data are not useful, there is no point in collecting and summarizing them.

"Could you do that one again—I think I missed a step."

At the beginning of training, it is often difficult—if not impossible—to collect data on every step.

CONCLUSION

People with mental illness vary in their need for assistance in learning jobs. Employment specialists who are familiar with a range of approaches to teaching job skills and the behavioral and adult learning theories that underlie those approaches will be able to provide more effective service at a level that is appropriate for the individual client's needs. Although some of these approaches involve mostly common sense, others use specific teaching technology and behavioral strategies that require the development of skill and expertise.

This chapter reviews some of the basic principles of teaching job skills to individuals who may need assistance. Barcus et al. (1987) and Powell et al. (1991) provide more detailed information about teaching techniques. Although written primarily for job coaches serving people with mental retardation, these manuals are an excellent resource for any employment specialist or mental health counselor who is new to supported employment training.

17

SPECIFIC TEACHING TOPICS

Although each worker and workplace has a unique set of issues, there are some challenges that many jobs have in common. Issues of independence, quality, speed, time management, and anger management often need to be addressed by the worker with the help of the employment specialist. In many cases the worker is able to deal with these challenges with only the off-site help of the employment specialist, whereas in other cases the worker will benefit from well-planned training and assistance on the job. Isbister and Donaldson (1987) reported that although many workers with mental illness acquired job skills quickly, production rates were often below criterion levels and jobsite intervention was required.

This chapter outlines some specific approaches employment specialists can use to help workers deal with worksite issues. Most of the approaches assume that the employment specialist is able to work with the worker at the jobsite. In situations where on-the-job training is not being provided, the employment specialist may still be able to assist the worker in thinking through problem situations on the job and identifying possible strategies for dealing with difficulties (see Chapter 19).

TEACHING INDEPENDENCE

The ability to work independently is a crucial characteristic for all workers. Supervisors in most businesses expect workers to maintain reasonable levels of production and quality without a lot of supervision or support. Table 1 lists approaches to teaching a worker independence.

Changing Tasks

One type of independence involves accurately assessing when it is time to move on to the next task and then correctly selecting and beginning that next task. Natural cues often available for this type of independence include clocks, the movement of other workers, the completion of a preceding task, and instructions from the supervisor. However, there are times when these natural cues are not strong or

Table 1.   Approaches to teaching independence

Model independent behavior.	Teach the use of self-monitoring.
Add and/or strengthen cues.	Teach the use of self-recording.
Provide reinforcement.	Teach the use of feedback.
Set limits.	Teach the use of self-cuing.

consistent enough to adequately prompt task changes, and the employment specialist may need to provide an alternative. Common examples include a written task list with criterion times, a timer or beeper, or reminder notes.

When a worker is having difficulty making task changes at appropriate times, the employment specialist must first determine whether the issue involves prioritizing tasks. Perhaps the task change is being missed because the worker is spending too much time on another, less important task. If this is the case, it might help to clarify the priority of each task and determine how much time should be allotted to it. This is done through the development of a job analysis and requires the involvement of the employer and possibly the co-workers.

It is important to determine whether the worker knows which task comes next and whether there is a clear and consistent cue to change tasks. If these areas are not the problem, the employment specialist must determine what is getting in the way of smooth task sequencing, and what (if any) reinforcers the worker gains from changing tasks at the appropriate time. Is the next task one he finds particularly arduous? Does he really know how to do the job and where to find the needed equipment? Is he having trouble completing the preceding task on time? The

"She has the best physical and verbal prompts of anyone I know."

Natural cues may not be strong or consistent enough to adequately prompt task changes, and the employment specialist may need to provide an alternative.

results of the observation and analysis of the situation will determine the course of action to be taken.

Completing a Task

Another type of independence involves the worker's ability to complete a task according to criterion standards while using the techniques specified by the employer. Task acquisition is the first step in this type of independence; the worker must at least be able to do the task with assistance from the employment specialist or co-workers before he can be expected to do it independently. Once this is achieved the employment specialist can begin to fade her presence and assess whether the worker can continue to complete the task accurately. The employment specialist may provide written or pictorial aids representing the steps involved in the task, which can be used by the worker as a reminder or final checklist.

When a worker is having difficulty completing tasks independently, the employment specialist may want to review the size of the steps being used to complete the task, the reinforcement levels, and possible alternate approaches to the task. If the worker is able to do the task only when the employment specialist is there prompting him, approaches such as written or pictorial aids, self-monitoring completion of each step, or verbal self-cues may help. It is also possible that the task and/or the work environment might be modified to cue appropriate independent performances. For example, a receptionist who did not file routine papers often enough could be instructed to use a very shallow tray to collect filing. The full tray would act as a cue to file the accumulated papers.

Staying on Task

A third type of independence, staying on task, comes into play after the employment specialist fades out of the employment site and the worker must independently maintain his attention on the task at hand. Even productive workers who are often off task will appear less valuable to the employer, while workers who are always on task will usually look productive whether they work quickly or not. People who experience hallucinations (e.g., hearing voices) and/or rely on psychotropic medication to control the symptoms of their illness often have difficulty learning to stay on task for extended periods.

Teaching a person to stay on task starts with setting clear definitions for the starting point and completion of tasks. It may be helpful to behaviorally define *on task* with regard to a particular employment situation. In one case being on task may mean the worker standing in one place with his body oriented to the conveyor belt and eyes fixed on the work going by, while in another it means walking through halls looking for trash to pick up or walls that need wiping and exchanging appropriate greetings with any guests who come by.

In some jobs it may be helpful to identify and teach specific extra tasks that can be used to keep a worker busy during any downtime. The resulting list of tasks can then be consulted by the worker when he has extra time. However, the appropriate way to handle downtime varies across worksites. On some jobs, the people who are caught up may head outside to smoke a cigarette and gossip with co-workers. On other jobs they may offer to help co-workers complete their tasks. These patterns are often governed by unwritten social norms that must be considered by the employment specialist. Teaching a worker to immediately start a downtime task when he has completed his tasks may cause resentment among co-workers who are used to sitting down and taking a break when the work slows.

Social Independence

A fourth type of independence is *social independence*: the ability to interact with co-workers at appropriate levels of intensity and frequency. Although in most work settings it is acceptable for co-workers to share information about their personal lives while doing their jobs, some people with long-term mental illness may have difficulty determining appropriate levels of interaction. It is not always appropriate for the worker to share every detail of his illness and subsequent treatment with every co-worker regardless of the co-worker's level of interest, or to use his co-workers as counselors to help him with nonwork issues. The employment specialist may need to work with the client to set specific limits and guidelines regarding the timing, frequency, and content of personal conversations at work. However, it is important to make sure that the worker has appropriate outlets (e.g., family, friends, community support, mental health counselors) for his concerns and personal conversation needs.

TEACHING QUALITY

Quality is essential in the American business community. Increased emphasis on continuous quality improvement and similar approaches sometimes contrast sharply with the loose quality standards expected in many prevocational experiences (e.g., some mental health day programs). Individuals with long-term mental

"So...this is how you stay on task!"

Staying on task is crucial because even productive workers who are often off task come quickly to the employer's (negative) attention.

illness may have difficulty adjusting to increased quality expectations as they move from more sheltered settings into competitive employment. Table 2 lists approaches to teaching quality.

Before an employment specialist can train a worker for quality skills, she must decide whether the issue is one of discrimination or motivation. Does the worker understand what the quality standards are and is he able to meet them under any circumstances? The employment specialist may need to operationally define what quality means for each task. Are water spots unacceptable on plates, or should the worker worry only about pieces of food? Do the pleats in the draperies have to be exactly in line or can they vary by an eighth of an inch? Does the printed material being collated and placed in envelopes have to be in a certain order? These quality standards (i.e., decision rules) need to be made clear.

In some cases it may be helpful for the employment specialist to "overteach" a particular task—for example, assisting the worker in learning to meet standards that are higher than those expected by the employer. This process leaves room for the worker to slide a bit on quality once the employment specialist fades, without going below an acceptable level.

Workers who are able to make good quality judgments but do not always do so, may need to have reinforcement directly tied to the quality of their work (or of their quality checking). In other cases it may be possible to modify the work procedure in order to minimize possible quality errors, especially where physical limitations (i.e., blurred vision, hand tremors) are present. One worker was taught to push one piece of an assembly back as far as it would go before using the power screwdriver rather than just aligning the pieces visually. This was an unobtrusive step that was not needed or done by co-workers, but it substantially decreased the worker's error rate.

Some workers may have difficulty maintaining quality standards while increasing production rates, and therefore it may be necessary to renegotiate the work schedule or production expectation with the employer. In this and other situations it is important that the employment specialist makes sure that all supervisors agree on quality and production standards so that the worker is not given conflicting information. At other times a worker may be having difficulty maintaining quality because he is preoccupied with nonwork issues happening on or off the job. These issues may include having difficulty getting along with another employee, experiencing increased psychiatric symptoms, or having problems with his landlord at home. The employment specialist may need to assist in arranging increased counseling or case management attention, checking medication levels, or providing any support and reassurance the client needs to work through the issue.

TEACHING SPEED

When faced with a situation in which a worker needs to work more quickly, the first question to be considered is whether the worker understands how to do the task at any speed. If not, then additional instruction may be needed. It is usually

Table 2.   Approaches to teaching quality

Provide and develop concrete cues.	Use competition during practice.
Overteach during initial period.	Strengthen feedback and reinforcement.
Modify procedures to minimize the issue.	Check for nonwork issues.

best to try to increase speed smoothly and slowly during task acquisition. Table 3 illustrates approaches to teaching speed.

If the worker knows how to do the task at a slower speed, the next question is whether medication levels, side effects, or physical limitations may affect his ability to work quickly. The worker may simply need more sleep or a different sleeping or medication pattern. Another possibility is that the person may not realize he is not working quickly enough and only needs more direct feedback about his work rate.

If the worker knows how to do the task, understands the importance of working more quickly, and is physically able to perform the task, the employment specialist should examine the procedures being used to ensure that they are the most efficient for that particular worker. The original task analysis may have resulted in a procedure that is no longer the most effective procedure, at least for the individual now doing the job. In some cases the procedures shown to the job coach and worker by the supervisor may not be the procedures actually used by others on the production floor, or the worker may have deviated from the procedure originally taught and may be using an approach that is not as efficient. In either situation, it may be possible to increase the worker's speed by increasing the efficiency of techniques. The employment specialist may need to provide a well-paced model through demonstration or have the client work alongside a co-worker who is performing at an appropriate pace. Practice sessions, either alone or with an employment specialist timing the production, can provide increased opportunities to develop skills and improve scores.

If the worker understands the task and uses the most efficient technique, the employment specialist should consider the cues and reinforcement being provided for working quickly. Is the worker cued to start the task at the right time? Is the cue reliable? Does it need to be stronger? If the cue seems adequate, what about the reinforcer? Issues of questionable "motivation" are often issues of reinforcement. It may also help to modify the work setting to reduce or remove distractions that may be present. As with quality, a preoccupation with nonwork issues may keep the worker from performing up to his potential speed.

People can often be motivated by making goals clearer and providing feedback on successive approximations of those goals. Having the worker contribute to setting his own goal may increase his investment. Employment specialists can often use competition to increase motivation. For example, many workers would enjoy a chance to go "one-on-one" with the employment specialist and try to surpass her performance. More frequent or even immediate reinforcers may need to be built in to reinforce improvement or maintain performance levels. For example, a worker may not be motivated to get the last mail delivery sorted by 4:30 P.M. in order to earn the reinforcer of continued employment or even a monthly paycheck because the reinforcers are not tied directly enough to performance on this particular task. However, the worker may be willing to work for any number of immediate reinforcers such as incentive bonus pay or extra break time, the satisfaction of beating

Table 3. Approaches to teaching speed

Model appropriate speed.	Provide physical prompts.
Use competition during practice.	Set goals.
Encourage self-recording.	Reward approximation.
Review and improve technique.	Arrange practice sessions.

the clock or a preset timer, meeting a personal goal, or receiving praise and attention from the employer. As with all interventions, the more natural the reinforcement strategies, the better they will be maintained.

During the period when the worker is increasing his speed, the employment specialist may need to make up missed production. It can be difficult to provide instruction while also doing part of the job, but the employment specialist has several options.

- The employment specialist may work alongside the worker, modeling appropriate technique and speed.
- The employment specialist may do the tasks while the worker observes.
- A co-worker may help the client learn the tasks while the employment specialist maintains production and oversees instruction.
- The worker may perform an independent task that is part of his usual routine, while the employment specialist catches up on the more difficult areas.
- The employment specialist may provide teaching efforts, while another staff member or a co-worker comes in to make up production.

In a situation where an employer is complaining that a worker is no longer able to complete a task in the assigned time despite his (and the employment specialist's) best efforts, it may be advisable to compare the worker's speed or production rates with those of his co-workers and with the speed criteria set during the original training period. The job volume or structure may have changed since the

*"Let's add a note to our training
package: Never clean the condor cage alone!"*

The original procedure may no longer be the most effective.

placement was made, and the production expectations may have changed over time. In one case, a hospital prep cook was expected to run baking sheets through a dishwashing machine for 15 minutes each day. After investigating the supervisor's complaints about this task taking much too long, the employment specialist discovered that the machine could only wash 3 sheets per minute and the worker was expected to process 90–100 sheets per day. The worker was doing his job as quickly as he could, given the limitations of the machine he was using, and the employment specialist was able to point out to the supervisor that the original schedule was no longer appropriate given the increased number of pans.

TEACHING TIME MANAGEMENT

Time management refers to the skills a worker needs to get to work on time and make time-related task changes appropriately and independently. Providing a schedule for job tasks that specifies when each task is to be started and completed may be helpful. Time management cues (e.g., clocks, bells, timers) should be provided or enhanced if needed. It may be necessary for the employment specialist to review on-task behavior and the sequence of job duties, as well as appropriate break and lunch times to make sure the workplace expectations are well understood. Table 4 is a list of approaches to teaching time management.

Workers who manage time poorly may need to have reinforcement made contingent on appropriate time management. Self-monitoring and recording task change times (with or without back-up reinforcement) may also help the worker manage his time independently. For example, if a worker kept a simple log of tasks done and times completed, he could then review the log in weekly meetings with the employment specialist and make plans for modifying any problem areas.

It is also possible that the worker misses task change times because he does not finish tasks within the time allotted, and therefore attention must be paid to the worker's speed and efficiency. Other situations may require adjustments in the original time criteria and work schedule.

The worker may need additional residential or counseling support to get up earlier or move more quickly through morning routines in order to ensure a timely arrival at work. Changes in transportation arrangements may also cause problems with time management.

Poor time management is often a sign of other problems, such as inappropriate scheduling, the lack of understanding of workplace expectations, and the need for improved skills. The employment specialist must first investigate and determine the source of the poor time management before choosing an intervention approach.

TEACHING ANGER MANAGEMENT

Being able to handle anger or frustration in appropriate ways is a crucial skill in maintaining employment. Workers who respond to frustrating situations by acting out, throwing temper tantrums, or yelling are not considered valuable employees regardless of their vocational skills. This may be an ongoing focus of mental health

Table 4.   Approaches to teaching time management

Provide concrete aids (written or pictorial).	Provide feedback and reinforcement.
Provide cue identification and enhancement.	Teach self-monitoring.

support efforts and/or a teaching issue addressed by the employment specialist. Table 5 lists approaches to teaching anger management.

The first step in teaching a worker to manage frustration and anger appropriately is to help him identify the kinds of situations that provoke anger and the way he feels when he *is* angry. The employment specialist may have to begin by pointing out the overt signs of the worker's frustration (e.g., tense muscles, loud voice) and helping the worker verbally label the fact that he is becoming upset. It may help to have the employment specialist or another person use role playing to help the worker practice identifying and labeling feelings.

Once the worker has learned to recognize and label his upset feelings, he can be taught appropriate ways of dealing with his feelings. Taking deep breaths, counting to 10, standing up and stretching, going to the bathroom and washing his face, writing comments in a journal, or leaving the work area briefly are examples of behaviors that workers can learn to substitute for angry outbursts. One worker used headphones to listen to a cassette tape of self-selected music and verbal instructions whenever he felt upset, which allowed him to continue with his job duties as he listened and got himself under control.

As the worker begins to use his new skills to deal with frustration or anger on the job, the employment specialist may provide feedback and reinforcement for gains made. The emphasis is not on remaining calm at all times but on handling frustration appropriately. During the early learning period, it may be helpful for the employment specialist to leave the work area with the worker for a time-out period to avoid affecting co-workers and to make the teaching process as discreet as possible.

It is also important for the worker and the employment specialist to examine the kinds of situations that are upsetting to the person, and if possible try to change or otherwise deal with them. If the frustrations are related to the work tasks, then changing the techniques used or just gaining skill over time may improve the situation. However, if there are interpersonal problems, the worker may need additional social skills. It also may be a situation in which the worker is being mistreated and needs to know how to seek help from the supervisor, or the frustration may be a result of the worker being placed in a job that is too demanding (or not demanding enough) for his current level of skill, and a change in jobs may be warranted.

In some cases, people act out angrily because of issues that have nothing to do with the job (e.g., family, issues of independence, problems in developing a social life, roommates, medication changes, difficulty in accepting a disability). Good communication with others on the worker's support team (i.e., medical personnel, mental health staff, family members) may help the worker identify an effective approach to minimizing anger problems.

CONCLUSION

Having a range of teaching skills and approaches at her disposal enables the employment specialist to support people with mental illness effectively as they

Table 5. Approaches to teaching anger management

Identify antecedents.	Model appropriate approaches.
Identify internal cues.	Provide feedback and reinforcement.
Role play.	Identify and teach appropriate alternatives.

learn job skills, rather than just removing tasks or responsibilities from the job as problems arise. The teaching approach assumes that most people *can* learn most needed skills with good instruction and support and that people are entitled to that chance to learn.

18

BEHAVIOR MANAGEMENT
AND SELF-MANAGEMENT

What is the difference between teaching skills and managing behavior? Teaching generally relates to new skills, whereas behavior management deals with the performance of skills already learned. There is a great deal of overlap between these two concepts and the distinction is somewhat arbitrary. The point of both behavior management and teaching skills is to enable workers to perform work tasks, social skills, and self-management skills that will support their success on the job.

Behavior management is an important topic for employment specialists serving individuals with long-term mental illness because the behavior patterns that may have served people well in the hospital or in day treatment may not be as useful once the person moves back into the community. Once a client has learned the necessary skills, she may still need help in performing them consistently in the natural environment.

THE ROLE OF BEHAVIOR MANAGEMENT

Human behavior is determined by learning and past experience, the current environment (including internal events, other people and their actions, and the physical environment), and the reinforcement or punishment that follows the behavior. This is true even when these factors may not be obvious or visible. For example, a person who makes delusional statements might be responding to a purely internal stimulus (e.g., a voice telling her that she is being controlled by the radio in the corner of the room). However, what looks like bizarre behavior may actually be a sensible and adaptive attempt to cope, given the person's unique internal environment and past history (see Chapter 1).

These internal stimulus and reinforcement factors are particularly important when working with a person with long-term mental illness because the illness may be causing her brain to process information in a way that is not typical or effective. It may take time and experience to determine which client behaviors are intentional and which are responses to illness or medication. The employment specialist is also encouraged to give careful thought to the question of which behaviors should be modified. Many behaviors that appear slightly bizarre may actually be well accepted in a particular workplace and are not worth spending time on (Meyer & Evans, 1989). For example, one individual who worked in a book repository felt that she needed to sprinkle baking soda and rice across the doorway each morning in order to keep the devil out. Because there was no customer traffic and very little staff traffic through the doorway, the employment specialist explained the behavior to the employer by saying that it was a "religious thing," and negotiated to have the worker arrive at the job early each day to fulfill her ritual and then stay a few minutes late each night to clean it up. Over time, the worker's dependability and excellent quality of work have more than offset her unusual habit. It may be a better use of the employment specialist's and client's time to try to strengthen general or specific work skills, rather than trying to modify unusual behaviors that are not a problem in the particular workplace.

Other behaviors believed to be problematic may actually be functional for the individual, and positive replacements will be needed if the problem behavior is to be eliminated. The person who has learned to get attention by talking to everyone about her symptoms will need to learn appropriate ways to seek interactions in addition to reducing the inappropriate conversation.

It is important to remember that behavior management programs aimed at reducing undesirable behaviors in particular situations should only be part of a long-term teaching and prevention approach that tries to develop confidence and skills.

CHARACTERISTICS OF BEHAVIOR MANAGEMENT PROGRAMS

When building plans for behavior change, interventions can involve changing the worker's base of experience (e.g., through preinstruction or graduated goals that provide successful experiences), changing the environment (e.g., adding and/or strengthening cues, providing prompts, removing distractions), changing the consequences (e.g., adding or removing reinforcing events contingent on the person's performance), or combining any of the above.

The use of structured, written behavior management plans may seem like unnecessary work to many employment specialists. It is true that it is not always necessary to write and use a formal plan. If the worker is able to learn and perform the needed skills by using simple instructions and feedback, there is no reason to set up a formal plan. Formal behavior management plans are only needed when the simple approaches have not worked or are inappropriate due to special worker needs. In these situations, a formal written plan is useful for the following reasons:

Written plans provide a detailed plan that can be referred to when making data-based decisions. It is always tempting to handle issues casually when on a job-site and not to take the time to document training efforts. However, for issues that do *not* respond quickly to an informal approach, a structured, data-based plan will often prove to be the most effective and efficient approach in the long run.

Written plans direct attention to and prioritize critical training issues. In some placement situations there are several issues that need to be addressed. The process of prioritizing such issues and writing plans for the most pressing of them ensures that critical issues are not being overlooked and that the worker is not being overwhelmed by trying to learn everything at once. The process of developing a written plan can also help the worker and the employment specialist clarify the problem and identify possible solutions.

Written plans promote training consistency across time, people, and places, and they facilitate communication among staff members. Turnover among employment specialists is a well-documented issue. There are also situations in which the responsibility for job support moves from the employment specialist to another professional (e.g., the case manager) at the point where the worker is stable on the job. Training details that do not seem worth writing down when a placement is made in 1995 may not be as obvious when a new person tries to help the worker make changes in 1997. In addition, providing coverage for another employment specialist is a much more manageable task when there are written, structured programs in place that are well documented. The substitute support person will also be able to provide more consistent support, which benefits the worker.

For funding agencies and program evaluation, written plans document that problematic behaviors are being addressed in a systematic way. Those who provide the financing for supported employment are often interested in seeing just what services have been paid for. Behavior management plans that are documented with written material and summarized with data are powerful evi-

"You've been talking back to your voices."

Behavior patterns learned in the hospital or day treatment may not be useful in the community.

dence that the employment specialist has approached his job in a thorough and professional manner. They also provide a resource for program evaluation and decision making. Table 1 lists characteristics of good behavior management programs.

DEVELOPING BEHAVIOR MANAGEMENT PLANS

Identifying the Problem

The process of developing a behavior management plan begins by identifying a discrepancy between what the worker is currently doing and what he or someone else thinks he should be doing. This draws on the model of the ideal employee developed earlier, comparing it against the worker's current performance.

It is important to consider first whether the discrepancy is significant enough in this particular environment to warrant an intervention, given the effort that will be necessary in order to make a difference. Ethical issues and training priorities should also be considered. Is this behavior a legitimate expression of the individual's personality? Is the issue one of style or substance? Is the behavior serving an important function for the individual, and therefore must it be replaced with a more acceptable behavior?

The next consideration is whether the worker's skills are adequate. Has the person been able to master the skill under any circumstances? Is this a generalization issue (i.e., the person is being asked to apply the skill in a setting other than the one in which it was learned)? Has the person forgotten how to do the skill? Perhaps a teaching approach is called for rather than behavior management.

If insufficient skills are not the issue (i.e., the person can do the skill under some circumstances), the next question is whether the person is being punished for doing the target behavior. For example, people who work quickly are often punished by being given more work to do. Is the worker being reinforced for not doing the target behavior or for doing something that is incompatible with it? A person working in a warehouse who is not completing her paperwork may have found that standing around smoking cigarettes with the other workers on the loading dock was much more reinforcing. Is the worker being adequately cued when it is time to do the task? Perhaps augmented cues would be more appropriate than behavior management. Is this skill or task one that is truly valued in the environment? The worker may be reacting to what is perceived as busy work. Are there obstacles to performance, such as inadequate equipment or physical or mental limitations? All of these questions provide information that will influence the type of intervention the employment specialist might choose.

Another area to investigate is environmental or other external influences. Such things as hunger, medical problems, boredom, crowding, noise, temperature, frustration, or fear may be contributing to the problem and must be taken into consideration in plan development (Powell et al., 1991). The best approach may be to modify the environment rather than to attempt structured behavior change.

Table 1.   Characteristics of good behavior management programs

They take a positive and structured approach to helping workers change their behavior.
They take into account the unique needs of the worker and the worksite.
They are written and involve the use of concrete data to assess progress.
They include a plan for fading the employment specialist and/or self-management.

The employment specialist may need to consider whether the skill is within the person's eventual capability. No amount of behavior management can make a trash collector out of a person who is 5 feet tall and weighs 95 pounds. Job or environmental modification can sometimes bring a specific task within reach or eliminate it from the job description.

Developing and Using Procedures

Once the situation is analyzed, specific procedures can be developed by specifying goals, selecting intervention procedures, and identifying consequences. In each case, selections should be made that are as unobtrusive as possible and that best encourage generalization of the behavior to different situations as well as maintenance of the behavior change over time.

Specifying Goals   Specifying goals includes defining target behaviors, describing how they will be measured, and determining how data will be recorded and summarized. Target behaviors should be described in objective, observable terms so that any two people can agree on whether or not they are happening.

Selecting Procedures   Selecting procedures involves specifying the intervention(s) that will be used to help the worker change her behavior. This could include cues, prompts, preinstruction, or self-management procedures.

Identifying Consequences   Identifying consequences involves using the person's idiosyncratic preferences and the things available in the environment to determine the reinforcers that will be provided to increase or decrease the target behavior. Consequences can be provided by the worker herself, the employment specialist, the employer, co-workers, or anyone else.

"You said be here early...1 P.M. is early!"

Target behaviors should be described in objective, observable terms.

Implementing the Program and Giving it Time to Work Behaviors important enough to warrant intervention on the job have often been developed over several years of experience. They may change quickly or they may take time to modify. A consistent commitment to following through with the program is crucial.

Collecting Data and Evaluating and Modifying the Program Based on the Results Every behavior change program should include a plan for measuring change, determining progress, summarizing data, and using those measures to assess the effectiveness of the plan. Behavior management plans are often very time consuming. People who are involved in these plans deserve to have information about whether their efforts are having the desired result.

It is often helpful to have a standard recording form for behavior management plans in order to encourage the careful development of plans and to provide a record for the worker and the employment specialist (and anyone else who is involved). Forms for behavior management plans summarize the following information:

- The current behavior (and information about the antecedents and setting in which it occurs)
- The behavioral goal (i.e., desired target behavior)
- The method and frequency of measurement
- The change technique to be used
- The target date for review

Figure 1 is a suggested format to summarize a behavior change program.

DEVELOPING AND USING CONTINGENCY CONTRACTS

A special kind of behavior management program, the contingency contract, is often used with workers whose cognitive abilities enable them to be active partici-

"Trust me! This job has some built-in feedback."

Identifying consequences involves identifying the person's idiosyncratic preferences and the things available in the environment.

BEHAVIOR CHANGE PROGRAM

Client: _____   Date started: _____

Staff: _____   Date ended: _____

1. Define the behavior to be changed. What is the problem?

2. How will you involve the client in developing this program? What does he or she have to say about the issue? Is he or she interested in changing?

3. Describe the circumstances in which the behavior occurs. Where? When? What is happening just beforehand? What happens afterward?

4. What do you hope this program will accomplish? Describe your long- and short-term goal(s) in observable, quantifiable terms. Describe the person's behavior if the program is successful.

5. Describe how, when, and by whom the behavior is to be measured. Some possibilities for measurement include counting how often it occurs in a given time period, measuring the length of time during which it occurs, counting or measuring the amount of work finished, or marking whether the behavior occurs in a given time period.

6. Describe the intervention you will try. Be specific about how you will change the environment, cues, or consequences (reinforcers) in order to help the person change his or her behavior.

7. When will this plan be reviewed?

Figure 1.   An example of a form used to summarize and provide a record of a behavior change program.

pants in changing their own behavior, which is the case with many people who have long-term mental illness. In these cases, the behavior plan is written as a contract between the worker and the employment specialist (and perhaps the employer or another third party), and signed by all involved. Table 2 lists some hints for successful contingency contracts.

An example of a contingency contract might involve a worker who would like to be placed in a different type of job but is inconsistent in her punctuality on the job she currently holds. Her contingency contract might specify that if she attends work on time each day for 2 weeks, the employment specialist will schedule 2 interviews for other jobs during the following week. Contingency contracts are effective only when the worker has the ability to perform the target behavior(s), the worker is interested in changing her behavior (or at least willing to give it a try), and the other party (e.g., employment specialist, employer) has something to offer or withhold that is of interest to that particular worker.

Furlong et al. (1994) suggested that the employment specialist seek a client's input when writing contracts by asking the client to complete the following thoughts:

> "I feel most proud at work when..."
> "The person from whom I most want a positive evaluation is..."
> "The thing that most motivates me to work well is..."
> "The best compliment I ever received for good work was..."
> "I would most like my co-workers to notice..." (p. 98)

Elements needed in a contingency contract include the following:

1. A statement of purpose as to why the contract is being written and why it is important
2. A description of the desired behavior
3. A description of the responsible people in the contract, including the worker, and specification of their responsibilities
4. Specification of any positive and negative consequences that will occur contingent on the worker's performance
5. A time line for completion and review
6. Signatures of all involved parties

Figure 2 is an example of a contingency contract.

DEVELOPING AND USING SELF-MANAGEMENT PROGRAMS

Self-management refers to the use of a procedure that lets the worker manage her behaviors or the events in the environment that were previously not under her control. Many employment specialists consider using a self-management approach only as they start to fade their presence in the workplace and are no longer able to maintain the programs they have arranged. In fact, self-management approaches should almost always be tried first so that the worker takes on as much of the responsibility for learning tasks and managing her behavior as she possibly can.

Table 2.   Contingency contracts: Hints for success

Always include the client. Have her write the contract if possible.
Keep the language simple and concise.
Be creative in positive consequences and in the techniques used.
Review the contract regularly so the client can see her progress.
Set a specific ending date.

CONTRACT BETWEEN JULIE M. AND RAY D.

Julie is currently working 4 hours per day at PetCo, restocking pet food and doing general clean-up work. Julie would like Ray to advocate with the employer to increase her hours to 6 per day. During the last 4 weeks, Julie has been late or absent from work 9 times (an average of twice per week).

Julie agrees that she is able to get to work on time because she has an alarm clock and transportation. This contract specifies that if Julie attends work every day during September (unless she is too sick to work), on October 1 Ray will begin negotiating with the employer for more hours. If Julie needs to take time off for medical reasons, she will call Ray (as well as PetCo) and let him know. If Julie misses work for other reasons or is more than 15 minutes late for work, Ray will not help her ask the employer for more hours.

Ray will visit Julie on the job every Monday and Wednesday to review her time card, and Julie will call Ray on Fridays. This agreement will end on September 30.

Date: August 18, 1995

Signed: Julie M.

Signed: Ray D.

Figure 2.   An example of a contingency contract between a worker and an employment specialist or employer.

Using self-management approaches both empowers the worker and makes the training more unobtrusive. Self-management is normalizing because everyone does it. People use alarm clocks to get up at the right time, reminder notes and appointment books to manage their time, shopping lists to make sure they buy the right groceries, and verbal reminders (i.e., talking to themselves) as they drive their cars.

Self-management is not necessarily an inborn skill, and it can be taught like any other behavior. Helping a worker learn to use self-management involves the same procedures used to teach a task such as filing (i.e., adding structure, adding or enhancing cues, providing information, and adding or enhancing consequences).

Self-management is measured by degree; it is not an all-or-nothing issue. The degree depends on how much the worker controls and how much someone else controls. For example, a checklist that is developed by the employment specialist and presented to the worker represents a low level of worker control, while a checklist developed and used by the worker (perhaps with support from the employment specialist) represents a higher level of worker control. The degree of control involved is determined by the level of the worker's ability and the demands of the job.

Approaches to Self-Management

Self-management programs must be individualized and must use cues and techniques the worker enjoys and can manage. In order to be unobtrusive, the techniques should match those used by others in the workplace when possible. As with all behavior programs, the ease of use for everyone involved will have a big impact on the program's effectiveness and durability. There are three basic approaches to self-management; each is discussed below.

Antecedent Cue Regulation   Antecedent cue regulation involves arranging or enhancing cues that will make the desired behavior more likely. Examples of this approach are appointment books, checklists, reminder notes, cassette tapes with instructions, wake-up calls, mental rehearsals, or strings tied to the little finger.

Self-Monitoring   Self-monitoring requires the worker to assess and document when, how often, or to what extent things happen or do not happen. Examples include tallying the frequency of an event, determining the amount, evaluating performance, or setting goals. This approach can be done by hitting a counter, recording the time a task is finished, marking cards or charts, or keeping notes.

Self-Determined Consequences   Self-determined consequences is an approach used by the worker to provide consequences at the appropriate time. Examples include the self-delivery of a reinforcer based on production or completion of items (i.e., a cigarette break when a certain amount of work is finished), participation in events or activities dependent on work performance, or eliciting self-recruited feedback and reinforcement (i.e., from a supervisor).

Variations of Self-Management

There are also three special variations of self-management programs that are particularly appropriate for many workers with long-term mental illness who may be dealing with variable symptom levels, low self-esteem, anxiety, or difficulty interpreting personal feelings or the behavior of others on the job.

Symptom Checklist   To use a symptom checklist, the worker and the employment specialist (and perhaps the mental health counselor) develop a list of symptoms or behavior change patterns that are associated with decompensation or

"They call it self-management,
but it looks like counting sheep to me."

In order to be unobtrusive, self-management techniques should match those used by others in the workplace.

hospitalization for that individual. The list is then used by the worker and perhaps family members, the employment specialist, the employer and/or co-workers, or anyone else in the worker's circle of friends to identify when the worker's illness seems to be getting worse. As part of the checklist development, the worker and the employment specialist also plan whom to contact and what to do when these key symptoms are noticed. Early intervention in the form of medication adjustment, increased counseling or other support, and/or temporary reduction of stressful activities may prevent decompensation or lessen its severity.

Journaling   Journaling teaches participants to write about their feelings, concerns, or symptoms such as hallucinations, which allows them to express themselves without interfering with work or seeking out a counselor immediately. Workers can be encouraged to use their journals on coffee breaks or at lunch, then discuss the issues or concerns raised with the employment specialist or counselor after work or at the next meeting. Sketching pictures of feelings and experiences can also be effective.

Self-Evaluation Form   A more structured form of journaling, the self-evaluation form, asks the worker to fill out a daily evaluation of her own work by completing the following four statements:

1. Three things I did well today were...
2. Compliments I received at work today were...
3. One thing about my work today that I would like to change was...
4. The replacement behavior I will try for the issue raised in #3 is...

The use of such a structured format encourages the worker to recognize the parts of the job that she is doing well rather than just focusing on the problems and also suggests a positive approach to dealing with any issues that are problematic. Some workers may benefit from developing a list of choices for each question so that filling out the form becomes more routine. This list may be changed at any time. For example, the employment specialist and the worker could identify 10 tasks or skills the worker usually does well, from which the worker would select 3 each day; four tasks or skills the worker needs to improve or change, from which one would be selected each day; and two or three replacement behaviors for each of the potential problem behaviors. As with other types of journaling, the self-evaluation form(s) can be reviewed with the employment specialist, the counselor, or even the employer, at intervals that can range from once a day to once a month.

CHANGING OR ENDING BEHAVIOR PROGRAMS

As mentioned above, it is important to give behavior change programs a chance to work before modifying or terminating them. Therefore, it is important to know what information should be used to decide whether it is time to make some changes.

Ideally, the program should be faded (if possible) once the worker is consistently meeting the goals that were originally set. This change might involve simply ending the program or fading its intensity by changing the intervals or criteria involved. The degree to which this is done depends on the time it took to change the behavior (i.e., the longer time periods warrant a longer fading period) and the cues and reinforcers that are available in the natural environment to maintain the behavior.

Other cues to reevaluate the program would be if the target behavior is not improving or is getting worse, if those involved in the program are having difficulty or getting careless in following through with the program, or if any of the participants are uncomfortable with the procedures involved.

Any structured behavior program should be reviewed at regular intervals to make sure it is still achieving its purpose and is worth the time being spent on it.

BEHAVIOR MANAGEMENT FROM A DISTANCE

A special challenge arises when the employment specialist is providing support only off site and the worker is handling her own task acquisition and integration on the job. Many of the behavior management approaches can be used off site to help clients improve their own performance on the job. Self-management approaches are very useful in these situations; the employment specialist assists the worker in identifying target behaviors and approaches to modifying them, while monitoring progress and providing additional reinforcement. It may also be possible for the employment specialist to use the supervisor or co-workers to provide assistance, either by working with them directly or by teaching the worker how to ask for such help.

An additional approach involves having the employment specialist provide feedback and reinforcement based on either self-report or information collected from the supervisor or co-workers. The specific approach chosen depends on the type of behavior targeted, the level of involvement the employment specialist has on the jobsite, and the needs of the worker (see Chapter 19).

CONCLUSION

The challenge of helping people with mental illness maintain the skills and behaviors needed for employment success can be daunting for the employment special-

"I think we may need to make some changes in our plan."

Reevaluate the program if the target behavior is not improving.

ist. The use of structured behavior management and self-management approaches, based on a solid understanding of the mechanisms by which behaviors become established, may make the task less daunting. This chapter reviews some of the basic principles of helping individuals manage their behavior. Meyer and Evans (1989) and Powell et al. (1991) offer more detailed information about behavior management and are excellent resources for any employment specialist who is new to the technology of behavior management.

19

NATURAL SUPPORTS, INTEGRATION, AND SOCIAL SKILLS

This chapter addresses some of the interpersonal issues involved in supporting people with long-term mental illness in jobs: natural supports, integration, and social skills. All three topics pertain to the degree to which the worker with mental illness is a part of the work team, becoming accepted as an individual as well as a part of the production effort. As supported employment has moved into the rehabilitation mainstream, social integration and support have become recognized as key aspects to successful placements. Unfortunately, they are among the most difficult aspects to objectively identify and manipulate because they depend on idiosyncratic and personal factors.

IDENTIFYING AND DEVELOPING NATURAL SUPPORTS

Several articles have examined ways in which co-workers can provide the support needed by workers with disabilities (Anderson & Andrews, 1990; Forest & Pearpoint, 1992; Hagner, Cotton, Goodall, & Nisbet, 1992; Murphy & Rogan, 1994; Nisbet & Callahan, 1988; Shafer, 1986). Although these efforts for the most part have involved workers with mental retardation, the guidelines they describe have implications for workers with other disabilities.

First, it is important to remember that enlisting co-worker support (or teaching the worker to do so) does not have to imply that the supported worker is unskilled or incapable. Most workers rely on their co-workers for support, advice, and assistance. The difference is that workers with long-term mental illness and their co-workers may need assistance in developing the usual relationships because of limited social skills, lack of information, or the stigma associated with the disability. The employment specialist's activities in this area are an attempt to compensate for any difficulties that exist in a given situation.

The best supports are those that occur naturally in the workplace and are available to all workers. These may be formal (e.g., new employee orientation and training) or informal (e.g., team members helping to keep an assembly line moving). The employment specialist's role in these situations involves helping workers gain access to existing support without overwhelming those involved.

Concern has been expressed in regard to relying on natural supports as the primary or only approach to use. DiLeo (1991c) listed the following four confusions about natural supports:

1. Not everything naturally found in the workplace will be supportive. It may be just as natural for others in the work environment to act in ways that are harmful as in ways that are helpful.
2. Natural support is not the same as dropping the worker off and hoping that everything will work out—the "place and pray" approach. People will need help to identify and use the supports that might be available.
3. Natural support is not the same as fading, promoting generalization, or maintaining skills. Developing natural support starts at the beginning of the placement and is an integral part of the employment specialist's role.
4. Using natural supports is not necessarily faster or less expensive and should not be seen as a solution to funding problems.

Griffin (1992) pointed out that although natural supports offer "incredible potential for consumer success, community integration, and reduced expenditures" (p. 1), implementing them requires dealing with complex social and organizational

"The computer does the prompting!"

The best supports are those that occur naturally in the workplace.

forces. He further pointed out that natural supports are easier to use if job analysis and matching are carefully done. Forest and Pearpoint (1992) wrote, "If natural supports, that is, the people most drawn to another person, are not organized systematically and intentionally, then we lose the momentum and potential" (p. 74).

Although in some cases valuable supports may develop without any effort on the part of the employment specialist, in other cases it may be necessary to provide the initial seed from which the supports can grow. The resulting support systems appear just like natural supports in the end, but might not have developed without discreet and judicious action by the employment specialist.

In most cases it seems clear that co-workers should be encouraged to provide suggestions, ideas, and support. Over time it may be possible to identify one or two people who have shown an interest in the worker, who work closely with him, and who might be encouraged to provide support on a more ongoing basis. The employment specialist should look for someone who has shown an interest in or affinity for the worker. Beyond that, it makes sense to look for someone who is well liked by other workers, who is an above-average worker (according to the supervisor), and who is stable. Furlong et al. (1994) suggested encouraging co-workers to take on a natural support role by mentioning the positive aspects of providing support and gaining supervisory experience.

PROFILE: TWO APPROACHES TO DEVELOPING NATURAL SUPPORTS

Sarah

After a couple of years as an employment specialist, Sarah is well aware of the value of helping develop natural supports in the workplaces of the people she supports. Because the people she works with generally need quite a bit of assistance in organizing and learning jobs, Sarah spends as much time as necessary working one-to-one with people over the first few weeks of the job. Sarah tries to make sure the job is done smoothly (by doing some of the work herself, if needed) so that others in the workplace are not inconvenienced and have a chance to get to know the supported worker on a positive basis. Meanwhile, Sarah keeps her eyes and ears open for co-workers whose work schedules and personalities seem to be a good match. Gradually Sarah encourages both the worker and the co-worker(s) to ask for and offer help to each other, purposefully moving into a secondary support role as she fades from the scene. In some cases she has assisted the supported worker in formally asking the co-worker if he or she would provide assistance such as giving routine feedback or being available as a resource for questions. More often the relationship is encouraged informally with Sarah's attention to the co-worker becoming one of the reinforcers maintaining the person's supportive behavior.

Jennie

Jennie and her agency take a different approach. Before the supported worker starts the job, Jennie works with the employer to set up a meeting or training session for all the co-workers. During this time Jennie shares general information about supported employment, about the disability experienced by the new worker, and (with the worker's permission) some personal information about the worker and effective ways to provide support. This meeting gives Jennie a chance to answer any questions or concerns people might have. If no one expresses any questions or concerns, Jennie brings them up herself by saying things like "You might be wondering..." or "One question a lot of people ask is...." She also explains that her role will be one of a consultant rather than a direct trainer. The training and orientation needed by the new worker is provided by the supervisor and/or co-workers, with Jennie there to give support and advice as needed. At the end of the meeting, Jennie asks if there is anyone who would like to take a role in training and supporting the new worker. Those who volunteer become part of a circle of support on the job.

Co-workers are often the most logical choice for providing natural support because they are more consistently available and most likely know more about the work tasks than the supervisor, and also because support among co-workers is a typical pattern in most workplaces. Co-worker support can take on several different forms.

Serving as a Model

An experienced co-worker can act as a model for vocational and social performance. This can happen on a formal basis with the co-worker deliberately demonstrating effective techniques for meeting task criteria or social expectations, or on an informal basis by encouraging the worker to observe the experienced co-worker and to act as he or she does.

Helping with Task Completion

A co-worker can help with task completion, providing support and assistance with completing work on a busy day or facing a difficult or unusual problem. This type of support is very common in most workplaces but may need to be deliberately developed for a supported worker, especially when the employment specialist has been providing support and training during the initial employment period.

Teaching Tasks and Skills

In most workplaces new workers are taught their tasks and skills by more experienced workers; this procedure should be followed in supported employment whenever possible. Although the employment specialist may have to provide training to augment that provided by the co-worker or may need to provide suggestions and support to the co-worker, the extra effort will be balanced by the increased investment by the co-worker(s) and the reduction in the stigma caused by having a special person (the employment specialist) provide all the instruction and support. In addition, the co-worker is likely to be available to support the worker long after the employment specialist has faded from the employment site.

Evaluating Work and Providing Feedback

Co-workers can provide formal or informal feedback on the work done by the supported worker. This might involve the co-worker coming by the worker's station a few times a day and doing a quick check on his work, having the co-worker(s) systematically give the worker feedback and praise for improvement on a specific task, or having the worker bring the task to the co-worker when he has a problem or a question. This may involve social skill issues (e.g., responding "You really handled Mary's complaints well today") as well as vocational issues (e.g., responding

"This list looks really good! Next time you might double-space this part to make it easier to read").

Providing Social Support

Many times social integration is enhanced by having a sponsor who will introduce the worker to others, let him know the unwritten social expectations of the workplace, and make sure he is included in social interactions.

Acting as an Advocate

An interested co-worker can advocate to protect the worker's rights (e.g., by preventing him from always getting stuck with the less desirable tasks, minimizing practical jokes, defusing any confrontations). It is important that all parties involved are aware of the confidentiality issues—both in terms of what information is given to that co-worker and what information he or she then passes on to others in the workplace.

Observing Target Behaviors

In some cases a co-worker might be asked to observe, record, or call attention to behaviors that the worker is trying to change. This may also mean involving a co-worker in using a symptom checklist to watch for signs of stress or decompensation. Early detection of symptom escalation enables the co-worker to prompt the worker to seek assistance with statements such as "I've been noticing that you're talking to yourself a lot the last few days. Are you feeling okay? Do you want to maybe give the employment specialist a call and see if she can drop by this week?"

FACILITATING INTEGRATION

Integration, along with wages and ongoing support, is one of the three criteria defining supported employment. As workers with disabilities become integrated in community jobs and increased numbers of community jobs become available, more attention is being paid to the quality of these jobs and the benefits they offer beyond wages. Integration is the opportunity to work alongside and interact with workers who do not have disabilities and is one benefit supported employment can offer.

The process of ensuring an integrated worksite begins with job development. Is the job a valued position and one for which others compete? Is the person currently in the position seen as a permanent member of the work team (e.g., on an assembly line) or as a temporary employee doing work that no one else wants (as in many, although not all, dishwashing positions)? Is the position one that the business typically recruits for or is it usually filled by applicants walking in off the street? All workers tend to take on the value of the jobs they hold. If a worker with mental illness is placed in a job that no one else wants, it will lower his perceived value and impede his acceptance as a co-worker.

The patterns of the workday can enhance or impede integration. Will the worker take breaks at the same time as others? Will he work with or near other workers? Are there other workers dependent on his production? Will he be the only person doing that job? Jobs that require contact with others (e.g., a photocopy machine operator) provide greater opportunities for integration than jobs that only offer incidental contact (e.g., a janitor).

When an employment specialist considers the integration potential of specific jobs, she must also consider the preferences of the individual worker. Some people, whether or not they have a disability, prefer to work alone, while others find it difficult to maintain motivation and interest in a job that offers little contact with others. Some workers may also choose to accept less than perfect job opportunities with the intention of upgrading in 6–12 months. Not every job must be considered a lifetime commitment or career. This may be particularly true for a worker who is new to the job market and who may anticipate working at several short-term jobs over a couple of years as a way of developing job skills and exploring possible long-term vocational goals.

The integration and socialization opportunities the worker has in his nonwork life must also be considered. Someone who has an active social life and good support outside of work may fare better in a relatively isolated job than someone who has little contact with others outside work.

THE ROLE OF THE EMPLOYMENT SPECIALIST
AS IT RELATES TO INTEGRATION AND NATURAL SUPPORTS

The role of the employment specialist with regard to integration and natural supports is a controversial one. Some authors believe that the employment specialist (or any other social service provider) should only assist co-workers and management, not directly train and support workers with disabilities (Anderson & Andrews, 1990). Others believe that although the ideal situation would be for the supervisors or co-workers to provide all the support needed by any employee (whether or not that employee has a disability), very few employment situations currently live up to that ideal (Nisbet & Hagner, 1988). As mentioned previously, others urge caution in jumping on the natural supports bandwagon, lest the days of "place and pray" return (DiLeo, 1991b; Griffin, 1992).

Some social service providers have a hard time believing that an employer could do a good job of teaching or supporting a worker with a disability (Anderson & Andrews, 1990). Many employers are not very experienced at *their* own jobs of supervising and managing, and benefit from the support and example provided by the employment specialist as she works with the person who has a disability. In addition, clients with long-term mental illness who are served by supported employment programs are generally those who have had difficulty in finding and keeping jobs on their own and need atypical levels of support. It is important for the employment program to be prepared to provide or help arrange any level of service and support that is needed by the individual, depending on his needs and the resources available on the job. The employment specialist therefore continues to have an important role in facilitating the development of natural supports and arranging or providing any support that is not available from the workplace. However, this role should be carried out as unobtrusively as possible given the needs of the worker and the workplace, and should draw as much as possible on any resources and relationships already available (Nisbet & Hagner, 1988). There is evidence that minimal social service intrusion in the workplace enhances the probability of the development of co-worker relationships (DiLeo, 1991b). The active presence of the employment specialist on the job may also call attention to the worker's disability and increase stigmatization, while interfering with the normal day at the workplace. Her presence may also foster dependency by the worker and the employer, which causes fading to be difficult. The on-site employment specialist approach is also expensive to maintain.

There are several ways an employment specialist can positively affect the eventual integration and social acceptance of a worker with a disability. The first and one of the most important, although not the most obvious, is to provide the training and support needed for the worker to become vocationally competent. Vocational competence, the worker's ability to perform tasks adequately as defined for each job, will contribute as much to acceptance as any social skill or natural support arrangement. Although the importance of providing any needed skill training may seem incompatible with the idea of keeping the employment specialist's involvement to a minimum, this contrast accurately reflects the challenge faced by the employment specialist: how to make sure all needed supports are provided while remaining invisible.

During the training period, the employment specialist may provide an example for the worker and the employer or co-workers by modeling appropriate interactions if needed. The employment specialist may also promote integration by using the most typical and nonintrusive training methods that will be effective. Therefore, if the worker is able to learn and maintain the needed job-related skills by using only the training methods and aids used by workers without disabilities,

"Psst! Job coach!"

It is important that support is provided as unobtrusively as possible.

those methods and aids should be used. Special reinforcement or cuing programs are reserved for situations where the typical systems are insufficient.

Hagner (1992) suggested that achieving integration remains "a work in progress" (p. 237) and recommended three strategies as useful to the employment specialist.

1. It is helpful to allow flexibility in tasks by leaving a few rough edges in the job design to be negotiated with co-workers over time and by allowing for interruptions and alterations in the work routine.
2. Interdependent jobs that require work-related interactions will encourage integration.
3. Training must include a focus on workplace customs (e.g., who brings the food to the coffee break) or the way in which routine tasks are informally rotated among staff members. The employment specialist may need to take an active role in identifying such customs and making sure the new worker understands them and has the skills to participate.

Table 1 lists ideas for promoting integration.

The employment specialist's role in facilitating integration and natural supports varies with the type of job and the abilities and desires of the worker involved. In some cases, the employment specialist may spend a great deal of time teaching job-related and social skills, or modifying the job to provide more opportunities for interactions and integration. In other situations, special skills training may not be required or integration may not be an issue. The needs and preferences of the worker and the employer should determine how much attention the employment specialist provides in this area. Providing effective assistance in the development of natural supports on the job requires that the employment specialist have both the skill to intervene when necessary and the grace to step out of the way when she is no longer needed.

Powell et al. (1991) pointed out that some of the "most powerful relationships are those normal friendships over which professionals have little control" (p. 125). Indeed, the personal relationships developed between co-workers may interfere with the relationship developed between the worker and the employment specialist as the worker becomes less dependent. Although this is a positive development for the supported worker, it may not always seem positive to the employment specialist who enjoys the close relationship she is able to develop with clients and sees them as one of the most positive aspects of her work. The employment specialist must work hard to ensure that her actions foster the strongest possible relationships between the worker and others on the job.

Table 1.   Hints for promoting integration

Help the worker learn the skills he needs to establish his relationships and then stay out of the way as the relationships develop.

Make it clear that the employer is the boss.

Teach the social expectations of the workplace, not just vocational skills.

Help identify interests shared by the worker and co-workers.

Do not use social services jargon in the workplace.

Use job restructuring to increase chances for integration.

Reinforce interactions that support the worker.

Act in ways that give permission and support to the worker, the supervisor, and the co-workers in developing their own unique relationships.

IDENTIFYING AND TEACHING SOCIAL SKILLS
THAT PROMOTE INTEGRATION AND JOB MAINTENANCE

The social skills required by a job vary with the type and location of the work and are not always the same as those taught in employment programs. In many cases, workers are given instructions on social greetings, sharing basic information, asking questions about work, and similar social skills. In contrast, a study by Henderson and Argyle (1985) listed the following as typical co-worker interactions (in order of frequency): 1) joking, 2) teasing, 3) helping with work, 4) chatting casually, 5) discussing work, 6) having coffee or meals, 7) discussing personal life, 8) asking or giving advice, and 9) teaching or demonstrating work tasks. Some of the most common workplace interactions such as joking or teasing may be very difficult for a worker with mental illness who has difficulty interpreting even the most straightforward of social interactions.

The significance of negative social behaviors varies with the job, the work setting, and the worker's vocational skill level. A worker who can assemble exercise bicycles very quickly and with excellent quality may be accepted despite her tendency to talk to herself, while a worker who has similar social problems but is a marginal producer may not be tolerated. In some jobs (e.g., a receptionist) good social skills are crucial, while in others (e.g., a solo warehouse worker) they are not of primary significance.

With so much variability among worksites regarding the types of social skills required, people sometimes question whether there is any sense in teaching social skills unless they are needed for a specific job. How much of social functioning is a product of the worker's natural personality and therefore must be respected, instead of modified, to fit an arbitrary norm? For example, should a shy person be taught to initiate conversations with co-workers just because society thinks it is something everyone should be able to do?

For people with long-term mental illness, social adjustment is a fairly good predictor of symptom relapses, rehospitalization, and long-term outcome; in other words, people with better social skills generally do better in the long run. In fact, improving social skills seems to reduce relapses and improve psychosocial functioning (Liberman et al., 1986). In addition, social skills have been shown to be a positive factor in successfully maintaining employment (Anthony, 1994b). Improving social skills can also reduce family stress and expressed emotion, which enables the family to provide more support for the worker.

There is good evidence that a highly structured behavioral approach is effective in helping people with mental illness improve their social skills (Meuser & Liberman, 1988; National Institute on Disability and Rehabilitation Research, 1989). How active a role the employment specialist takes in teaching social skills depends on the needs of the worker and the other resources available (e.g., through the mental health center). The employment specialist may rely on the mental health providers to teach social skills, while possibly providing feedback to the worker on the job. Another option is for social skills to be taught only on the job, with no involvement of others. Alternatively, both the employment specialist and the mental health provider could provide instruction and practice opportunities on the same skills, both on the job and off, which is probably the most powerful way to improve skills because it provides both rehearsal and practice in a neutral site and practice and feedback on the job.

There are some vocationally related social skills that have been identified by employers as important for workers in entry-level jobs (Rusch, Shutz, & Agran, 1982). Table 2 lists these desirable work-related social skills. These skills can and should be assessed and taught by the employment specialist just as she would teach any other vocational skills.

As part of the job development and analysis process, the employment specialist should track the types of interactions required for the particular job and verify that the worker either already has the needed skills in his repertoire or will receive training in those areas. The employment specialist may also be able to adjust work patterns to allow for more interactions with co-workers or the public, if that is desirable.

It is important to note that although the skills listed above have been identified as desirable by employers, it is possible to be successfully employed without having all of them. For example, it is possible for an individual with poor skills at following verbal instructions to work in a job that is very routine or with an employer who is willing to give instructions in writing or through modeling. The match between the skills of the worker and the demands of the job is more significant than either of the two variables alone. It is also important to remember that social competence means adequate social performance, not exceptional social performance.

There is some evidence that social skills are not easily acquired by casual contact and must be specifically taught. Activities such as group meetings or social events engage people in social interactions but do not necessarily teach skills (Mueser & Liberman, 1988). It is more effective to deliberately teach social skills in the same way that a vocational skill might be taught. The steps usually recommended include the following:

- Identifying the target social behavior. What is it? How often does and should it happen? With whom? In what environment and with what cues?
- Specifying training goals based on the target behavior.
- Using direct instructions, modeling, shaping, coaching, and role playing to identify and practice desired behaviors.
- Using repeated trials and many practice sessions to produce the fastest acquisition.

This instruction and practice may take place in several environments including on the job, at the workplace but away from the job, at the mental health center, or at some other nonwork location. Family members, co-workers, and other clients with mental illness can be involved as models or role players. Learning usually is most durable when it takes place across many settings. At this point it seems clear

Table 2.   Desirable work-related social skills

Reciting identification information on request
Responding to and following verbal instructions
Accepting correction or criticism
Handling frustration
Asking for assistance when needed
Getting information before starting
Offering to help co-workers

Source: Rusch, Schutz, & Agran (1982).

that social skills training is an important part of employment support for many workers with long-term mental illness and should not be left to chance.

CONCLUSION

Natural supports, integration, and social skills are all important aspects of successful placements. Undoubtedly, as knowledge about the world of work and the capabilities and preferences of workers with long-term mental illness expands, the role of interpersonal issues in the workplace will be reinforced.

"Try it again...when I ask you about your weekend, I mean last weekend, not November 5th, 1983."

Instruction and practice in social skills can take place on or off the job.

20

FADING FROM THE JOBSITE

T he job coach model of supported employment, which is often used for individual placements, requires the employment specialist (or job coach) to initially spend a significant amount of time training and supporting the worker. At some point it becomes necessary and appropriate for the employment specialist to begin fading his presence and testing the systems that will maintain the worker's performance once she is working independently. Fading requires a delicate balance between spending enough time on site to ensure that training is complete and the needed support systems are organized, while making sure that the worker and employer do not become dependent on the employment specialist's presence. The need to fade intensive support and the difficulties inherent therein are considered to be a major weakness of the job coach model and have provided much of the impetus for the development of alternative placement models involving natural supports.

For many people with long-term mental illness, fading from the jobsite is not an issue because the employment specialist will not have done any training on the jobsite. This chapter discusses situations in which the employment specialist *has* been involved in providing on-site training and support because it was needed or desired by the worker. This support ranges from being informal and brief to being as structured and extensive as support provided to workers with mental retardation. The level of difficulty associated with successfully fading the employment specialist's presence while maintaining job performance will vary with the intensity of the training provided, the needs of the worker, and the characteristics of the job.

Fading decisions are particularly difficult for the new employment specialist who is anxious to have everything perfect before he begins to fade and who ends up making the worker and employer thoroughly dependent on his presence. However, fading precipitously (the falling-off-a-cliff approach) or fading according to a preset schedule that is not determined by the worker's needs may not provide the needed support for stable ongoing performance.

Systematic, data-based fading provides the employment specialist with opportunities to assess the worker's independent performance on individual tasks or for time periods while the specialist is still available to intervene if needed. It provides guidelines for the employment specialist to use in planning when to fade and when to remain on site. It also enables the employer and worker to increase their direct interactions with each other, while having access to the employment specialist as a resource.

The amount of job-related support that is needed off site from the employment specialist, residential staff, family members, service coordinators, and others is another consideration in determining fading schedules. Residential changes, family problems, or medication changes may indicate a need to delay fading even if the job performance is stable (Wool, 1990).

DECIDING WHEN AND HOW TO FADE

There are many areas to consider when deciding when and how to fade from a job-site. Careful attention to these areas will increase the worker's chances of maintaining stable employment beyond the period when the employment specialist is directly involved. From the beginning of the placement, the employment specialist should design his teaching approaches in a way that will make fading as easy as possible.

External Parameters and Initial Considerations

Funding restrictions or multiple demands on the employment specialist's time may need to be considered when developing a fading plan. The employment spe-

"I've just never seen a job coach fade!"

Systematic, data-based fading provides opportunities to assess the worker's independent performance.

cialist may need to make another placement or his time on site may be funded only for a specified period. The level of ongoing support available after the initial training period may also be limited by policy or work load pressures. These are important parameters to keep in mind both before and during the fading period.

The other issues that are considered in initial fading have to do with how well the training period is going. Is the worker developing the skills needed? Is the worker managing her symptoms? Is there effective communication between the worker and the employer?

The employment specialist must be careful to keep both the worker and the employer informed about the fading schedule, including times when he expects to be with the worker and times when he will be away from the worksite. Good communication is particularly crucial during this time of transition.

Transfer of Control

As discussed previously, the employment specialist should design his approaches in a way that will make fading as easy as possible. This means choosing teaching techniques that are the most unobtrusive, the least structured, and the most independent given the needs of the individual. This usually involves starting with a combination of verbal instruction and social reinforcement because both techniques are generally used to teach workers without disabilities and will likely be the procedures available after the employment specialist has faded out. Only if these typical approaches are ineffective should more structured programs be designed and implemented.

It should be easy for the employment specialist to fade from the worksite when the worker is able to learn and maintain needed skills through instruction and social reinforcement. However, it is not as easy in situations in which the worker needs structured programs to provide cues and/or reinforcement. In this situation, the employment specialist must either transfer the responsibility of providing cues or reinforcement to the worker by using a self-management approach or find someone else in the work environment to provide the needed support. If transferring control is necessary, the employment specialist must examine the ongoing interactions between the supervisor and the worker (e.g., giving instructions and feedback, teaching a new skill, asking questions, dealing with symptoms), and between the worker and her co-workers. Transfer of control might also involve the employment specialist turning over his support role to another professional (e.g., the case manager), rather than to the worker, supervisor, or co-workers. In any case, good team-building and communication efforts are the foundation of the fading process.

Data-Based Fading

In situations where fading is necessary, the employment specialist should use training and performance data to determine which tasks the worker is able to do independently. He can then systematically leave the worker alone on the job for increasing periods of time, starting with tasks the worker is performing correctly while the employment specialist is present. This process often begins by having the employment specialist leave the immediate work area during times when the targeted task(s) is being performed, but remain on the worksite to check proper completion of the task. If performance is maintained, the employment specialist can then begin leaving the worksite during those tasks.

In some cases (i.e., when the worker is doing basically the same task throughout most of her shift), the employment specialist will need to use a different method of fading. As the worker begins to perform her task independently for brief periods of time, the employment specialist begins to fade by standing farther away from the worker and providing the minimum number of cues. As the worker increases her independence, the employment specialist moves out of sight for set intervals of 5, 10, or 15 minutes, returning at the end of each interval to check the work and provide feedback and reinforcement. The length of time between checks is gradually lengthened until the employment specialist is able to leave the worksite between checks.

A data-based approach to fading requires the employment specialist to continue seeking feedback on the worker's performance in order to assess whether existing support systems adequately maintain the worker's performance without the employment specialist's presence. The employment specialist gradually either increases the amount of time the worker is independent or reintervenes on problem areas, depending on the information gained from the worker, employer, and/or co-workers.

Setting Up Supports

Setting up supports is a part of the fading process that examines the long-term supports the worker will need in order to maintain employment. Such things as a plan for decompensation, a plan for providing support and reinforcement to the employer for his efforts, and a proactive schedule of checks with the employer and worker should be in place before the fading period ends.

"I'll be there in a minute—you go ahead and go back to work."

As independence continues to increase, the employment specialist moves out of sight for set intervals of time, returning periodically to check the work and provide feedback and reinforcement.

In some situations, particularly those where the worker needs more assistance and support on the job, it may be useful for the employment specialist to leave brief written summary instructions with the supervisor and/or co-workers. In many jobs, there is a high turnover of supervisors or several people have supervisory responsibilities (Kirsner et al., 1994). Brief (i.e., index card size) instructions for communicating with a worker who needs special considerations such as small words, slower instructions, and repetition may help transfer responsibility to the supervisor and encourage a consistent approach across supervisors, while helping develop an employer–employee relationship. The written format provides concrete, visible instructions for the supervisor to refer to when the employment specialist is not there and may prompt a management style that works with other employees as well. Simple examples may also be useful. For example, the employment specialist may recommend that the supervisor verify the worker's understanding of his instructions by having her repeat them back to him. Figure 1 is a fading worksheet that outlines many crucial issues that should be considered by the employment specialist as he plans and works through the fading period.

MEASURING MAINTENANCE OF PERFORMANCE

During and after the fading period, the employment specialist must use any resources available to continue assessing the worker's performance. Potential resources include the following:

- Self-report or self-measurement by the worker (e.g., counting and recording the number of packets collated in a set time period, writing down the time the waiting room was cleaned)
- Formal or informal observation by a co-worker or supervisor (e.g., noting if the worker "kept up" during a rush period, recording the incidence of inappropriate self-talk during a shift)
- Formal written performance evaluations completed by the employer and/or co-workers
- Observation and checking by the employment specialist

It is often difficult for the employment specialist to get accurate feedback about the supported worker from employers and co-workers. Many people are reluctant to appear critical of an individual with a disability and will therefore hide their concerns about the individual's performance until they can no longer be hidden and action must be taken. A written evaluation form that requires the employer to assess the worker in a number of areas will encourage the employer to give accurate feedback. Giving the employer several different means in which to communicate (e.g., written form, verbal interview) increases the chance of receiving good feedback. However, in the long run it is often up to the employment specialist to establish the kind of relationship with the employer and co-workers that facilitates honest feedback and then to ask repeatedly for information and follow up on it when it is given.

WHAT TO DO WHEN FADING GETS STUCK

There are times when it seems as though the employment specialist will never be able to completely fade from the worksite. For example, the worker just cannot quite get the work done, the worker slows down as soon as the employment spe-

FADING WORKSHEET

Worker: _____   Date: _____
Employment site: _____

Part 1: Parameters

1. What are the time limits for your on-the-job training and support activities?

2. What is the *maximum* level of continuing support *you* can provide on an ongoing basis once the initial training phase has ended?

Part 2: Setting the stage

1. Is communication between the worker and the boss effective? How about with co-workers?

2. Are vocational skills improving at a satisfactory rate?

3. Is the worker managing symptoms in a satisfactory manner?

4. Does the worker routinely get clear and sufficient feedback?

5. Are natural supports developing?

6. Are the worker's social interactions becoming positive?

7. Is the employer becoming invested in the worker's success?

_____
(continued)

Figure 1.   A fading worksheet that outlines many of the crucial issues the employment specialist should consider as he plans and works through the fading period. (Adapted by permission from John P. Dineen [1990].)

Figure 1. *(continued)*

8. Are existing agreements with family, significant others, and other agencies working out well?

9. Who else needs to become involved?

Part 3: Transfer of control

1. Has the supervisor assumed full management responsibilities for the worker? Does the supervisor consult with you as if you were now maintaining the job instead of teaching it?

2. Have you observed the supervisor providing critical feedback to the worker? Was it effective?

3. Have you observed the supervisor teaching or training the worker on a new skill? Was it effective?

4. Is the supervisor prepared to deal with the worker's more intense symptoms?

5. Have you observed the worker asking for help?

   Asking for clarification of an instruction?

   Disagreeing with the supervisor in a respectful manner?

6. Does the worker have a co-worker to whom he or she can turn for help or support?

(continued)

Figure 1.   *(continued)*

7.   Is the worker using self-management strategies successfully?

8.   If there is to be a handing over of the worker to a caseworker or other follow-along provider, is that person assuming his or her responsibilities?

9.   Use this section to outline significant transfer problems:

     Principal players:

     What things seem to be problematic?

     Is this a result of (please check the answer that best applies):
     _____ A lack of skills (does not know *how* to assume control)
     _____ Poor discrimination (does not know *when* to assume control)
     _____ Low motivation (does not *want* to assume control)

     What do you want to happen?

     Describe your intervention strategy:

Part 4: Data-based fading

The following measures may be useful in measuring the employment specialist's involvement with the worker:

Minutes of help   For each shift of work, total the number of minutes you have assisted the worker to complete the job. You want this measure to drop to zero.

Total prompts   For each shift, tally the number of instructions, directives, and cues you have given the worker. You want your prompts to approach zero, and the boss and co-workers to take up their normal level of support.

Task sequencing   A job analysis provides a sequential list of tasks. By noting each time a new task is begun independently, you track the worker's improvement as a percentage of tasks independently sequenced. You want this measure to reach 100%.

(continued)

Figure 1.   *(continued)*

Task completion   Using the same list of tasks, note each task the worker does *without* any instructions from you. You want this measure also to reach 100%.

Work rate   Note each task the worker completes on time. You want this percentage to reach 100%.

1. Is the worker able to sequence tasks correctly, even with interruptions?

2. Is the worker working with few or no instructions from the employment specialist?

3. Is the worker completing tasks at the expected rate?

4. Are other measured behaviors now at the desired levels?

5. Do the data suggest low variability in performance?

6. Do the data suggest stability in performance?

7. Does the employer rate the worker as performing the job satisfactorily?

8. Does the employment specialist rate the worker as performing the job satisfactorily?

Part 5: Setting up supports

1. Has the employer endorsed a plan for fading? For follow-up services?

2. Could any additional support be given to the employer for his or her continuing cooperation?

(continued)

Figure 1. *(continued)*

3. Do supervisors and co-workers understand their roles in supporting the worker's attempts at symptom management?

4. Is additional education on mental illness needed for the supervisor or co-workers?

5. Do the employer and the worker have an agreement on how vacations will be earned and scheduled?

6. Does the worker understand how future promotions or pay increases will be earned and scheduled?

7. Is there a means for tracking the above benefits to ensure that promised perks will be delivered?

8. Is the worker clear on how the job will affect Social Security payments?

9. Is there a proactive plan for checks with the employer and the worker to catch problems before they get out of hand?

10. If the job becomes threatened, will someone call you? Who?

11. Is there a plan for handling decompensation?

12. Have most or all agreements with the support network been tested and found to be adequate? Are all parties routinely communicating?

13. Are case notes and other pertinent information organized in a manner that allows a new employment specialist to follow the successful and not-so-successful strategies in placing and maintaining this worker?

cialist leaves, the employer keeps adding responsibilities to the task list, or the employer does not follow through on giving the worker opportunities to learn all the tasks involved in the job. When fading gets stuck, one of three things is usually happening: 1) the worker has not yet reached criterion on a task, 2) the worker has grown dependent on the employment specialist's attention to maintain performance, or 3) the employer is making changes in the original employment agreement. Possible solutions are offered below.

The Worker Never Reaches Criterion on a Task

In situations where the worker never reaches the speed or quality criterion on a task, the employment specialist must determine whether retraining on the task is needed. The problem may be in the complexity of the steps involved in the task or in the level and schedule of reinforcement. It may be that the task must be broken down into simpler steps, more frequent reinforcers must be provided, or different reinforcers should be used. Is the worker using the most efficient method of doing the task? Can the work station be modified to make the work flow more smoothly? Does the worker understand what she should to be doing and what the criteria for speed and quality are?

If the employment specialist believes that the worker is performing at her best possible level on the task, it may be possible to negotiate the criterion level with the employer. In many situations, the employment specialist believes the worker is not producing enough, while the employer is actually satisfied with the worker's production or is willing to accept a slightly lower level of production in exchange for the worker's other strengths. If the criterion is not negotiable, the employment specialist may suggest exchanging the problematic task for a different task that is currently done by another employee.

There are times when nothing seems to work. The employment specialist has given training the worker his best effort (including perhaps getting advice from someone else), and the employer has declined to modify the expectations of the job. At some point the employment specialist may have to go the employer and make it clear that the worker is performing as well as she is able and the employer must decide whether he is satisfied with the worker's performance. This may seem like forcing the issue but if the employer is going to fire the worker because she cannot keep up with the work, it might as well happen sooner rather than later. It is also important to remember that the employment specialist cannot always predict how the employer will react. At times the desperate employment specialist has said, "It's the best she and I can do, so take her or leave her," and the employer has in fact chosen to retain the worker for many years afterward.

The Worker Depends on the Employment Specialist

It is not uncommon for the quality of a worker's performance to decline as the employment specialist fades from the worksite, indicating dependency on the cues and reinforcers provided (deliberately or inadvertently) by the employment specialist. Building support in the workplace throughout the initial placement period will lessen the likelihood of long-term dependency on the employment specialist. Approaches to consider include identifying others in the workplace who can provide attention and reinforcement, investigating whether this attention will be provided routinely or whether the worker must ask for it, and testing whether the worker can monitor her own work and provide herself with reinforcement.

Another important approach to this problem is to make the employment specialist's attention contingent on *good* performance, not on the worker's mistakes. This allows the worker to earn attention from the employment specialist (perhaps away from the workplace) whenever she meets an agreed-upon performance measure. For example, the worker might earn a chance to have lunch with the employment specialist if she makes it to work on time 5 days in a row. This approach assumes that the worker has the supports she needs to make it to work on time and that the employment specialist's attention is actually a reinforcer for which the worker would be willing to work.

The Employer Keeps Changing the Requirements of the Job

The employment specialist must be clear to the employer that if the employer keeps changing the requirements of the job (or does not follow through on providing opportunities to learn all the tasks), problems will arise. The employer may not understand that long-term training and support on the job do not mean eternal training and support on the job. At some point the intensive training must end because the employment specialist must move on to another placement, funding is no longer available, or the worker is tired of having the employment specialist around and wants to work independently. In addition, the employer who is still changing the work schedule after 8 weeks is probably going to continue making changes after the employment specialist has faded out, which will cause future problems for the worker. Meeting with the employer, reviewing progress to date, and agreeing on a date for the training to end may modify the employer's behavior.

If meeting with the employer and explaining the problem does not work, the employment specialist may need to make a written agreement with the employer outlining how much longer the employment specialist will be providing training and specifying any commitment the employer has made (e.g., rotating the worker through another production line). In fact, written fading agreements can often facilitate the fading and transfer process and should be considered as a proactive approach. Written agreements may also help clarify the worker's expectations about the employment specialist's continued involvement on the job. Because most mental health services are not time limited, the concept of having the service provider leave a client and reduce the level of support provided may be both unfamiliar and anxiety producing to a worker who has been in the mental health system for any length of time. A written plan that details the procedures for fading and long-term support may assuage the worker's concerns, while setting guidelines for the employment specialist's continued role. Figure 2 is an example of a fading agreement.

CONCLUSION

It should be remembered that the course of rehabilitation rarely runs in a linear or predictable fashion when people with mental illness are involved. Many people will experience daily, weekly, or monthly fluctuations in their symptoms and their functioning level. For this reason, fading from a jobsite may have to occur on a schedule that corresponds with the varying needs of the worker, rather than on the predictable schedule often used with workers who have mental retardation. Whereas a fading schedule for working with a person with mental retardation might be to plan on being on site 25% of the time in the sixth week, then 15% in

---

EXAMPLE FADING AGREEMENT

Employer: Fred's Roofing
Contact: Jack Employer
Address: 574 Dayton Avenue North
Telephone: 783–0000

Employee: Keisha Employee
Employment specialist: Gary Coach
Telephone: 543–0000

Date: March 14, 1995

Keisha Employee has now been working as a roofer's helper at Fred's Roofing for approximately 5 weeks. As stated in the employment agreement, a fading agreement is to be developed once Keisha's production stabilizes and all work skills are taught and mastered. Data have been kept on Keisha's progress and shared with Jack, and all involved parties agree that Gary should begin to fade from the jobsite.

To this point, fading has consisted of changing the type of prompts used to assist Keisha. Other employees have observed the various support procedures and seem comfortable in continuing to support Keisha. Simple indirect prompts such as, "Keisha, what's next?" are usually enough. Gary will continue to work with the staff in this area.

This week Gary will begin to leave Keisha alone for increasingly longer periods each day. He will continue to check with Keisha and Jack at the end of each day to monitor production rates and quality and will provide additional training as necessary. He will also be available to answer questions, but will be changing his role to one of consulting with the staff rather than spending most of his time working directly with Keisha. Any days Keisha is out sick will be covered by other employees of Fred's Roofing, as per the original employment agreement.

When Keisha no longer needs Gary's assistance more than once a week, an evaluation of her work will be completed by Keisha, Jack, and Gary. This will probably happen in about 3 weeks, depending on how things go. After the training period has ended, Gary will continue to check in with both Keisha and Jack as well as being available by telephone and can provide additional training or support if it is needed. It is important for Keisha and/or Jack to let Gary know if his assistance is needed for any reason. Adjustments to this fading agreement can be initiated by all involved parties.

Figure 2.   A fading agreement between an employment specialist and a client.

the seventh week, and 10% in the eighth week, the employment specialist supporting a worker with mental illness may need to be on site 10% of the time during the sixth week, 50% in the seventh and eighth week because of an increase in symptoms and support needs, and then 5% in the ninth week when the worker is stable. Many professionals say the only thing predictable about mental illness is unpredictability. The employment specialist must remember to make plans for fading and transferring support that are flexible enough to accommodate changing client needs.

V
STAYING EMPLOYED

21

Ongoing Support

Ongoing support is one of the keystones of supported employment. As employment specialists in early placement programs found themselves needing to return to placement sites repeatedly over time, it became apparent that many people with disabilities could be successfully employed in the community if there were no expectation of eventually withdrawing all support. This is true for workers with mental illness, as well as for people with mental retardation. One study found that ongoing contact with a support person was the best single predictor of job retention for workers with mental illness (Bond & McDonel, 1991). Cook and Rosenberg (1991) also reported that people who received continuous support were significantly more likely to be employed 6 months after placement.

The ongoing support or follow-up period begins once the worker is stable on the job (i.e., he has learned the necessary tasks, gotten to know the people he works with, and developed on- and off-site support arrangements). The key to good follow-up is the proactive aspect; it should not be equivalent to crisis intervention.

It is hard to identify a standard format or schedule for long-term follow-up because of the variability in workers and workplaces. Follow-up may be provided by the employment specialist who did the original placement, by a follow-up specialist, or by the mental health counselor or case manager. It may involve troubleshooting, crisis management, retraining, advocacy, or marshaling resources to help a worker avoid decompensation and rehospitalization. Follow-up should involve whatever support is needed by the worker to stay employed, whether it is 2 hours per month for a year or 10 hours a week for a month.

WHY ONGOING SUPPORT?

One thing that seems clear is that both work and nonwork issues can affect job retention. In order for a worker to maintain employment, eight factors must remain in balance. Changes in any one of these areas can threaten job retention. Therefore, the employment specialist needs to work with the client to develop skills and/or resources in each area.

Issues in the Match Between the Job and the Worker

The match between the job requirements and the worker's skills and support needs may change over time, affecting job stability. Three important characteristics of the job–worker match are the following:

1. The structure and feedback provided by the job
2. The reinforcement provided by the job
3. The adequacy of the worker's skills to meet job demands

Changes in these areas can affect the worker's ability to maintain the job. For example, a new supervisor may not carry through on meeting briefly with the worker each morning, depriving the worker of the feedback and reinforcement on which he has come to depend; or the tasks assigned to the worker may have changed and he is no longer able to do them adequately.

Issues Outside the Workplace

Changes in the worker's life outside the workplace can also have an impact on job stability. Common issues include the following:

4. The level of home support toward employment
5. The stability of the worker's health
6. The worker's interest and motivation to maintain employment

"Oops!"

Follow-up is not the same as crisis intervention.

The type of home support enjoyed by workers can have a strong impact on their ability to remain employed. Coiner (1990) conducted a study of supported employment participants who had mental illness and found that participants living with other clients were much more likely to drop out of supported employment programs than were clients who lived with family members. Another positive influence on continued employment is the availability of recreational and social activities that are consistent with employment.

The worker's health, both physical and mental, can also affect employment stability. Many people with mental illness have physical problems (e.g., high blood pressure, dental problems) that are not routinely assessed or treated that affect the person's ability to continue with employment. The issue of worker interest and motivation is tied in with other issues, including reinforcement on the job, home support, stability of symptoms, and competition from other activities.

Issues in the Availability of Work

The following two characteristics of the job can have an immediate impact on stable employment:

7. Work continues to be available.
8. Work continues to be accessible.

Availability issues (e.g., businesses closing, cutting back staff) and accessibility issues (e.g., changes in transportation arrangements, changes in residence, changes in shifts where the worker no longer has access to a bus) are usually beyond the influence of the worker or the employment specialist, but may need to be addressed during the follow-up period.

A proactive follow-up plan can enable the employment specialist and the worker to identify changes on the job or in the support system before the situation deteriorates beyond redemption. The plan can also serve as a prompt to the employer to continue noticing the tasks the worker is doing correctly. Often employers have the perception (true or false) that workers with disabilities are performing at a level below that of other employees and consequently workers with disabilities are under more scrutiny and are expected to live up to higher expectations (Rusch, 1986). A proactive follow-up plan can teach the employer to recognize and value the contribution being made by the worker with mental illness.

The continued attention of the employment specialist can also serve as a reinforcer for both the worker and the employer by encouraging them to continue their efforts. Visits and attention from an employment specialist have convinced many supervisors to retain individual workers far beyond the point that they otherwise would have been retained.

HOW TO PROVIDE ONGOING SUPPORT

Some programs use written employer evaluation forms and follow-up schedules to structure their ongoing support; others just have the employment specialist and worker meet informally away from the jobsite. The exact structure and format of follow-up is less important than providing it in a consistent manner and not waiting until problems occur before making contact. The style and tools used depend on the need of the worker, the atmosphere of the workplace, and whether the employment specialist has been directly involved at the workplace up to this point.

Like other types of support, follow-up services should be as unobtrusive as possible. This often means meeting during nonwork times and away from the worksite. Besides the follow-up initiated by the employment specialist, plans should also be in place that allow the worker and perhaps the employer to request support for work or nonwork issues.

The employment specialist may need to check and support a self-management program (e.g., journaling, symptom checklist), reinforce co-workers who are acting in structured supportive roles, or help maintain and review production data. However, for other workers it may only be necessary to make a general probe into current conditions. It is often useful to keep track of pay raise dates, benefits accrued, and current hours scheduled to assist in advocacy efforts when needed.

Because of the variability inherent in long-term mental illness, follow-up services must be available on a flexible basis. A person who may need no extra support one month may need quite a lot of support the next month because his symptoms intensified, his rent went up, his supervisor changed, and his girlfriend walked out on him. Common follow-up approaches are on-site visits, telephone calls, written evaluation forms, off-site meetings, and peer support groups.

On-Site Visits

In situations in which the worker is comfortable with having the employment specialist involved at the workplace, on-site visits can maintain the personal contact and rapport developed during the initial training period. The supervisor and co-workers serve as an early warning system that alerts the employment specialist to changes in the worker's performance or behavior. Observing and interacting with the worker in his work environment can give the employment specialist further information about things that are going well and things that need modification. As mentioned previously, having the employment specialist visit the jobsite can be reinforcing to some workers who have a chance to show off their progress and accomplishments. It can also be reinforcing to the supervisor and co-workers, who appreciate a chance to share their opinions with someone who will listen with interest and respect.

Ideally, on-site visits should involve spending time with the worker as well as his supervisor and co-workers, giving him a chance to bring up any concerns or changes. It is important that the employment specialist discusses strengths as well as problems during her on-site visits. Rusch (1986) suggested that employment specialists look for both subjective evaluative information about the worker's performance and social comparisons (i.e., how the worker's performance compares with that of his co-workers). Co-workers often have more accurate information than supervisors because they work more closely with the person. However, the supervisor is generally the one who decides whether the worker continues to be employed.

The disadvantages of making on-site visits are the expense involved (i.e., in terms of the amount of time), the labeling effects, the possibility of interrupting the workday, and the potential obtrusiveness. However, in many circumstances on-site visits can be a powerful tool throughout the follow-up phase.

Telephone Calls

There are times when a telephone call to the worker, a co-worker, and/or the supervisor is a cost-effective way to keep tabs on what is happening. In addition, telephone calls are usually more discreet and therefore less obtrusive than personal visits. However, telephone calls are also usually less powerful and in most cases should be used between, rather than instead of, on-site visits.

Written Evaluations

Some employment specialists use written work performance evaluation forms to collect and document information from the employer, co-workers, and sometimes even from themselves. These generally cover such areas as dependability, cooperation, task completion, consistency, independence, personal appearance, and communication. In some cases feedback is also requested about the agency services from the employer or supervisor. Asking if the employment specialist provides enough support or if the employer would like to meet with the employment specialist provides valuable information to the agency. Written evaluations provide a way for employment specialists to identify trends in employer satisfaction (or the lack of satisfaction) and to improve retention by disclosing problematic changes quickly. They can also help shape the kind of feedback the employer gives the employment specialist (and perhaps the worker) by describing performance issues in concrete, behavioral terms.

Guidelines for using written evaluations are the following:

1. Include the strengths of the worker as well as issues that might be problematic. This allows the employment specialist to teach the employer to notice things that are going well.
2. Explain to the worker and the employer why the items are included in the form and how the information will be used.
3. Go over the evaluation form item by item with the employer so that there is a clear understanding of the meaning of each item.
4. Respond as quickly as possible to any problems mentioned in the evaluations to avoid having the employer feel that it is just more paperwork that will be filed and forgotten.
5. The process should be made convenient for the employer by keeping the form brief and sometimes leaving it with a return envelope, rather than waiting for the employer to complete it or making a return trip to pick it up. In general, written evaluations should be used *along with*, rather than *instead of*, personal visits.
6. The process should be made personal by including evaluation items that are pertinent to that worker and that workplace. A basic format can easily be customized on a computer.
7. The worker should be involved in reviewing written evaluations.
8. To measure consistency and changes over time, the employment specialist should have the same person complete the evaluation each time; or if that is not possible she must understand that different evaluators may produce very different ratings of the same performance level.

Botterbusch (1989), Fadely (1987), and Moon et al. (1986) offer examples of work evaluation formats in their job coaching manuals.

Off-Site Support

When the employment specialist is not involved on the jobsite or with the employer, long-term support may involve meeting at the agency or at home, going for a walk or for coffee, talking with the worker at the clubhouse, or picking the worker up at his job and giving him a ride home. Although this type of support is less direct than on-site support and may seem less important, for many workers it is necessary and sufficient for job maintenance. Off-site support can also be used along with on-site visits to extend the employment specialist's involvement with the worker without being a constant presence at the workplace.

Off-site support can also be provided through others in the worker's environment (e.g., family members, friends). In these situations, the employment specialist's role is one of supporting others in their efforts to help the worker maintain employment.

The line between long-term support and case management grows very unclear at times. If the case manager is not the person responsible for job follow-up, ideally she is in close contact with the employment specialist so that their efforts can be coordinated (see Chapter 22).

Peer Support Groups

Many agencies find it valuable to sponsor peer support groups for clients who are employed. These may be called job clubs, employment dinners, or transitional employment dinners. Ongoing participation in a worker's support group can encourage a client's continued relationship with agency staff and other clients in a setting that is consistent with his new role as an employed person. Besides providing peer support in a positive atmosphere, groups give the employment specialist a chance to maintain contact with clients and stay on top of changes in behavior, increased symptoms, changes in living arrangements, difficulties on the job, or other issues.

Groups typically meet weekly or every other week and are scheduled at times when they will be accessible to the most workers. They may meet at the mental health center, at the rehabilitation facility, or in another location such as a church or coffeeshop. Meetings usually begin with each participant sharing what is happening on the job—both successes and problems. These discussions allow participants to learn that others in the group are dealing with similar challenges on and off the job and provide an opportunity for concrete approaches to be developed through brainstorming and discussion.

After each participant shares his story, a staff member or participant usually makes a brief presentation on a topic previously selected by group members. Topics include such things as problem solving, planning leisure time, and talking with co-workers about mental illness. Meetings generally end with some kind of social exchange, such as a meal, refreshments, or casual conversation. Staff members play varied roles. In some groups they take the major responsibility for recruiting members and coordinating and facilitating meetings, while in others they participate on an advisory basis while group members are responsible for the activities listed above.

Some agencies find it works well to include job seekers in the group with people who are currently employed because the workers act as role models for those who have not yet moved into employment. Other agencies find it works better to include only those individuals who have successfully moved into employment. In these groups, participants identify themselves as workers rather than clients and may be reluctant to identify with or include those who are still largely in a patient role (Botterbusch, 1989). Peer support groups can be an effective and efficient way for agencies to enhance the support available to clients who become employed.

CONCLUSION

Having access to ongoing support following the initial placement period enables many workers with mental illness to maintain stable employment. This support may be provided on or off the job and may involve the employer, co-workers, family members, the case manager, peers, and neighbors as well as the employment specialist. Although the intensity and format will vary with the needs of the worker and the workplace, ongoing support is always a proactive answer to the changes that inevitably occur on the job.

22

TEAM BUILDING

One essential issue that arises when discussing supported employment for people with long-term mental illness is the need to work cooperatively with other professionals and community members in building support teams. One reason this is so important is because the mental health and vocational rehabilitation systems (and the people who work in them) approach people with mental illness in very different ways (see Chapter 8). In some communities, the two agencies have never worked together before and have a difficult time finding common ground. In addition to the vocational rehabilitation and mental health issues, there are several other reasons that solid team building is often a necessary part of the employment specialist's job.

THE IMPORTANCE OF TEAM BUILDING

One person often cannot provide all the support that is needed by an individual with long-term mental illness. This may be a result of limited time available for any one client, a lack of expertise in a given area, or the need to provide time-limited services (e.g., when an employment specialist provides the initial placement and then turns the worker over to the mental health system for long-term support) (Woy & Dellario, 1985).

People with long-term mental illness are often involved in complicated service systems before they become involved in employment. Therefore, many people may already be involved with a client, including medical and mental health personnel, family members, residential support providers, or Social Security representatives. These other individuals often have the power to prevent or support efforts toward rehabilitation, and they may or may not value employment.

Unlike people with mental retardation who have had a disability for all or most of their lives, some people with mental illness have had the disease interrupt a complex and rewarding life as a spouse, friend, parent, and employee or employer. Others who are regularly involved with these individuals (e.g., family, friends, employees) may need the structure and encouragement of being part of the support team so that they in turn can assist the person who has a mental illness. In addition, the effects of mental illness usually cut across all areas of functioning, reaching beyond employment into issues of residence, social and recreational activities, medical needs, and daily living skills. Therefore, people with mental illness may need to receive support from various sources in all of these areas.

Vocational service providers may interact with a person over a relatively brief period of time and in a limited topic area. In other words, the employment specialist may spend 1–3 years helping the person become stable in employment, but her parents will interact with her for the rest of their lives. It is imperative that these two systems work cooperatively.

Increased participation in supported employment by people with long-term mental illness has challenged some service providers to change their roles—a change that may require education and support from other professionals. For example, some mental health case managers have agreed to do long-term follow-up on the job without understanding that they need to leave their offices in order to provide such follow-up. Residential providers who usually work with people participating in flexible day treatment programs may have to learn to help participants schedule haircuts and shopping trips around working hours rather than assuming the person will be available whenever it is convenient. Much of the mental health system is set up to accommodate and treat "patients," not people who are employed.

"It's your case manager, she's calling collect!"

Case managers sometimes agree to do long-term follow-up without understanding that they need to leave their offices.

Team building can also build continuity during an age of high turnover. Bourbeau (1990) reported that in studies there was a 70%–200% turnover annually for people in job coaching positions. Having support coordinated and provided by a cohesive team means the worker will receive effective support even if a member of the team moves on.

INTERAGENCY RELATIONSHIPS

Most employment specialists will at some time or another end up in a situation in which they have to work with another agency (e.g., a group home, day treatment) whose staff or policies seem to obstruct clients' efforts to achieve vocational goals. For example, the Social Security representative may refuse to approve any PASS applications, or the psychiatric nurse may only take appointments during the hours when a client is employed. Although advocating on an individual client's behalf remains an important role for the employment specialist, it may also be helpful for the staff of the two agencies in question to establish a good working relationship separate from activities that center around a particular client. This is also true for two units of the same agency (e.g., the day program and employment units of a mental health center). In fact, the negotiations between units of the same agency are often more complicated and difficult than those between two separate agencies. The territory and mistrust issues that sometimes develop can seriously interfere with the support that is available to clients.

The Issues

Coordinating services is not easy to accomplish. There are several issues involved that can cause problems if they are not adequately addressed.

Lack of Agreement on Goals and Priorities   One of the biggest interagency issues is a lack of agreement on goals and priorities. The vocational provider may believe that clients should have access to the type of employment they prefer, while the residential provider may believe that clients should be employed only during the day (if at all) because working during evening hours interferes with recreation and activities of daily living (ADL) training.

Communication   A second problem area is communication, both in terms of clearly expressing what is needed and desired and in informing others about changes in arrangements or routines. For example, the employment specialist may tell the case manager that Lynn will be working every afternoon from 1 A.M. to 6 P.M., but the case manager may assume that Lynn can still take time off every Tuesday for the peer support group because the employment specialist was aware that Lynn had been in the habit of doing so for several months and had not said otherwise. Or the doctor monitoring Lynn's medication may decide to try a lower dosage for her during the same week that the employment specialist is placing Lynn in a full-time job. Poor communication in each case makes it more difficult for Lynn to make a smooth transition into employment.

Roles and Responsibilities   A third common area of disagreement is on the roles and responsibilities of each person. In the example described above, people may all agree that Lynn needs support to get to work on time. However, the residential provider believes that the employment specialist should be responsible, while the employment specialist believes that the case manager should pressure the residential provider to do it. The result is that no one does it, at least with consistency, and Lynn loses her job after repeated tardiness.

Team-Building Guidelines[1]

In order to build a relationship with another agency or branch, an employment specialist must begin by developing a clear picture of the ideal situation. What would this agency or unit be doing if it were perfect? What kind of services would be provided? What kind of support? What kind of follow-through? How would the two agencies interact? Although this ideal may not be achievable, it will provide a framework for change. Table 1 lists approaches for developing a relationship with staff of another agency or branch.

It is important to work at building a relationship with the other agency separate from cooperating on behalf of specific clients. This process is not unlike doing job development, where the employment specialist must get to know an employer and his business before he begins discussing specific jobs and workers. Spending time with other professionals and learning about the needs and challenges they are facing is an excellent way to begin the process of developing a cooperative relationship that can provide a foundation from which to begin negotiating for a specific client.

Sharing information in many forms—articles, stories, reports, and anecdotes—helps agencies interact across a common database. For example, working with day program staff who are not convinced their clients can be successfully employed may require the production of a great deal of evidence to the contrary. This evidence includes sharing the successes achieved by clients or former clients, which may include showing as well as telling (e.g., visiting employed clients and hearing about their experiences as well as those of employers and co-workers).

Identifying where agency goals do overlap and emphasizing those areas initially may provide a positive starting point. However, this may take some work because areas of disagreement are much easier to identify than areas of agreement.

It is often more effective to support and empower clients to deal directly with the other agency than to act as the go-between. The case manager may not place much credence in the employment specialist saying that Lynn is interested in and entitled to employment because that is presumably the employment specialist's role. But if Lynn repeatedly says she wants a job (perhaps with coaching from the employment specialist) and other clients are saying it too, the case manager (or program manager or agency director) will eventually start hearing that message.

When the leaders and staff from both agencies agree on the reasons for and the process of change, the changes work best. To the degree that it is possible to get directors and supervisors involved with the team-building process (along with direct-service staff), the change will be easier to make and longer lasting.

The employment specialist may find it helpful to relate theories to specifics, so that instead of talking about "changing from a medical to a rehabilitative approach" or "moving everyone out of the day program into the community," he talks about specific changes such as moving two staff members out of day treatment and into employment, or working with five clients who are interested in employment over the next 6 months. Often people are fearful because they are pic-

---

[1]This discussion has been adapted by permission from Marrone, J. (1990). *Supported employment for persons with long-term mental illness.* St. Paul: Minnesota Division of Rehabilitation Services Support Employment.

Table 1. Building a relationship with another agency or branch

Picture the ideal relationship.	Identify overlapping goals among all those involved.
Develop a relationship between agencies.	
Empower and work through the clients.	Relate theories to specifics.
Share information with all involved participants.	Involve the management.
Show or share success with all involved participants.	Jointly solve problems.
	Expect change to be slow.

turing a different reality, one that may require frightening changes. It is important for the other agency's staff to understand exactly what is being suggested.

It is also important for employment specialists to understand that other agencies may lack the resources, skills, or manpower to provide what is needed. As the employment specialist begins to visit other agencies and gets to know the other professionals, he can identify possible approaches to joint resource development.

Organizational change happens slowly, and there are often environmental pressures (e.g., competition for funding, contracts that require incompatible outcomes) that interfere with the development of interagency cooperation. However, if the result of that cooperation will be that more people with mental illness will achieve their vocational goals, then it is well worth investing the time and effort.

Working Effectively as a Team

Marrone (1990) developed the following guidelines to help team members work effectively:

- Team activities should be approached with the assumption that everyone has things to *learn from each other*, rather than assuming the employment specialist

*"Yesterday they fought about what's 'important,'
today they are fighting about what's 'reasonable.'"*

One of the biggest interagency issues is a lack of agreement on goals and priorities, or even on what is reasonable.

knows everything and is there to educate the others. This encourages and supports full participation by all team members.

- Effective teams have a *networking* function by which the members expand the knowledge base available in the team by reaching out to other people and entities that may be useful. Thus, the power of the team reaches beyond the individuals who are actively involved.
- *Avoiding turf issues,* those related to maintaining the status quo and minimizing any changes in one's own operations, is a necessary step to providing good support. Positive collaboration involves identifying client-related problems that need to be addressed and finding ways to ensure that everyone can assist without looking for ways to exclude other players or to avoid responsibility.
- Everyone involved in a support team must learn to *accept ambiguity* because client issues are often complicated and may not all be resolved at the same time. No one can work effectively as part of a team while expecting clear answers to all the questions about roles, funding, and client needs before feeling comfortable in moving ahead.
- A functioning team is built on *relationships among people,* not among agencies. In other words, to the degree that the employment specialist believes there is a VR counselor that he can count on to understand what the client is trying to accomplish, the employment specialist will believe that he has a good working relationship with vocational rehabilitation. Whether the employment specialist's agency and the vocational rehabilitation agency have an official working agreement is much less important than the personal relationship between the individual practitioners. Maintaining these relationships can be a challenge when working in a field in which there is high turnover. Frequent contacts, even brief ones, are probably more useful in maintaining relationships than longer, more infrequent visits.
- Although it is important to cultivate personal relationships with other team members, the team must remember that *client gains are the most important issue.* If the emphasis is on good relationships among team members, there is a tendency not to want to put the other professionals in a difficult spot or to push them too much. There may be a desire to avoid testing the relationship by working with clients who are considered marginal in one or both systems. For example, an employment specialist has been cultivating a relationship with a particular mental health case manager. At this point the employment specialist wants to find a job for a client named Sue, but the case manager believes that Sue is not yet ready for competitive employment. How hard can the employment specialist push the case manager to support Sue in a job without jeopardizing the relationship he has been developing? How does he balance his responsibility to Sue with his need to continue to work with the case manager?
- It is important to *define whose need is being met by a given action.* Although the majority of the team's actions should support the needs of the client, there are times when the needs of a given agency or support team member need to take precedence. For example, VR counselors must have a certain number or percentage of successful closures over time. Even counselors who are willing to take chances on clients with more severe disabilities must have some successful placements for balance. Therefore, when considering which client to offer a job opening to, the employment specialist may decide to prioritize a client who has a very good chance of success over another client who has been waiting longer

but has a lower chance of being successful, because the last three clients referred to vocational rehabilitation were high risks and not successful. This is not to say that the client who is a higher risk should never have a high priority for a job opening. There are simply times when agencies and service providers make decisions that may not be the first choice of a given client at a given time, but will keep their agency healthy and stable in order to continue providing services.

BUILDING AND USING INDIVIDUAL SUPPORT TEAMS

What Is an Individual Support Team?

There are several things that define the kind of support team needed by many people with long-term mental illness. The people on the team hold a common purpose: to assist the client in achieving her goals. Each team member possesses particular expertise and is responsible for making individual decisions. Whether all team members ever meet together, they share knowledge and information from which plans are made, actions are determined, and future decisions are implemented.

Team members are often recruited individually and their services provided one-to-one rather than in group meetings. Therefore, a client can have a support team without ever having all the people involved together in one room. Group meetings can be useful to share information efficiently, to give a feeling of progress and effort, and sometimes to overcome resistance through information and encouragement. However, they are often logistically difficult to arrange and may overwhelm the client or others involved.

Working in teams should not be a way to avoid individual responsibility, delay action, or stake out agency turf. Rather, using a team approach makes it possible to share responsibilities and resources, take advantage of individual strengths, and expedite action.

Support Team Guidelines

Start with the Existing Informal Support System   The client may already have a strong or potentially strong informal support system on which a support team can build. When support teams are in the initial stage of development, those involved tend to think *first* about paid service providers such as the employment specialist, the mental health counselor, and the residential provider. In some cases paid service providers may be the only ones available to provide support because the client may not have relationships with others in the community. However, in other cases the client may need only better coordination of those already involved.

A Variety of People Should Be Involved   Unless there is no other choice, paid service providers should not be the only participants in the support team. Most people without disabilities do not look to paid providers when in need of support, relying instead on their friends, family, co-workers, and neighbors to pitch in and do what is needed. In developing teams to provide support to an individual with mental illness, every effort should be made to include families and other community-based resources.

Support Teams Must Be Client Centered   Ideally, support teams are client centered and allow the client to take the directive role in encouraging and directing the team's operations. At the very least, the client should be encouraged and taught to be active in planning and managing the activities of the support team.

Decide Who Should Take the Lead Role   Because most people who are involved in supported employment are not able to manage their own support, it is usually necessary for someone else to take the lead role. This person could be the employment specialist, the case manager, or a family member. This team manager takes responsibility for supporting the client in identifying and operationalizing goals. Although active management is often necessary for productivity, the best team managers use only as much authority as necessary. They also play an important role in providing reinforcement to all team members and encouraging the client to do the same.

Who Should Be Included in an Individual Support Team?

Involvement of other team members depends on the individual situation and may include any or all of the following people.

Family Members   Family members often have a lifetime association with the client and may provide powerful support, or they may be a significant obstacle to the client's employment. Although some people with long-term mental illness are estranged from their families, many others continue to have contact with family members and are strongly influenced by them.

Vocational Rehabilitation Counselors   Vocational rehabilitation counselors are generally involved with clients for only a brief period (at least in comparison to mental health providers) and limit their involvement to vocational activities. They are, however, valuable resources for information about employment issues and may have financial resources for employment efforts.

Job Coaches   The job coach is generally a person who provides job placement and training during the initial period and brings specific vocational expertise to the team. He may be funded by vocational rehabilitation, by the client through a PASS, by a block mental health grant, or through Title 19 Medicaid dollars.

Mental Health Case Managers   The case manager is often a key figure in terms of making decisions and providing support. He may eventually be the person who provides long-term support once the job coach or employment specialist has faded out. Many case managers are most familiar with the medical model of treatment

Family members can provide powerful support.

for mental illness and may need education and reinforcement to become committed to employment as a rehabilitation activity. They may also have large caseloads, which make it difficult for them to provide intensive and broad-based support or to be preventive rather than reactive.

Mental Health Counselors   Mental health counselors provide psychological support and therapy. Like case managers, counselors may or may not be familiar with a rehabilitative approach to services and may be concerned about the possible destabilizing effects of employment.

Medical Personnel   Medical personnel (e.g., nurses, physicians, psychiatrists) may be involved to monitor and adjust medication. This person may or may not be associated with the mental health center. Medical personnel may not value work and may be more interested in helping their clients to avoid stress. However, the right medical person can assist in adjusting medication for the highest benefit and the lowest side effects and in making adjustments in medication as challenging events arise.

Friends   Friends who are themselves employed and have an understanding of what it takes to maintain employment can offer emotional support, strategies for dealing with obstacles, and social and recreational opportunities that are compatible with employment.

Employers and/or Co-workers   Employers and co-workers may be involved, especially when employment is being resumed after a period of illness. Each client will need to determine how comfortable she is asking for support from people at work.

Social Security Representatives   Social Security representatives are not often thought of as active members of a support team. However, they can make an important contribution in helping develop plans for future support and working with disincentives. Given that a fear of losing benefits is one of the biggest obstacles to employment experienced by many people with long-term mental illness, it is very important to begin to include Social Security as an integral part of support teams.

Residential Providers   People who live in group homes (congregate care facilities), adult foster homes, tenant support, or other residential programs will benefit from the inclusion of residential providers on the support team because the kind of support people receive at home can "make or break" employment efforts. Assistance in preparing for work, managing medication, and rescheduling other activities around work can be crucial.

Community Resources   People who are involved in recreation, education, religion, and other areas of the community may provide important activities and support. This could involve adult literacy, supported education, representative payees, or a variety of other types of support.

Peer Support Groups   Peer support groups are usually sponsored by the mental health center and can be invaluable through periods of transition. Clients often are more comfortable with others who have experienced mental illness because they are peers facing similar challenges.

Significant Others   Who else is important in this person's life? Any significant person in the client's life may be an important component of the support team.

Managing Individual Support Teams

As the team manager, the employment specialist has the responsibility to ensure that the client receives the support she needs to be successful. Managing a support team is not much different from any other type of behavior management—the employment specialist needs to understand the environment, specify the desired behavior, and make sure that reinforcement follows. The following key approaches (see Table 2) will help the employment specialist in his task.

Stay Creative   The team manager must stay creative when enlisting and working with team members. He must not get so comfortable working with the same practitioners that he overlooks possible supporters from the work, home, and other environments. The best person to provide a particular type of support may be a neighbor, the minister, or the guy behind the counter at the donut shop, rather than a paid service provider.

Have Clear Goals   The team manager must have clear medium- and short-term goals. These goals should be developed by, or at least with, the client to the extent possible and remain subject to change. The team manager must remember that clients may need assistance in learning how to determine and set goals. Once these goals are set, it is important that all the team members know them and are updated immediately when a change occurs.

Understand the Issues   The team manager must understand the goals, agendas, and reinforcers affecting other team members. For example, the vocational rehabilitation counselor may be most interested in a successful closure. The mental health counselor wants the client to be stable, whether or not she is employed. The residential provider wants an empty house during the day. The client's wife may want to maximize the income coming to the family. These goals may or may not coincide with what the client wants to do, but they all need to be recognized and incorporated if possible. A good starting place for team activities may be to identify goals that are clearly already shared by team members.

Be Clear and Specific About Responsibilities   The team manager should be clear and specific about what each team member needs to do to achieve the agreed-upon goal. These responsibilities should be put in writing after the meeting or telephone call and sent to all the team members involved. It often happens that different people in the same meeting will come away with different understandings of what is to happen, or someone involved will forget that he or she agreed to do something. Written follow-up serves both as a reminder and as documentation.

Assign Small Steps   It may be necessary to assign small steps to team members if they have a great deal to learn and experience. The vocational rehabilitation counselor who is wary of working with people with long-term mental illness may need to start with clients who are very likely to be successful before moving on to those who are more challenging.

Table 2.   Managing individual support teams

Stay creative in using team members.
Have clear goals.
Understand the issues that affect other team members.
Be clear and specific about responsibilities.
Assign small steps if necessary.
Provide feedback and reinforcement.
Model good team-member skills.
Use facilitation skills.
Deal gently with resistance.
Deal directly with poor follow-through.
Maintain the team's energy.
Plan for relapses and other setbacks.
Stay focused on the goal of client achievement.

Provide Feedback and Reinforcement   The team manager must provide feedback and reinforcement to team members or help the client learn to do it. The ultimate reinforcer is seeing the client achieve her goals, but meanwhile any progress toward that goal should be recognized and reinforced. It is important to celebrate even small achievements.

Model Good Team-Member Skills   The team manager should use good team-member skills to model supportive behavior. Habits such as rushing in late or leaving early, insisting on a particular agenda, never having a chance to gossip or exchange small talk, often talking about the pressures he or his agency is under, not returning telephone calls promptly, or making every request to do something seem like a major imposition are all signals that the other members of the group are not valued.

Use Facilitation Skills   Good facilitation skills should be used with other team members. The typical employment specialist has excellent skills in dealing with other people because of his experiences with clients, employers, and family members. However, employment specialists sometimes forget to use these excellent skills on their fellow service providers. These skills include such things as showing empathy, accepting who and where the other person is, actively listening, being available, being clear on objectives for each meeting or conversation, being specific and using behavioral descriptions, sharing feelings, and choosing language appropriate to each person's style.

Deal Gently with Resistance   The team members must remember that resistance has its function. People use it to protect things they value (e.g., their self-image, comfortable paradigms), to keep from letting themselves be overloaded, or to allow themselves to make clearer choices by narrowing what they are willing to consider. It is not effective to deal with resistance through threats, coercion, selling, reasoning, deflecting, ignoring, attempting to induce guilt, or dismissing it as unimportant. Below are four effective ways to work with resistance:

1. The first step is to try to get the person to talk about the resistance, making expression as safe as possible. If people are resistant to the goals or activities of the support team, that resistance will be there whether it is made public or not. If the resistance and the reasons are open, the team may be able to determine what approach to take.
2. The next step is to listen and gain information, not only about what the resistor wants but also about who he is. Team members must acknowledge the resistance and affirm the right to resist: "I see how that could be a problem for you" or "You certainly have a right to be concerned." It is important to remember that showing an understanding of what someone is saying is not the same as agreeing with it.
3. It may be useful to explore the resistance by determining whether it really has to do with the issue at hand or if it originates from other things, such as resentment of authority or a need for attention. Team members should clarify the objection by trying to get the resistor to state it clearly. If the objection remains fuzzy despite repeated attempts at clarification, it is probably not related to the issue at hand.
4. The final step is to clarify desirable alternatives. This means asking, "What would you prefer?" A sincere attempt should be made to try to arrive at a solution or approach with which everyone can live.

Once resistance is at a workable level, the team manager should thank the resistor and move on. It is important not to try to persuade the resistor to like the proposed change. It is enough that the resistor is willing to agree to it. Team members should keep in mind that the positive side of resistance is the energy it brings to the proceedings. People who care enough to actively resist change can be a powerful proponent once they feel comfortable in moving to the other side.

Deal Directly with Poor Follow-Through Just as he would with a behavior change program that was not working as planned, the team manager may need to examine why a team member is not following through with agreed-upon action steps. Are the steps too big? For example, maybe the family member is not ready to help the client fill out job applications, but he could help her develop a list of possible employers. Is there no agreement on a goal? For example, maybe the case manager has not followed through on a referral to vocational rehabilitation because he does not really agree with the goal of employment for this client. Are there competing reinforcers, or are the reinforcers too small? For example, the physician may not care if the client gets a job, and therefore it is not worth the time he would have to put in to identify the lowest possible medication dose. Are there circumstances that make it difficult for the person to do what he has agreed to do? For example, the vocational rehabilitation counselor may truly like to provide financial support, but he has just been informed that his funding is exhausted for the rest of the year. If the possible reasons have been identified and remedied where possible and a team member still is not following through, it may be necessary to work around or replace that person. Are there others on or off the team who could provide that particular type of support? Are there other practitioners in that agency who could take over the client?

Maintain the Team's Energy The team manager and client must understand that it will take energy to maintain the team, because even desired changes are not always enough to keep up the effort. An effective team manager often functions as a promoter and public relations specialist, sharing successes and providing reinforcement.

Plan for Relapses or Other Setbacks Support teams must plan for relapses or other setbacks, especially at the point when the client is stabilized and the support team moves into the long-term follow-up phase. The plan should identify who is called for support and assistance, how other team members will be brought in, who is responsible for keeping the team members up-to-date, what action should be taken if other team members are the first to become concerned (family members often notice symptoms of impending decompensation), and who will be the ongoing contact to arrange support. These questions should be answered by and for team members.

Stay Focused on the Goal of Client Achievement Teams must be client centered and remain focused on the goal of client achievement. This focus will make it possible to minimize disputes over control and responsibility and maximize the potential strengths to be found among team members. They can stretch and coordinate scarce resources and support the movement toward using paid providers to augment and coordinate resources already available in the community. Most importantly, well-managed teams can best provide coordinated and consistent support, increasing the chance that people with disabilities will be able to achieve their employment goals.

CONCLUSION

Although active interdisciplinary support teams can be a lot of work to arrange and maintain, they are immensely valuable because the whole is greater than the sum of the parts. Support teams can contribute both to client progress and to the education of other professionals about the value of employment as a rehabilitation focus.

23

TROUBLE IN PARADISE

For the last 6 months Matt had been employed at the local gourmet coffee store. He enjoyed his job duties, which included restocking the shelves with gift items and the bins with freshly roasted coffee beans, assembling and wrapping the gift baskets, weighing and packaging bulk coffee, and helping customers when things got busy. The initial concerns of the shop owner, Jean, had been alleviated by Matt's excellent attendance and quality of work. The fact that Matt needed reassurance and praise several times a day seemed like a small price to pay.

One day Terry, the employment specialist who helped Matt and Jean during the first few weeks of the job, received a frantic telephone call from Jean. "Matt's not at work, and he was not here yesterday either. I tried to call him but there's no answer. I really need him here at the shop, and besides I'm worried about him. He's been working really slowly lately, talking to himself a lot, and snapping at us when we tried to tell him he needs to work faster. What's going on?"

"Beats me," thought Terry to herself as she mentally ran through a list of the possible problems. Problems with the girlfriend? Decompensating? Less reinforcement from Jean? Not getting along with the person who works at the counter? Bored with the job? Changes in the job expectations—maybe the shop's getting busier? "Whatever it is," she thought, "the first thing I need to do is find Matt and see what he has to say."

Not even the worker most well matched with a job can be expected to work happily in that same job from graduation to retirement. Wool (1990) pointed out that instability in employment is to be expected and is a part of healthy career growth for everyone. Unfortunately, workers with long-term mental illness often find that changes in the work environment, physical health, job tasks, or other work or nonwork areas may adversely affect job performance, work relationships, or the ability to tolerate stress. In addition, these individuals typically struggle with the unpredictable financial, residential, transportation, and child care problems that challenge all those who live at or below the poverty line.

The long-term support that is by definition part of supported employment can assist individuals with mental illness in dealing with problems that arise after placement and stabilization. In many cases, routine follow-up systems (see Chapter 21) assist in identifying and avoiding potential problems, but in some cases issues will slip past the early warning system and the employment specialist will be called on to troubleshoot, to deal with an ongoing crisis, or to assist a client in moving through and beyond a job loss.

TROUBLESHOOTING

The Success Through Employment Program (STEP), a supported work program serving people with mental illness, in St. Paul, Minnesota, has identified the following four common problem areas faced by clients who have a long-term mental illness (Botterbusch, 1989):

1. Problems dealing with co-workers (especially misinterpreting social behavior)
2. Learning to recognize signs of decompensation and taking action to circumvent it
3. Managing medication
4. Managing nonwork problems in a way that enables continued employment

Developing problems may be signaled by work avoidance (e.g., tardiness, absences); changes in the language or nonverbal behavior used by the employer, the co-workers, or the worker; or changes in the job environment or routine.

*"Ralph, you've worked for this company
for 50 years...what on Earth is wrong with you?"*

Not even the most well-matched worker can be expected to work happily in the same job from graduation to retirement.

A more general list was cited in Fadely (1987), who listed six problem areas often experienced by people with various disabilities who were working in supported employment programs. These include the following:

1. Low work rate and/or quality
2. Poor time management on the job
3. Tardiness or absenteeism
4. Poor social interactions
5. Poor grooming
6. Change in management on the job

No matter what the issue is, the employment specialist's first task is to assist the worker and employer to accurately identify the problem. It is important to start by getting those involved to be as specific as possible. What exactly is the concern? When is it happening (or not happening)? How often? Under what circumstances? Each person who is party to the situation may have a different opinion about the issue and the reasons for it. The real problem may not be the first one mentioned. For example, when Jean called the employment specialist to say she was worried about Matt's stress level she may have actually been even more concerned about his very low productivity and the effect that it was having on others in the workplace.

When possible, it is often useful for the employment specialist to spend time in the environment where the problem is occurring (whether at the workplace or somewhere else) to observe the current situation and note any changes that have occurred since the initial job acquisition period. However, there will be times when the employment specialist will be troubleshooting from a distance because

"Bob...exciting news...
we're all pitching in to send Doris on vacation!"

The real problem may not be the first thing that is mentioned.

the worker has acquired and learned the job independently, possibly without disclosing his disability. This can be frustrating for the employment specialist, especially after trying to deal with repeated job difficulties with only the worker's account of the problems. The employment specialist may end up trying to encourage the worker to let the employment specialist get involved on site, or eventually trying to take a more active role in the next job placement for that individual.

Once the problem(s) has been isolated and identified, the worker and employment specialist (and perhaps the employer) work together to develop a plan to improve the situation. Fadely (1987) suggested the following guidelines for plan development:

Examine any underlying causes. What are the environmental circumstances? What is going on in other parts of the client's life or in other parts of the job? What has changed besides the client's job performance and/or behavior?

Prioritize the problems that need attention. Often there are several things that need attention and it may be necessary to choose which to intervene on first and address others at a later time.

Know the client. Knowledge of the worker's history, cognitive and verbal ability, emotional makeup, strengths and limitations, available support, and short- and long-term goals will assist the employment specialist in developing an effective approach. If the client is new to the employment specialist, perhaps because he was transferred from another agency for long-term support, the employment specialist must try to get information from previous support providers and spend time with the client (on the job if possible). The way in which this knowledge is gained depends on the functional level of the client, the availability of referral information, and the relationship of the employment specialist to the jobsite.

Know the employer and the jobsite. The more the employment specialist knows about the jobsite and employer, the more assistance she can provide to the employer and worker. In some cases, the employment specialist may know only what the worker has shared with her, while in other cases she may be able to work closely with those on the worksite to make a plan.

Be aware of limitations. The employment specialist must be aware of time and attention demands that compete with the current needs of the client. In some cases, the employment specialist may not have the expertise or ability to intervene in a given area (e.g., medication management). In these cases, good interdisciplinary team building is necessary, and the employment specialist must be able to enlist the support and efforts of other service providers, advocates, and/or family members.

Remember that it is the match between the worker and the job that is problematic, not necessarily the worker's behavior. In some cases, the employment specialist may be able to help the worker to change his behavior in order to maintain the job. At other times, it may be most beneficial to assist the worker to negotiate changes in job requirements or to help him leave his current job and obtain another one.

Creativity may be required. A thorough knowledge of the worker's assets and potential support systems as well as of the demands of the job will allow the employment specialist to come up with creative, individualized solutions to difficult situations. Often the best solutions are entirely idiosyncratic; that is, they would only work in this particular situation because of the unique individuals and demands involved.

Dealing with problem employment situations can involve any of the teaching or behavior change approaches (see Chapters 15–17). It may also be helpful to restructure the job or certain tasks involved, to provide advocacy on or off the job, or to use counseling-type strategies (i.e., active listening, "I" statements) to help the worker analyze and change his own behavior. Contracts may also be used effectively with many workers.

Figure 1 is a post-fading intervention worksheet, which may be useful in analyzing problem areas and selecting an intervention strategy. Powell et al. (1991) also suggested that before choosing a decision-making approach the employment specialist should consider whether the plan needs to be 1) made quickly, 2) of high quality, or 3) implemented by a group of people.

CRISIS INTERVENTION

For employment specialists who are unfamiliar with mental health issues, one of the most worrisome aspects is the possibility of having to deal with a full-blown crisis on the job. Although this happens far less often than many people assume, the variable nature of long-term mental illness makes it a possibility for some clients. Fortunately, a proactive approach will enable the employment specialist and the worker to act on most problems before they become crises.

Work with the Client

First, the employment specialist should work with the client to make sure he has support for nonwork issues. What would happen if he had a fight with his girlfriend and had to move out of their apartment? If he failed to get his Social Security check? If his car broke down? An employment specialist must remember that not all crises faced by workers with mental illness are related to their mental illness. Helping people develop a strong system for dealing with nonwork issues will result in fewer of those issues affecting the job.

Set Up an Early Warning System

Second, the worker and the employment specialist should set up an early warning system to watch for changes in mental health or illness management. In most cases, crises are preceded by increased tension, anxiety, nervousness, and other similar symptoms. Very few people decompensate with absolutely no warning. Developing and using a symptom checklist or other assessment approach can help the worker and those around him be sensitive to the early signs of change. Encouraging the person to continue to participate in medication management, mental health counseling, or support groups makes it even more likely that early changes will be noticed and the needed support will be provided.

Understand the Individual's Behavior Patterns

Third, it is important to understand the behavior patterns unique to each client. What happens when this person decompensates? Some people may become agitated or aggressive, while others may simply refuse to get out of bed. The type of

POST-FADING INTERVENTION WORKSHEET

Part 1:   Identifying the problem

1.   Who has identified that there is a problem? What does that person say is wrong?

2.   What do others say about the situation? Have you considered checking with the supervisor, co-workers, or family members (with the worker's permission)?

3.   How do current job demands compare with those outlined in the original job analysis? Are the expectations identical?

4.   Is the volume of work identical to that outlined in the original job analysis? Look for increased work loads with no changes in the time to complete them.

5.   Has the worker recently made any significant changes at work (e.g., additional tasks, new machinery, additional responsibilities)?

6.   Have there been changes in key supervisors or co-workers since the problem began? Are new individuals aware of worker characteristics and any ongoing support arrangements?

7.   Do you sense underlying social interaction difficulties between the consumer and other individuals at work? Could they be contributing to the situation?

8.   Is the worker clearly aware of employer expectations for job performance? Look for subtle changes in what the consumer believes to be adequate performance compared with earlier times?

9.   Is the feedback the consumer receives for job performance sufficient to distinguish among unacceptable, barely acceptable, and outstanding work?

(continued)

Figure 1.   A post-fading intervention worksheet for an employment specialist who finds herself in a crisis situation. (Adapted by permission from John P. Dineen [1990].)

Figure 1. *(continued)*

10. Is the feedback on job performance the consumer receives sufficient to motivate him? Would a change in feedback/reinforcement levels contribute to solving the situation?

11. Would direct data gathering further clarify the situation? Have you considered:
    Observing the worksite?
    Collecting descriptive data on co-workers?
    Checking written records (e.g., production)?

12. Does the consumer seem less able to perform the job? Could this be due to:
    Changes in health?
    Reaction to stress?
    Loss of motivation?
    Problems outside work?
    Medication changes?
    Disability-related changes?
    Substance abuse?

13. Everybody eventually needs job changes. Could the worker be ready for a different job?

14. Restate the problem as you now understand it.

Part 2: Developing strategies

1. Is there a need to provide additional training to the worker on the job? If yes, what is the projected amount of time required?

2. Would social skills training facilitate better co-worker or supervisor interactions?

3. Would efforts aimed at improving the worker's ability to participate in social activities at the employment site help resolve the situation?

(continued)

Figure 1. *(continued)*

4. Are there problems in the worker's life outside work that need to be addressed? If yes, who will do it?

5. Is there a need for the worker to become involved in ongoing, outside support activities such as counseling, recreational activities, or peer support groups?

6. Are there changes in the client's work schedule or responsibilities that can be negotiated with the employer?

7. Does the worker require additional or improved feedback?

8. Does the employer need more training in methods of supporting the worker?

9. Could co-workers be taught better methods of supporting the worker?

10. Could efforts toward better integration of the worker be rewarded and/or supported?

11. Would better interagency cooperation or coordination reduce the effects of the issue?

12. Would it be helpful to work on the attitudes and assumptions of the worker's mental health providers, family, or residential service providers?

Part 3: Selecting a strategy

1. Based on the information available, what steps could be taken to resolve the situation?

(continued)

Figure 1.   *(continued)*

2.   Are there too many potential solutions to implement at once? If yes, prioritize them.

3.   Is there a way of measuring or assessing the success of a solution?

4.   Will participants need additional training to implement the situation? If so, how will they get it?

5.   How long will the strategy be used before it is evaluated for its effectiveness? Be cautious about abandoning potential solutions before they have a chance to work.

6.   What options are available if the proposed strategy fails?

Part 4: Maintaining your successes

1.   Does the success of the strategy depend on a single individual? If so, how might the responsibility be spread out or additional individuals be taught what to do?

2.   Are communication channels open and functioning well among significant individuals in the successful strategy?

3.   Are significant individuals committed to maintaining the change? What types of feedback or reinforcement could maintain *their* participation?

4.   Did you document your efforts in a manner that will help the next employment specialist avoid your mistakes?

5.   Is there a schedule of checks with or on the worker that will catch future problems before they become job threatening?

behavior that is most likely will determine the plan that is developed for dealing with crises. The behavior that has precipitated the crisis may have little to do with the person's illness. Matt may be having trouble expressing anger appropriately because he has poor skills, not because he is decompensating.

Know the Policies and Procedures

Fourth, the employment specialist should know her agency's policies and procedures for dealing with crises on the job. When does the employment specialist deal with it herself? When does she call for backup from another employment specialist or the case manager? When does she call 911? Talking through these issues ahead of time will help everyone deal with them if they arise.

Additional Training May Be Needed

Fifth, an employment specialist who is providing support to individuals with a past history of aggressive behavior may want to get some training in physical restraint and release approaches such as the Mandt System.[1] Knowing that she can handle a physically challenging situation will increase the employment specialist's confidence.

Negotiate with the Employer in Advance

Sixth, it is often wise to negotiate with the employer ahead of time about the potential need for the worker to take a brief leave of absence should his illness become worse. Will the job remain open for the person? For how long? Will it need to be covered? Having these issues discussed in advance will mean one less thing for the worker and the employment specialist to worry about if a crisis *does* arise.

When the early warning system fails and the employment specialist is called in to deal with a full-blown crisis on the job, the short-term goal is to resolve the situation in such a way that no one is injured and the worker can leave the work situation as gracefully as possible in order to maintain his access to the job. Although a crisis can eventually lead to growth, the middle of the crisis is not the time for troubleshooting or behavior change. A person who is in crisis is unable to deal with the environment in the usual way and needs reassurance that control exists, even if he cannot demonstrate it at the moment.

People who are in crisis often respond best to limited eye contact, a calm voice tone, and repetitive speech using short words. It may help if the employment specialist validates feelings using statements such as "It's okay to be upset," but in general it is best for her to remain somewhat formal rather than being extremely warm and friendly. Offering threats, promises, and deals is usually not helpful.

Table 1 summarizes five stages of crises and appropriate strategies for each.

COMMON PROBLEMS AND REASONS FOR JOB LOSS

There is little research on the reasons people with long-term mental illness lose or leave community-based jobs. Many of the early employment programs were intentionally designed to be short term (i.e., transitional employment) or to provide flexible working conditions that could accommodate variable productivity levels (e.g.,

---

[1]Additional information on training in physical restraint and release approaches such as the Mandt System is available from David Mandt and Associates, Post Office Box 1921, Richardson, Texas, 75080; 214-495-0755.

Table 1. Crisis stages and strategies for an employment specialist

Behavior level	Cues	Strategies
Anxiety—intense feelings of fear or dread	Stuttering, giggling, talking a lot, withdrawing, pacing, rocking, changes in body language	Supportive reassurance: Be positive, smile. Increase self-esteem. Allow release of feelings. Encourage participation in other support (e.g., counseling, peer groups). Have medication levels checked.
Changes in verbal and/or physical behavior	Sarcasm, refusal, name calling, blaming, interrupting, faster breathing, darting eyes, staring, increased pacing, pointing fingers	Validate feelings with clear, direct "I" statements. Disengage—give the person some space. Use voice and tone to control. Decrease stimulation. Distract.
Attacking or agitated—not responding to reason, at risk	Protesting, challenging, threatening, throwing things, pushing	Give him space. Protect yourself. Set enforceable limits. Do not negotiate. Know when to back down. Use silence until reinforcement comes.
Release/cool down	Remorseful, belittling of self, softer, slower speech, tired, decrease in eye contact	Do not rush to solve the problem.
Reflection—developing a plan for change	Acceptance, willingness to talk, repentant, increased eye contact, positive body language	Reflect on thoughts, actions, and feelings. Problem-solve. Plan for the future.

Fairweather Lodges, other entrepreneurial and sheltered work). There has been quite a bit of data collected on participants involved in the state systems-change grants, and subsequently in vocational rehabilitation–funded supported employment, but only 8%–12% of those participants have a primary diagnosis of mental illness. Job retention for workers with mental illness, although a crucial variable, has gotten little experimental attention (Bond & McDonel, 1991).

Fabian (1992) looked at "survival analysis" data for workers with mental illness and examined the rate at which people lost or left their jobs over time. The data showed that the largest percentage of job loss occurred in the first month of placement, when 16% of those placed lost their jobs. About one third of the group was still working at the same job after 2 years.

Anthony (1994b) reported that it is not a lack of vocational skills that most often causes job loss, but rather poor work adjustment skills (e.g., getting along, doing the job, being dependable). In contrast, Wehman et al. (1990) looked at 89 individuals with long-term mental illness in five different states who were placed into 205 community-based jobs. The most common reason for job loss was medical problems (i.e., mental or physical), which was credited for 15% of the losses. Following that, the reasons were quitting to take a better job (13%), deciding not to work at all (12%), poor job matching (10%), attendance/tardiness (8%), low-quality work (6%), layoffs (5%), working too slowly (5%), and eight other categories each representing less than 5%. Although the relatively small number of clients involved in this study makes it difficult to confidently assume that these are universal issues, it is interesting that poor work behavior accounted for a relatively small number of job losses. Cook (1992) had similar findings looking at the reasons 252 adults with mental illness left jobs; the most common reason was advancement to a better job (19%), followed by symptom recurrence (18%), inability to do job tasks (18%), poor job environment (16%), and poor motivation (10%).

It is important to remember that job loss, while it may have a negative effect on the vocational agency, can actually be a positive move for the worker. Many workers with long-term mental illness are beginning their career development a decade or two behind their peers, and to some degree can be expected to go through the same progression of relatively short-term, unskilled jobs before perhaps settling into a more advanced position (MacDonald-Wilson, Revell, Nguyen, & Peterson, 1991). The employment specialist may be able to assist an unskilled or reluctant employer in terminating a worker in a way that is as positive as possible; that is, the worker is both reinforced for his efforts and given clear information about the reasons for termination.

It has been noted by several researchers that increased effort in the career development and job identification phase of supported employment may result in improved long-term retention. Mcloughlin et al. (1987) pointed out that many people with disabilities have little choice as to the type of work they might prefer—

"This is not a good sign!"

It is also important to understand the behavior patterns unique to the individual.

often the only choice is to take any job that is open or stay in day treatment. There are some cases when a worker will express his preference by becoming a regular job placement failure until the job he really wants comes along.

It is worthwhile for employment programs to keep some records on reasons for job loss, listing all the factors that seem to have been contributors as well as the timing of the termination. This information can lead to the identification of unmet support needs or insufficient skills on the part of individual workers as well as pointing out program design issues. Discovering that most clients leave their placements to take better jobs would be wonderful news; discovering that most clients lose their jobs within the month after the employment specialist turns the person over to the case manager for follow-up would indicate a need for change in the way things are done.

Whether leaving a job is the decision of the worker or the employer, it is important to remember that job loss is a common part of the workplace for workers without disabilities as well as for workers with disabilities. Conceptualizing the employment process as long-term, focusing on job loss as a learning experience, and helping the client apply what has been learned to the next vocational goal or step will greatly reduce the trauma of job loss.

MATT, PART 2

Terry tracked Matt down at his girlfriend's house, and they spent a long time talking. Matt said that the job had gotten too busy, the new person who worked

"Johnson, I want to contribute to your education...you're fired!"

Focusing on job loss as a learning experience will greatly reduce the trauma of job loss.

at the counter kept telling Matt to do things that he didn't think he should have to do, and Jean was so busy with the new staff that she didn't have time to talk to Matt anymore. Matt started off saying that he wanted to quit, but agreed to return to the job if Terry would come with him for a few days. The next day Matt, Jean, and Terry sat down and talked, and with Matt's permission Terry shared some of his concerns. They reviewed Matt's job duties, and Jean agreed to review them with the counter staff. Terry helped Jean clarify how to measure whether Matt was working fast enough by specifying the amount of work she thought was reasonable. Jean and Matt also set three specific times every week, Monday and Friday mornings and Wednesday at lunchtime to have coffee and talk about how things were going.

CONCLUSION

Troubleshooting, crisis intervention, and dealing with job loss are important parts of the employment specialist's job. Understanding the issues involved in these activities will enable the employment specialist to provide better assistance in helping the worker maintain stability in employment. Recording and analyzing data on the reasons for job problems and job loss will enable employment program staff to improve the effectiveness of their program design.

BIBLIOGRAPHY

Akabas, S.H. (1994). Workplace responsiveness: Key employer characteristics in support of job maintenance for persons with mental illness. *Psychosocial Rehabilitation Journal, 17*(3), 91–102.

American Psychiatric Association. (1994). *Diagnostic and statistical manual of mental disorders* (4th ed.). Washington, DC: Author.

Americans with Disabilities Act of 1990 (ADA), PL 101-336. (July 26, 1990). Title 42, U.S.C. 12101 et seq: *U.S. Statutes at Large, 104,* 327–378.

Anderson, B., & Andrews, M. (1990). *Creating diversity: Organizing and sustaining workplaces that support employees with disabilities.* Sitka, AK: Center for Community.

Andreason, N.C. (1984). *The broken brain: The biological revolution in psychiatry.* New York: Harper & Row.

Anthony, W.A. (1982). Explaining "psychiatric rehabilitation" by an analogy to "physical rehabilitation." *Psychosocial Rehabilitation Journal, 5*(1), 61–65.

Anthony, W.A. (1994a). Characteristics of people with psychiatric disabilities that are predictive of entry into the rehabilitation process and successful employment outcomes. *Psychosocial Rehabilitation Journal, 17*(3), 3–14.

Anthony, W.A. (1994b). The vocational rehabilitation of people with severe mental illness: Issues and myths. *Innovations and Research, 3*(2), 17–24.

Anthony, W.A., & Blanch, A. (1987). Supported employment for persons who are psychiatrically disabled: An historical and conceptual perspective. *Psychosocial Rehabilitation Journal, XI*(2), 5–23.

Anthony, W.A., & Blanch, A. (1989). Research on community support services: What we have learned. *Psychosocial Rehabilitation Journal, 12*(3), 56–81.

Anthony, W.A., Buell, G.J., Shannatt, S., & Althoff, M.E. (1972). Efficacy of psychiatric rehabilitation. *Psychological Bulletin, 78,* 447–456.

Anthony, W.A., Cohen, M.R., & Danley, K.S. (1988). The psychiatric rehabilitation approach as applied in vocational rehabilitation. In J.A. Ciardello & M.D. Bell (Eds.), *Vocational rehabilitation of persons with prolonged psychiatric disorders* (pp. 59–80). Baltimore: The Johns Hopkins University Press.

Anthony, W.A., Cohen, M., & Farkas, M. (1990). *Psychiatric rehabilitation.* Boston: Center for Psychiatric Rehabilitation, Boston University.

Anthony, W.A., Cohen, M.R., & Vitalo, R.L. (1978). The measurement of rehabilitation outcomes. *Schizophrenia Bulletin, 4,* 365–383.

Anthony, W.A., Howell, J., & Danley, K. (1984). Vocational rehabilitation of the psychiatrically disabled. In M. Mirabi (Ed.), *The chronically mentally ill: Research and services.* New York: SP Medical & Scientific Books.

Anthony, W.A., & Jansen, M.A. (1984). Predicting the vocational capacity of the chronically mentally ill: Research and policy implications. *American Psychologist, 39*, 537–544.

Azrin, N.H., & Besalel, V.A. (1980). *Job club counselor's manual*. Baltimore: University Park Press.

Azrin, N.H., & Phillips, R.A. (1979). The job club method for the job handicapped: A comparative outcome study. *Rehabilitation Counseling Bulletin, 23*, 144–155.

Barcus, M., Brooke, V., Inge, K., Moon, S., & Goodall, P. (1987). *An instructional guide for training on a job site: A supported employment resource*. Richmond: Rehabilitation Research and Training Center, Virginia Commonwealth University.

Barker, J.T. (1988). Coordination of efforts between vocational rehabilitation and mental health systems. *1988 Switzer Monograph*, 48–61.

Beck, A.T., Freeman, A., & Associates. (1990). *Cognitive therapy of personality disorders*. New York: Guildford Press.

Bell, M.D., Milstein, R.M., & Lysaker, P.H. (1993). Pay and participation in work activity: Clinical benefits for clients with schizophrenia. *Psychosocial Rehabilitation Journal, 17*(3), 173–176.

Bellamy, G.T., O'Connor, G., & Karan, O.C. (Eds.). (1979). *Vocational rehabilitation of severely handicapped adults*. Baltimore: University Park Press.

Bellamy, G.T., Rhodes, L.E., Mank, D.M., & Albin, J.M. (1988). *Supported employment: A community implementation guide*. Baltimore: Paul H. Brookes Publishing Co.

Bingham, W.C. (1988). A vocational psychology perspective on rehabilitation. In J.A. Ciardiello & M.D. Bell (Eds.), *Vocational rehabilitation of persons with prolonged psychiatric disorders* (pp. 137–149). Baltimore: The Johns Hopkins University Press.

Black, B.J. (1988). *Work and mental illness*. Baltimore: The Johns Hopkins University Press.

Blatt, B. (1987). *The conquest of mental retardation*. Austin, TX: PRO-ED.

Bond, G.R. (1987). Supported work as a modification of the transitional employment model for clients with psychiatric disabilities. *Psychosocial Rehabilitation Journal, XI*(2), 55–73.

Bond, G.R., & Boyer, S.L. (1988). Rehabilitation programs and outcomes. In J.A. Ciardiello & M.D. Bell (Eds.), *Vocational rehabilitation of persons with prolonged psychiatric disorders* (pp. 231–263). Baltimore: The Johns Hopkins University Press.

Bond, G.R., & McDonel, E.C. (1991). Vocational rehabilitation outcomes for persons with psychiatric disabilities: An update. *Journal of Vocational Rehabilitation, 1*(3), 9–20.

Botterbusch, K.F. (1989). *Understanding community based employment and follow-up services*. Menomonie: Research and Training Center, Stout Vocational Rehabilitation Institute, University of Wisconsin–Stout.

Bourbeau, P. (1990). *Empowering facility employed supported employment personnel*. Presentation at first national conference of the Association for Persons in Supported Employment (APSE), Denver, CO.

Brown, M.A., & Basel, D. (1989). Understanding differences between mental health and vocational rehabilitation: A key to increased cooperation. *Journal of Psychosocial Rehabilitation, 12*(2), 23–33.

Buckley, J. (1990). *Training and support mechanics outline*. Seattle, WA: Center for Continuing Education in Rehabilitation, Seattle University.

Burnham-Thornton, P., & Graham, N. (1988). *Job development: Finding the right job for each individual*. Seattle: Office of Rehabilitative Studies, University of Washington.

Campbell, J.F. (1989). Employment programs for people with a psychiatric disability: An overview. *Community Support Network News, 6*(2), 1–11.

Campbell, J.F. (1991). The consumer movement and implications for vocational rehabilitation services. *Journal of Vocational Rehabilitation, 1*(3), 67–75.

Campinha-Bacote, J. (1991). Community mental health services for the underserved: A culturally specific model. *Archives of Psychiatric Nursing, V*(4), 229–235.

Coiner, R. (1990). *Supported work employment services summary evaluation report*. Salem: State Mental Health Division, Oregon Department of Human Resources.

Cook, J.A. (1992). Job ending among youth and adults with severe mental illness. *Journal of Mental Health Administration, 19*(2), 158–169.

Cook, J.A., Razzano, L.A., Straiton, D.M., & Ross, Y. (1994). Cultivation and maintenance of relationships with employers of persons with psychiatric disabilities. *Psychosocial Rehabilitation Journal, 17*(3), 103–116.

Cook, J.A., & Rosenberg, H. (1991). Predicting community employment among persons with psychiatric disability: A logistic regression analysis. *Journal of Rehabilitation Administration, 18*(1), 6–22.

Cook, J.A., Solomon, M., Jonikas, J., & Frazier, M.A. (1990). *Supported competitive employment program for youth with severe mental illness: Final report to the U.S. Department of Education.* Unpublished manuscript.

Cooper, L. (1993). Serving adults with psychiatric disabilities on campus: A mobile support approach. *Psychosocial Rehabilitation Journal, 17*(1), 25–38.

Danley, K., & Mellen, V. (1987). Training and personnel issues for supported employment programs which serve persons who are severely mentally ill. *Psychosocial Rehabilitation Journal, XI*(2), 88–102.

Danley, K.S., & Anthony, W.A. (1987). The choose-get-keep model: Serving severely psychiatrically disabled people. *American Rehabilitation, 13*(4), 6–9, 27–29.

Danley, K.S., Rogers, E.S., & Nevas, D.B. (1989). A psychiatric rehabilitation approach to vocational rehabilitation. In M.A. Farkas & W.A. Anthony (Eds.), *Psychiatric rehabilitation programs: Putting theory into practice* (pp. 81–131). Baltimore: The Johns Hopkins University Press.

Davis, D. (1990). Antisocial personality disorder. In A.T. Beck & A. Freeman (Eds.), *Cognitive therapy of personality disorders* (pp. 147–175). New York: Guilford Press.

DiLeo, D. (1991a). Corporate-sponsored supported employment increasing. *Supported Employment InfoLines, 2*(2), 1–3.

DiLeo, D. (1991b). Helping to solve on-the-job conflict: When supported employees and coworkers don't get along. *Supported Employment InfoLines, 2*(6), 4–5.

DiLeo, D. (1991c). Natural supports and integration: Beyond the buzz words into reality. *Supported Employment InfoLines, 2*(6), 1–3.

DiLeo, D. (1991d). Working with families to build support for SE experiences. *Supported Employment InfoLines, 2*(5), 1–3.

DiLeo, D. (1993). *Enhancing the lives of adults with disabilities: An orientation manual* (2nd ed.). St. Augustine, FL: Training Resource Network.

DiLeo, D., & Langton, D. (1993). *Get the marketing edge! A job developer's toolkit for people with disabilities.* St. Augustine, FL: Training Resource Network.

Dineen, J.P., Ford, L.H., & Oswald, S.I. (1994). *Meaningful career choices through community assessment.* Presentation at the Association for Persons in Supported Employment National Conference, San Francisco, CA.

Dougherty, S., Hastie, C., Bernard, J., Broadhurst, S., & Marcus, L. (1992). Supported education: A clubhouse experience. *Psychosocial Rehabilitation Journal, 16*(2), 91–104.

Douglas, R. (1994). The Americans with Disabilities Act after three years: Where are we? *Journal of Vocational Rehabilitation, 4*(3), 153–157.

Education for All Handicapped Children Act of 1975, PL 94-142. (August 23, 1977). Title 20, U.S.C. 1401 et seq: *U.S. Statutes at Large, 89,* 773–796.

Eisenberg, M.G., & Cole, H.W. (1986). A behavioral approach to job seeking for psychiatrically impaired persons. *Journal of Rehabilitation, 52*(2), 46–49.

Evans, K., & Sullivan, J.M. (1990). *Dual diagnosis: Counseling the mentally ill substance abuser.* New York: Guilford Press.

Fabian, E.S. (1992). Longitudinal outcomes in supported employment: A survival analysis. *Rehabilitation Psychology, 37*(1), 23–35.

Fabian, E.S., Luecking, R.G., & Tilson, G.P. (1994). *A working relationship: The job development specialist's guide to successful partnerships with business.* Baltimore: Paul H. Brookes Publishing Co.

Fabian, E.S., Waterworth, A., & Ripke, B. (1993). Reasonable accommodations for workers with serious mental illness: Type, frequency, and associated outcomes. *Psychosocial Rehabilitation Journal, 17*(2), 163–172.

Fadely, D.C. (1987). *Job coaching in supported work programs.* Menomonie: Materials Development Center, Stout Vocational Rehabilitation Institute, University of Wisconsin–Stout.

Farkas, M.D., Anthony, W.A., & Cohen, M.R. (1989). Psychiatric rehabilitation: The approach and its programs. In M.A. Farkas & W.A. Anthony (Eds.), *Psychiatric rehabilitation programs: Putting theory into practice* (pp. 1–27). Baltimore: The Johns Hopkins University Press.

Fifteenth Institute on Rehabilitation Issues. (1988). *Enhancing the rehabilitation of persons with long–term mental illness.* Fayetteville: Arkansas Research and Training Center in Vocational Rehabilitation.

Fisher, D. (1994). New vision of healing: A reasonable accommodation for consumers/survivors working as mental health service providers. *Psychosocial Rehabilitation Journal, 17*(3), 67–82.

Floyd, M. (1982). Employment problems of ex-psychiatric patients. *Employment Gazette, 90,* 21–27.

Ford, L.H., Dineen, J.P., & Codd, N. (1993, July). *Career development through supported employment for persons with long-term mental illness.* Unpublished manuscript from the Association for Persons in Supported Employment national conference presentation, Baltimore.

Ford, L.H., Dineen, J.P., & Hall, J.A. (1985). Is there life after placement? *Education and Training of the Mentally Retarded, 19,* 291–296.

Forest, M., & Pearpoint, J. (1992). Families, friends, and circles. In J. Nisbet (Ed.), *Natural supports in school, at work, and in the community for people with severe disabilities* (pp. 65–86). Baltimore: Paul H. Brookes Publishing Co.

Frey, J.L. (1994). Long term support: The critical element to sustaining competitive employment: Where do we begin? *Psychosocial Rehabilitation Journal, 17*(3), 127–134.

Furlong, M., Jonikas, J.A., Cook, J.A., Hathaway, L., & Goode, S.L. (1994). *Providing vocational services: Job coaching and ongoing support for persons with severe mental illness.* Chicago: Thresholds National Research and Training Center on Rehabilitation and Mental Illness.

Garner, J.B. (1989a). Going where the jobs are: Working within the business community. In M. Callahan (Ed.), *Supported employment training project manual III: Direct services* (pp. 57–69). Lexington: Interdisciplinary Human Development Institute, University of Kentucky.

Garner, J.B. (1989b). Issues in planning: A focus upon the needs of the individual. In M. Callahan (Ed.), *Supported employment training project manual III: Direct services* (pp. 1–28). Lexington: Interdisciplinary Human Development Institute, University of Kentucky.

Garner, J.B. (1989c). Ongoing support services: A question of commitment. In M. Callahan (Ed.), *Supported employment training project manual III: Direct services* (pp. 82–89). Lexington: Interdisciplinary Human Development Institute, University of Kentucky.

Gold, M. (1976). Task analysis of a complex assembly task by the retarded blind. *Exceptional Children, 43*(20), 78–84.

Gorman, J.M. (1990). *The essential guide to psychiatric drugs.* New York: St. Martin's Press.

Government Accounting Office. (1993). *Vocational rehabilitation: Evidence for federal program's effectiveness is mixed* (PEMD Publication No 93-19). Gaithersburg, MD: Author.

Griffin, C. (1992). Time and a studied approach needed for natural job supports. *Supported Employment InfoLines, 3*(2), 1–3.

Hagner, D.C. (1992). The social interactions and job supports of supported employees. In J. Nisbet (Ed.), *Natural supports in school, at work, and in the community for people with severe disabilities* (pp. 217–239). Baltimore: Paul H. Brookes Publishing Co.

Hagner, D.C., Cotton, P., Goodall, S., & Nisbet, J. (1992). The perspectives of supportive coworkers: Nothing special. In J. Nisbet (Ed.), *Natural supports in school, at work, and in the community for people with severe disabilities* (pp. 241–256). Baltimore: Paul H. Brookes Publishing Co.

Harding, C.M., Zubin, J., & Strauss, J.S. (1987). Chronicity in schizophrenia: Fact, partial fact, or artifact? *Hospital and Community Psychiatry, 38,* 477–486.

Henderson, M., & Argyle, M. (1985). Social support by four categories of work colleague: Relationships between activities, stress, and satisfaction. *Journal of Occupational Behavior (6),* 229–239.

Herz, M.I. (1984). Intermittent medication and schizophrenia. In J.M. Kane (Ed.), *Drug-maintenance strategies in schizophrenia* (pp. 51–68). Washington, DC: American Psychological Association.

Howie the Harp. (1994). Empowerment of mental health consumers in vocational rehabilitation. *Psychosocial Rehabilitation Journal, 17*(3), 83–90.

Human Services Research Institute. (1994). Survey of SE program administrators. *Supported Employment InfoLines*, 5(1), 7.

Hyde, A.P., & Goldman, C.R. (1993). Common family issues that interfere with the treatment and rehabilitation of people with schizophrenia. *Psychosocial Rehabilitation Journal*, 16(4), 63–74.

Idaho Easter Seal Society/Goodwill Industries. (1987). *Community supported employment—Job coach model*. Boise: Author.

Infants may give signs of schizophrenia. (March 30, 1992). *Seattle Times*, p. B1.

Isbister, F. (1992) Final OSERS SE rules. *Supported Employment InfoLines*, 3(7), 7.

Isbister, F., & Donaldson, A. (1987). Supported employment for individuals who are mentally ill: Program development. *Psychosocial Rehabilitation Journal*, 11(2), 45–54.

Jacobs, H.E., Kardashian, S., Kreinbring, R.K., Ponder, R., & Simpson, A. (1984). A skills-oriented model for facilitating employment among psychiatrically disabled persons. *Rehabilitation Counseling Bulletin*, 28, 87–96.

Jansen, M.A. (1988). The psychological and vocational problems of persons with chronic mental illness. In J.A. Ciardiello & M.D. Bell (Eds.), *Vocational rehabilitation of persons with prolonged psychiatric disorders* (pp. 35–46). Baltimore: The Johns Hopkins University Press.

Johnson, T.W. (1988). A family approach to rehabilitation. In J.A. Ciardiello & M.D. Bell (Eds.), *Vocational rehabilitation of persons with prolonged psychiatric disorders* (pp. 104–119). Baltimore: The Johns Hopkins University Press.

Judd, L.L., & Rapaport, M. (1994). A new antipsychotic medication for the treatment of schizophrenia. *Innovations & Research*, 3(1), 1–7.

Kane, J.M. (1988). The role of psychotropic medication in vocational rehabilitation. In J.A. Ciardiello & M.D. Bell (Eds.), *Vocational rehabilitation of persons with prolonged psychiatric disorders* (pp. 181–195). Baltimore: The Johns Hopkins University Press.

Kaufman-Rosen, L., & Springen, K. (1994, November 7). Who are the disabled? *Newsweek*, p. 80.

Kirsner, M.L., Baron, R.C., & Donegan, K. (1994). *Employer participation in employment programs for persons with long-term mental illness: A three year research study of employer involvement in transitional and supported employment services*. Philadelphia: Matrix Research Institute.

Koehler, F., & Ellis, J. (Eds.). (1990). *Project WIN: Work incentives network training manual*. Richmond, VA: The Association for Persons in Supported Employment (APSE).

Kregel, J., & Sale, P. (1988). Preservice preparation of supported employment professionals. In P. Wehman & M.S. Moon (Eds.), *Vocational rehabilitation and supported employment* (pp. 129–143). Baltimore: Paul H. Brookes Publishing Co.

Lefley, H.P. (1990). Culture and chronic mental illness. *Hospital and Community Psychiatry*, 41(3), 277–285.

Liberman, R.P., Mueser, K.T., Wallace, C.J., Jacobs, H.E., Eckman, T., & Massel, H.K. (1986). Training skills in the psychiatrically disabled: Learning coping and competence. *Schizophrenia Bulletin*, 12(4), 631–644.

MacDonald-Wilson, K.L. (1994). Using impairment related work expenses (IRWEs) and other deductions from earnings. *Community Support Network News*, 10(1), 5–6.

MacDonald-Wilson, K.L., Mancuso, L.L., Danley, K.S., & Anthony, W.A. (1989). Supported employment for people with psychiatric disability. *Journal of Applied Rehabilitation Counseling*, 20(3), 50–57.

MacDonald-Wilson, K.L., Revell, W.G., Jr., Nguyen, N., & Peterson, M.E. (1991). Supported employment outcomes for people with psychiatric disability: A comparative analysis. *Journal of Vocational Rehabilitation*, 1(3), 30–44.

Mancuso, L.L. (1990). Reasonable accommodation for workers with psychiatric disabilities. *Psychosocial Rehabilitation Journal*, 14(1), 3–19.

Mancuso, L.L. (1992). Questions frequently asked about the ADA by workers with psychiatric disabilities. *Community Support Network News*, 8(2), 4–13.

Marrone, J. (1986). Job placement techniques for counselors working with persons with psychiatric disabilities. In L.J. Katz (Ed.), *Psychiatric rehabilitation training program: Vol. III. Career counseling and job development strategies* (pp. 101–113). Pittsburgh, PA: Western Psychiatric Institute and Clinic.

Marrone, J. (1990). *Supported employment for persons with long–term mental illness.* St. Paul: Minnesota Division of Rehabilitation Services Supported Employment Project.

Marrone, J. (1993). Creating positive vocational outcomes for people with severe mental illness. *Psychosocial Rehabilitation Journal, 17*(2), 43–62.

Marshall, C.A. (1989). Skill teaching as training in rehabilitation counselor education. *Rehabilitation Education, 3,* 19–26.

Mastboom, J. (1992) Forty clubhouses: Model and practices. *Psychosocial Rehabilitation Journal, 16*(2), 9–23.

McCue, M., & Katz-Garris, L. (1983). The severely disabled psychiatric patient and the adjustment to work. *Journal of Rehabilitation, 49,* 52–57.

McGurrin, M.C. (1994). An overview of the effectiveness of traditional vocational rehabilitation services in the treatment of long term mental illness. *Psychosocial Rehabilitation Journal, 17*(3), 37–54.

Mcloughlin, C.S., Garner, J.B., & Callahan, M. (1987). *Getting employed, staying employed.* Baltimore: Paul H. Brookes Publishing Co.

Meinz, R.I. (1988). *VR counseling with the personality disordered client: An accommodation model.* Edmonds, WA: Author.

Menchetti, B.M., & Rusch, F.R. (1988). Vocational evaluation and eligibility for rehabilitation services. In P. Wehman & M.S. Moon (Eds.), *Vocational rehabilitation and supported employment* (pp. 79–90). Baltimore: Paul H. Brookes Publishing Co.

Menchetti, B.M., & Udvari-Solner, A. (1990). Supported employment: New challenges for vocational evaluation. *Rehabilitation Education, 4,* 301–317.

Mental Health Law Project. (1992). *Mental health consumers in the workplace: How the Americans with Disabilities Act protects you against employment discrimination.* Washington, DC: Author.

Mental Retardation Facilities and Community Mental Health Centers Construction Act of 1963, PL 88-164. (October 31, 193). Title 42, U.S.C. 2670 et seq: *U.S. Statutes at Large, 77,* 282–298.

Meyer, L.H., & Evans, I.M. (1989). *Nonaversive intervention for behavior problems: A manual for home and community.* Baltimore: Paul H. Brookes Publishing Co.

Mueser, K.T., & Liberman, R.P. (1988). Skills training in vocational rehabilitation. In J.A. Ciardiello & M.D. Bell (Eds.), *Vocational rehabilitation of persons with prolonged psychiatric disorders* (pp. 81–103). Baltimore: The Johns Hopkins University Press.

Mintz, J., Mintz, L.I., & Phipps, C.C. (1992). Treatments of mental disorders and the functional capacity to work. In R.P. Liberman (Ed.), *Handbook of Psychiatric Rehabilitation* (pp. 290–316). New York: Macmillan.

Moon, M.S., Goodall, P., Barcus, J.M., & Brooke, V. (1986). *The supported work model of competitive employment for citizens with severe handicaps: A guide for job trainers* (rev. ed.). Richmond: Rehabilitation Research and Training Center, Virginia Commonwealth University.

Moon, M.S., Inge, K.J., Wehman, P., Brooke, V., & Barcus, J.M. (1990). *Helping persons with severe mental retardation get and keep employment: Supported employment issues and strategies.* Baltimore: Paul H. Brookes Publishing Co.

Muller, L.S. (1992). Disability beneficiaries who work and their experience under program work incentives. *Social Security Bulletin, 55*(2), 2–19.

Murphy, S., & Rogan, P. (1994). Involving co-workers to support training employees with disabilities. *Supported Employment InfoLines, 5*(6), 4–5

National Alliance for the Mentally Ill (NAMI). (1994). *NAMI Advocate, 15*(3).

National Council on Disability. (1993). *A report to the president and Congress.* Washington, DC: Author.

National Institute of Mental Health. (1986). *Plain talk about the stigma of mental illness.* Washington, DC: Author.

National Institute of Mental Health. (1993, July). *National Institute of Mental Health UPDATE.* Washington, DC: Author.

National Institute on Disability and Rehabilitation Research (NIDRR). (1989). *Rehab brief: New strategies in psychiatric rehabilitation.* Washington, DC: Department of Education, Office of Special Education and Rehabilitative Services.

Nikkel, R., & Fujita, B. (1991). *Training manual in dual diagnosis: Mental illness and substance abuse.* Seattle, WA: Center for Continuing Education in Rehabilitation, Seattle University.

Nisbet, J., & Callahan, M. (1988). *Assessing the quality of supported employment services.* Durham, NH: Institute on Disability.

Nisbet, J., & Hagner, D. (1988). Natural supports in the workplace: A reexamination of supported employment. *Journal of The Association for Persons with Severe Handicaps,* 13(4), 260–267.

NISH. (1993, December). Congressional study finds VR program results "mixed." *NISH News,* 18(12), 10–12.

Noble, J.H., Jr., & Collignon, F. C. (1987). Systems barriers to supported employment for persons with chronic mental illness. *Psychosocial Rehabilitation Journal, XI*(2), 26–54.

O'Mara, S. (updated by Pellegrino, C.). (April, 1993a). *Understanding and using the PASS work incentive.* Richmond: Employment Support Institute (ESI), Virginia Commonwealth University.

O'Mara, S. (updated by Pellegrino, C.). (April, 1993b). *Understanding Social Security benefits.* Richmond: Employment Support Institute (ESI), Virginia Commonwealth University.

Owen, E. (1982). *Connections: A self–help and resource guide for patients, professionals, and families.* Seattle: Washington Advocates for the Mentally Ill.

Parrish, J. (1992). Reasonable accommodations for people with psychiatric disabilities. *Community Support Network News,* 8(2), 8.

Pelissier-Shelton, M.A., & Wong, H. (1989). *Job coaching roles in supported employment projects: A national study.* Carbondale: Rehabilitation Institute, Southern Illinois University.

Pope, H.G., & Lipinski, J.R. (1978). Diagnosis in schizophrenia and manic-depressive illness. *Archives of General Psychiatry, 35,* 811–828.

Powell, T.H., Pancsofar, E.L., Steere, D.E., Butterworth, J., Itzkowitz, J.S., & Rainforth, B. (1991). *Supported employment: Providing integrated employment opportunities for persons with disabilities.* New York: Longman.

Pretzer, J. (1990). Borderline personality disorder. In A.T. Beck & A. Freeman (Eds.), *Cognitive therapy of personality disorders* (pp. 176–207). New York: Guilford Press.

Rayton, M.R. (1993). The federal courts speak. In *Fifth annual employment law update: The winds of change.* Seattle: Ryan, Swanson, & Cleveland.

Razzano, L. (1993). *Impact of psychiatric rehabilitation programs on rehospitalization.* Chicago: Thresholds National Research & Training Center.

RehabACTion Advocacy Network. (1992). *In the Public Interest, 1*(6).

Rehabilitation Act of 1973, PL 93-112. (September 26, 1973). Title 29, U.S.C. 701 et seq: *U.S. Statutes at Large, 87,* 355–394.

Rehabilitation Act Amendments of 1986, PL 99-506. (October 21, 1986). Title 29, U.S.C. 701 et seq: *U.S. Statutes at Large, 100,* 1807–1846.

Rogan, P., & Hagner, D. (1990). Vocational evaluation in supported employment. *Journal of Rehabilitation, 56*(1), 45–51.

Rusch, F.R. (Ed.). (1986). *Competitive employment issues and strategies.* Baltimore: Paul H. Brookes Publishing Co.

Rusch, F.R., Schutz, R.P., & Agran, M. (1982). Validating entry–level survival skills for service occupations: Implications for curriculum development. *Journal of The Association for Persons with Severe Handicaps,* 8(3), 32–41.

Russell, H., & Associates. (1985). *Development of staff roles for supported and transitional employment programs* (Contract No. 300-85-0094). Washington, DC: U.S. Department of Education.

Ruth, D., Hill, M., & Wood, W. (1990). *Fee for service manual: Establishing fee-for-service rates for individual placement models of supported employment.* Richmond, VA: The Association for Persons in Supported Employment (APSE).

Rutman, I. (1994). How psychiatric disability expresses itself as a barrier to employment. *Psychosocial Rehabilitation Journal, 17*(3), 15–36.

Schultheis, A.M.M., & Bond, G. (1993). Situational assessment ratings of work behaviors: Changes across time and between settings. *Psychosocial Rehabilitation Journal, 17*(2), 107–120.

Shafer, M. (1986). Utilizing co-workers as change agents. In F.R. Rusch (Ed.), *Competitive employment issues and strategies* (pp. 215–224). Baltimore: Paul H. Brookes Publishing Co.

Shafer, M.S., Parent, W.S., & Everson, J.M. (1988). Responsive marketing by supported employment programs. In P. Wehman & M.S. Moon (Eds.), *Vocational rehabilitation and supported employment* (pp. 235–250). Baltimore: Paul H. Brookes Publishing Co.

Shaw, J., & Associates. (1987). *Dual diagnosis training: Assessing and treating the client with both an alcohol and drug and a mental health diagnosis (Participant's Manual Vols. I and II).* Salem: Oregon State Office of Mental Health, Bureau of Education and Training.

Social Security Administration. (1991). *Working while disabled—A guide to plans for achieving self-support while receiving Supplemental Security Income* (SSA Report No. 05-11017). Washington, DC: Author.

Social Security Administration. (1992). *Red book on work incentives—A summary guide to Social Security and Supplemental Security work incentives for people with disabilities* (SSA Report No. 64-030). Washington, DC: Author.

Social Security Administration. (1993). *Quarterly report on SSI disabled workers and work incentive programs: June 1993.* Baltimore: Office of Supplemental Security Income, Division of Property Management and Analysis.

Solomon, P. (1988). Racial factors in mental health service utilization. *Psychosocial Rehabilitation Journal, 11,* 3–12.

Solomon, P., Gordon, B., & Davis, J.M. (1986). Reconceptualizing assumptions about community mental health. *Hospital and Community Psychiatry, 37,* 708–712.

Stanton, A.H., Gunderson, J.G., Knapp, P.H., Frank, A.F., Vannicelli, M.O., Schnitzer, R., & Rosenthal, R. (1984). Effects of psychotherapy on schizophrenia: I. Design and implementation of a controlled study. *Schizophrenia Bulletin, 10,* 520–563.

Stephens, J.H. (1978). Long-term prognosis and follow-up in schizophrenia. *Schizophrenia Bulletin, 4,* 25–47.

Sue, S., McKinney, H., & Allen, D.B. (1976). Predictors of the direction of therapy for clients on the community mental health center system. *Community Mental Health Journal, 12,* 365–375.

Sullivan, P. (1994). Recovery from schizophrenia: What we can learn from the developing nations. *Innovations & Research, 3*(2), 7–16.

Tashjian, M.D., Hayward, B.J., Stoddard, S., & Kraus, L. (1989). *Best practice study of vocational rehabilitation services to severely mentally ill persons: Vol. 1. Study findings.* Washington, DC: Policy Studies Associates.

Tilson, G.P., Jr. (1991). Essential functions of the job: A critical aspect of ADA. *Supported Employment InfoLines, 2*(7), 1–3.

Toms Barker, L. (1994). Community based models of employment services for people with long term mental illness. *Psychosocial Rehabilitation Journal, 17*(3), 55–66.

Torrey, E.F. (1988). *Surviving schizophrenia: A family manual* (rev. ed.). New York: Harper & Row.

Torrey, E.F., Erdman, K., Wolfe, S.M., & Flynn, L.M. (1990). *Care of the seriously mentally ill: A rating of state programs* (3rd ed.). Washington, DC: Public Citizen Health Research Group and National Alliance for the Mentally Ill.

Unger, K. (1990). Supported postsecondary education for people with mental illness. *American Rehabilitation, 16*(2), 10–14.

Unger, K. (1993). Creating supported education programs utilizing existing community resources. *Psychosocial Rehabilitation Journal, 17*(1), 11–24.

Unger, K. (1994). Access to educational programs and its effect on employability. *Psychosocial Rehabilitation Journal, 17*(3), 117–126.

Unger, K., Anthony, W.A., Sciarappa, K., & Rogers, E.S. (1991). A supported education program for young adults with long-term mental illness. *Hospital and Community Psychiatry, 42*(8), 838–842.

U.S. Department of Labor, Employment Standards Administration (Wage and Hour Division). (1993). *Statement of principle.* Washington, DC: Author.

Vischi, T.R. (1988). *Financing community services for persons with severe and disabling mental illness.* McLean, VA: International Association of Psychosocial Rehabilitation Services (IAPSRS).

Wehman, P. (1988). Supported employment. Toward zero exclusion of persons with severe disabilities. In P. Wehman & M.S. Moon (Eds.), *Vocational rehabilitation and supported employment* (pp. 3–14). Baltimore: Paul H. Brookes Publishing Co.

Wehman, P. (1989). Supported employment implementation in 27 states: An introduction. In P. Wehman, J. Kregel, & M.S. Shafer (Eds.), *Emerging trends in the national supported employment initiative: A preliminary analysis of twenty-seven states* (pp. 1–14). Richmond: Rehabilitation Research and Training Center on Supported Employment, Virginia Commonwealth University.

Wehman, P. (1993). 250,000 by 1998? *Journal of Vocational Rehabilitation, 3*(4), 1–2.

Wehman, P., & Melia, R. (1985). The job coach: Function in transitional and supported employment. *American Rehabilitation, 11*(2), 4–6.

Wehman, P., Kregel, J., Shafer, M.S., & West, M. (1989). Supported employment implementation: I. Characteristics of persons being served. In P. Wehman, J. Kregel, & M. S. Shafer (Eds.), *Emerging trends in the national supported employment initiative: A preliminary analysis of twenty-seven states* (pp. 46–74). Richmond: Rehabilitation Research and Training Center on Supported Employment, Virginia Commonwealth University.

Wehman, P., Revell, W.G., Kregel, J., Kreutzer, J., Callahan, M., & Banks, P.D. (1990). Supported employment: An alternative model for vocational rehabilitation of persons with severe neurologic, psychiatric, or physical disabilities. In J. Kregel, P. Wehman, & M.S. Shafer (Eds.), *Supported employment for persons with severe disabilities: From research to practice* (pp. 101–114). Richmond: Rehabilitation Research and Training Center on Supported Employment, Virginia Commonwealth University.

West, M.D., Kregel, J., & Revell, W.G. (1994). A new era of self-determination. *TASH Newsletter, 20*(7), 11–12.

Wingerson, D. (1994). Risperidone brings new hope in the medication treatment of schizophrenia. *Innovations & Research in Clinical Services, Community Support, and Rehabilitation, 3*(1), 12–13.

Wool, P. (1990). Vocational stabilization for persons with psychiatric disability (or square holes and round pegs). *The Advance, 1*(4), 1–3.

Woy, J.R., & Dellario, D.J. (1985). Issues in the linkage and integration of treatment and rehabilitation services for chronically mentally ill persons. *Administration in Mental Health, 12*(5), 155–165.

Yudofsky, S.C., Hales, R.E., & Ferguson, T. (1991). *What you need to know about psychiatric drugs: The most comprehensive consumer guide to over 100 current prescription drugs.* New York: Ballantine Books.

Zemke, R., & Zemke, S. (1988). Thirty things we know for sure about adult learning. *Training: The Magazine of Human Resources Development, 25*(7), 57–62.

INDEX

Page numbers followed by "f" indicate figures; those followed by "t" indicate tables.